American Wines
of the Northwest

Northwest Wine Regions

Legend:

- Mountains
- Yakima Valley
- Snake Valley
- Columbia Valley
- Walla Walla Valley
- Southern Oregon
- Umpqua Valley
- Willamette Valley
- Southwestern Washington
- Columbia Gorge

Map labels: SEATTLE, SPOKANE, YAKIMA, PASCO, WALLA WALLA, PORTLAND, SALEM, EUGENE, BOISE, ROSEBURG, MEDFORD

AMERICAN WINES
of the NORTHWEST

A Guide to the Wines of
Oregon, Washington, and Idaho

CORBET CLARK

QUILL
WILLIAM MORROW
NEW YORK

It is the policy of William Morrow and Company, Inc., and its imprints and affiliates, recognizing the importance of preserving what has been written, to print the books we publish on acid-free paper, and we exert our best efforts to that end.

Library of Congress Cataloging-in-Publication Data

Clark, Corbet.
  American wines of the Northwest: a guide to the wines of Oregon, Washington, and Idaho/Corbet Clark.
    p. cm.
  Originally published: 1st ed. New York: W. Morrow, © 1989.
  Includes index.
  ISBN 0-688-11276-5
  1. Wine and wine making—Pacific, Northwest. I. Title.
TP557.C52   1992
641.2'2'09795—dc20   91-34080
                                                         CIP

Printed in the United States of America

        2 3 4 5 6 7 8 9 10

FOR JEFF,
whose friendship and encouragement
made this book possible

WASHINGTON

48°

SEATTLE

Columbia R.

Snake R.

46°

PORTLAND

Willamette R.

44°

OREGON

Umpqua R.

Rogue R.

42°

BOISE

IDAHO

Snake R.

Principal
Growing
Areas

38°

Sonoma Valley

Napa Valley

SAN
FRANCISCO

35°

Latitude North

CALIFORNIA

PACIFIC OCEAN

Wine Growing Areas
of the
Pacific Coast

FOREWORD

Corbet Clark is an amateur when it comes to wine. This may sound strange to you, but I say this because the term *amateur* comes from the Latin *amator,* which means "lover." An amateur is one who does something for the sheer love of it. A professional does it for cash. Corbet is an amateur.

Don't misunderstand me. Father Clark is a well-trained authority on wine, but he is not to be mixed up with the stuffed-shirt professional types who are inclined to act as if they had some secret wine knowledge that you and I would never understand. Corbet knows wine intimately, and he is willing to share his knowledge with anyone.

Clark has enough degrees to mark him as an authority on several subjects. He has a Bachelor of Arts from Harvard, a Master of Arts in history from Yale, and a Master of Divinity from General Theological Seminary in New York. I suppose you could say he makes his living by teaching, but wine remains a basic love.

Wine tasting and appreciation go back to his childhood, when his father, a well-known Seattle lawyer and wine enthusiast, offered Corbet wine in a very nonchalant and matter-of-fact manner. I am saddened that Irving Clark did not live to see this volume, since he would have been proud that his son has become such an ardent evangelist for the most blessed of fluids.

Corbet and I have drunk wine at the most wonderful and difficult of times. I have tasted wine in his home, and he has done the same in mine. We tasted too much of the grape while preparing a book on cooking with wine, and we shared a bottle of wine on the birth of his firstborn, a son that remained in an incubator for weeks. We drank wine together because it was healing and because wine is, for the both of us, a clear symbol that God loves us and wants us to be happy. That son, by the way, is now five and likes a bit of wine now and then himself.

The priestly author has put together a volume that is based on joy, insight, and experience. He is honest about his task when he says, "I do not pretend this is a scholarly book, and it is based unashamedly on my own preferences and views." Those views will be helpful to both the amateur wine fan and the professional, since this is the most complete and intimate discussion of Northwest wines yet to be published. Clark knows the personalities behind the Northwest wine industry, and he openly gossips about them in an affectionate manner. The sections on history help us understand that winemaking in the area goes back a long time—perhaps prior to the plantings in the Napa Valley.

And he writes in a witty manner. I found myself sitting in bed reading this volume until late into the night, and enjoying same with a good dry sherry, of course. This is a terrific volume.

The largest part of the book deals with Corbet's judgments on the many wineries to be found in the Pacific Northwest. You can look up a winery, and he will give his opinion on the bottle you have in your hand. He is also anxious to have his volume accompany you as you tour this wonderful wine region, which is now becoming known worldwide.

I really have to laugh. Had you told me twenty years ago that I would one day be writing a foreword to a book about Northwest wines, I would have refused to talk with you. I was raised in the Fremont district of Seattle and had a paper route in a rather depressed area. I would deliver papers in the darkness of the early morning and smell the remains of the Washington wine that was spilled about in the corridors of the cheap one-night hotels where my clients resided. Corbet has taken me through the history of the wine industry in this area, a history that has moved from those terrible fortified and stinky wines of the 1950s to wines that have been judged among some of the best in the world. You will appreciate his discourse on this movement.

This book is a directory, a guide, a purchasing help, and a source of insight into serious appreciation of the wines of my beloved Pacific Northwest. But most of all, it is a volume written by an amateur, a priest and teacher who writes out of love, and he knows his loves very well, very well indeed.

JEFF SMITH

ACKNOWLEDGMENTS

I must acknowledge my debts to an enormous range of people, starting with winery owners, managers, and winemakers. As if tending vineyard and winery were not enough, they must put up with nagging questions from wine writers, an eccentric lot, and they do so very graciously. I thank all those who have given me hours of their time, drawn off wine from tank and barrel, tramped through vineyards, and opened innumerable bottles of wine for me, often extending the hospitality of table and bed as well. To some I owe a particular debt, because they have patiently but persistently tried to disabuse me of bad ideas and wrong notions and have shared freely of their great store of experience, always with good humor. These include Rob Griffin, David Lake, Joel Klein, Mike Wallace, Don Mercer, Joan Wolverton, Rick Small, Stan Clarke, Myron Redford, John Paul, and David Lett.

My writing colleagues in the Northwest have also shared with me extensively of their knowledge. Ronald and Glenda Holden deserve thanks for starting the Washington Wine Writers—a most congenial group. In particular I thank Chuck Hill, with whom I have shared the road as well as much information and many ideas; Ted Jordan Meredith, whose scholarship on Northwest wine is unequaled and whose research enlightened me on many points; Lynn Crook, who does wonderful things with Northwest wine and food; and Noel Bourasaw, whose work on Northwest wine history has been very helpful.

Those who work to promote the whole industry have also been generous with time and information: Simon Siegel and the Washington Wine Institute, the Oregon Winegrowers' Association, the Oregon Wine Advisory Board, and Jack Watson and the Extension Service of the Agriculture Department of Washington State University.

Those whose work is selling and promoting these wines have also given their aid in discussing markets and consumers; in particular, Lila Gault, Elizabeth Purser, and Stuart Friedman.

I have tasted and compared notes with many people, but I especially wish to thank those who helped me sort through the wines for this book, including Patty Smith, Gary Habedank, Bill and Phyllis Gill, Ron and Harriett Fields, David Dahl, Michael Stagg, and Sandy and (most particularly) Ronn Johanson, whose palate has proved a foil for my own for many years.

Barbara Ensrud read the manuscript and made a number of useful suggestions. Michele Laboda created the maps.

Finally, my family. Myra, Philip, and Margaret have accepted the long hours devoted to this book with patience and with love. I am grateful.

Acknowledgments

CONTENTS

INTRODUCTION

My best friend when I was growing up lived next door to a University of Washington professor whose normal rationality, we decided, left him in the fall. This poor, deluded man's falls were given over to the frenzy of the grape crush, the mad hauling, smashing, pumping of fly-covered fruit to try to make wine of it. We knew, with the confidence that adolescents have, that this was evidence of madness because this man and his friends were trying to do all this with grapes from our own state, Washington. I knew from the bittersweet experience of summers spent bundled in sweaters, sailing boats in chill winds under gray skies, that beautiful as it was, this was not a place to grow grapes. Apples, yes, but not grapes. Grapes came from sunny lands to the south, carefree places where children spent the summers in their swim trunks, scratching their peeling skin.

The poor man in question was Lloyd Woodburne, a founder of Associated Vintners, one of Washington's first premium wineries. He had the last laugh, since I have spent the last ten years trying to keep up with a wine industry in the Northwest growing at a dizzying pace both in size and in quality. I have visited at least three quarters of the 135 or so wineries now in Washington, Oregon, and Idaho. I have talked with the men and women who grow the grapes and make the wines, sampled from bottle and barrel, and tried to convey something of the excitement of these efforts to consumers through a regular wine column, wine classes, and a couple of books.

This book grows out of a conviction that Northwest wine has come of age. It's no longer a matter of dedicated amateurs making small lots of wine in basements and garages, or struggling to get a few vines through their first winter.

The Northwest wine industry is one of the few in the world devoted almost exclusively to the making of premium European vinifera wines, it is doing so on a scale to contend nationally for consumers' attention, and the wines have demonstrated their ability to compete with the best from California and Europe. I don't have to suggest anymore that Northwesterners should drink the wines because they're Northwestern; now I suggest that any wine lover should drink them because they're good—and different from the wines of California.

Indeed, if there is a theme to this book, it is that Northwest wines, although they have their own style, owe as much to the European wine traditions as to California's. Wine lovers familiar with the flavors of French Bordeaux and Burgundy, German Rheingaus and Mosels, will have flashes of recognition when they try Northwest wines, as have wine professionals from Europe. This should not be surprising, as the climate of the Northwest is strikingly similar to that of northern Europe.

Northwest wines are now seeking and getting a national audience, and this book seeks to inform that audience. I have tried not only to introduce the wines of the Northwest to consumers who have no familiarity with them, but also to help consumers distinguish among the increasing abundance of labels and varietals. I do not pretend this is a scholarly book, and it is based unashamedly on my own preferences and views. It is simply an introduction to what I am convinced will be recognized within the next generation as a *great* wine region of the world.

ORGANIZATION OF THE BOOK

You will find this book divided into two basic parts. The first is general: I have attempted to provide an overview of what wine people are up to in this region, with a brief history of wine in the Northwest. Here you will also find a discussion of the region's various growing areas, the grapes particular to each area, and how the wines are being made. Several short essays on certain aspects of wine in the region have been included because they are of particular interest or significance.

The second part is a winery-by-winery review of Northwest wines. I have attempted to make this as user-friendly as possible, providing ratings, descriptions, and a guide to prices of the wines. Each winery description can stand alone, to provide the essential information on the wines of that producer, but if you want to explore a certain varietal, or a region, in more depth, turn to the appropriate section in the first part. A separate introduction to the second part of the book may be found on page 135.

The appendixes include a quick-reference guide to recommended wines in each varietal category, as well as a partial listing of awards received at Northwest wine competitions in 1988.

Columbia, Yakima
and Walla Walla Valley
Growing Regions

Part One

THE NORTHWEST WINE REGION

1

PEOPLE & PLACES

The wine business is a people business. True, a modern winery, particularly a large one, is packed with gleaming steel equipment, and the art of winemaking relies heavily on the instruments of the chemist. In the end, though, even for a mammoth producer like Gallo, the product seems so often to depend on the personality of grape grower, winemaker, and cellarmaster. Wine is a friendly, if very competitive, business, perhaps because almost everyone first got involved in it on account of some creative urge that could be satisfied only in vineyard and cellar, and wine folk admire that in one another. Wineries habitually share equipment, trade vine cuttings and yeasts, and band together to work on common problems, such as the weather, recalcitrant state regulators, disease, or unhelpful local farmers. It's a shirt-sleeve business in which deals are still often struck with just a handshake, gossip is endemic, and the wine gets made not by computerized plan but often just by sheer hard work and force of personality. If every wine is linked with the particular geography that shaped its origins, it is also indelibly marked by the men and women who helped make it. They are part of its fascination.

Bill Preston has the weathered and determined look of someone who might have been a farm equipment salesman in the eastern Washington desert—which he was. And a very successful one, too. His success at selling Ford tractors led to numerous junkets to the Bay Area, where he was wined and dined in the finer establishments. He and his wife took rather easily to the good life, San Francisco style, including a taste for fine California wines, which they developed on forays into the Napa Valley. Eventually, he says, Preston began to wonder why he should be spending his time in California when he could have been making his own wine in Washington. Very much a man of action, he up and sold the tractor business and started a spread of grapes in the arid flatland outside Pasco; mind you, this was in the mid-seventies, when "Washington wine" still conjured up images of sagebrush and winos. For a number of years, Preston Wine Cellars was the second-largest winery in the state, after Ste. Michelle.

The desert around Pasco sure doesn't look like wine country. Approaching Preston on the road outside Pasco, one gets a sense of how water has transformed the landscape. Mile after mile of flat brown rangeland gives way with sudden starkness to acres of dark green vineyard, with rows of elevated sprinkler heads spraying a fine shower constantly, keeping the vines cool and lush. From the elevated tasting room this green island stands out dramatically against the intensely blue sky and the mousy hills. The Columbia and Snake rivers have provided both the water and the electricity to make this paradise, cultivated with fervor. (There are no lawns as green as those grown in the desert.)

In some ways the times have passed Preston by. Newer wineries are run as buttoned-down businesses, with a careful eye to slick marketing (one winery owner remarks that the wine business is one-third winemaking and two-thirds marketing). If Bill Preston was a wine pioneer, a man who started his enterprise not with a sharp pencil but with a sharp desire to do something new, maybe the pioneer days are already over.

David Lett, whose whisker-covered face, perpetual turtlenecks, and broad grin make him look a bit like a grizzled sea captain, runs a fastidiously kept little winery in the capital of the Oregon wine country, McMinnville. He was, he says, "young and stupid" when he decided that Oregon would be the next great wine region and that people would flock to his support to make that happen. He had sites picked out and ambitious plans laid, "but no one would loan me any money." So he found a ramshackle former turkey-processing plant in a seedy section of McMinnville, near the railroad tracks, renting for $25 a month. He's still there.

McMinnville has been little changed by the Oregon wine industry's newfound fame. Although in the summer of 1987 it played host to the first International Pinot Noir Conference, which attracted wine professionals from as far away as Australia, there's still no first-class wine shop in town, and the classiest restaurant, Nick's Italian Café, which does have first-rate food and an excellent wine list, is a slightly spiffed-up diner where most folk come in jeans and open shirts. On Saturday nights outside Nick's on the main drag, teenagers still cruise slowly up and down in aging cars, a ritual from the fifties, while the sidewalks are loaded with gawkers. There's a new computer plant outside town, but the businesses are still mostly oriented toward farming, and the houses and churches and the local college have a comfortably worn New England look.

Lett's Eyrie winery is not ordinarily open to the public, but an exception is Thanksgiving weekend, when all the local wineries have special hours and entertain thousands of visitors from Portland and beyond, stocking up for Christmas and the winter. Lett presides behind a pouring table, looking terribly imperturbable (except when he detects the odor of cigar smoke in the air and takes off to find the culprit). While the current wines are being snapped up at $15 to $20 a bottle, a look round the winery reveals its humble origins, in a day when no one cared about what was happening in Oregon's vineyards. On display is a tiny, antique crusher-stemmer, which a sign says left the operator plenty of time for coffee breaks while it was laboriously eating up small amounts of grapes. Also on display is Lett's homemade punching-down tool, needed to stir under the solid cap of fermenting Pinot Noir grapes, now supplanted by a "modern" French device that looks like an oversize plumber's helper. Lett has learned to cope patiently with the vagaries of nature, Oregon style. In 1984, when the rains went on for weeks, he waited until nearly the end of November to finish harvesting the Pinot Noir and then put his grapes under a giant drier designed for the local filberts in order to get some of the moisture out of the fruit. His '84 Pinot Noir, as always, was one of the better ones.

Lett's manner is modest, but he has the convictions of the solitary prophet who has survived many years in the wilderness and emerged to popular acclaim. For many years, before the wine groupies began to flock to his winery, he hit the road selling textbooks for part of the year in order to underwrite the vineyard. The longtime public neglect of what he was trying to do has inured him to both the hoopla and any criticism. A comment about any of his wines gets a quick and confident response: Doesn't the '85 Pinot seems more closed than the '86? No, the '86, still recovering from bottle shock, is definitely the more closed. Having almost single-handedly established the state's reputation for Pinot Noir, he's working hard to build up a name for Pinot Gris, a grape related to Pinot Noir that produces some of Alsace's finest white wines. His '85 Pinot Gris was truly exceptional, and he had planned to release it as a reserve—he kicks himself that he let his local distributor dissuade him because the latter found the wine odd. He still thinks of himself as primarily a viticulturist (that's what his UC Davis degree was in): "If I were going to replant," says Lett quietly, "I would plant just those sister grapes—Pinot Noir and Pinot Gris."

Salishan Vineyards' location owes more to life's practicalities than to careful viticultural planning. When Lincoln and Joan Wolverton were contemplating a vineyard of their own, inspired by the newborn Oregon wine industry, they were both pursuing professional careers in Seattle. Having decided not to move immediately, they looked for a location close enough to Seattle so they could drive down for weekends, and close enough to the Willamette growing area to produce fine Pinot Noir and Chardonnay. They picked a hilltop near La Center, Washington, about thirty miles north of Portland, and planted a dozen acres in 1971. With their award-winning 1978 and 1979 Pinot Noirs they proved that southwest Washington could produce excellent wine, and other small vineyards have been developed in the area.

Joan Wolverton doesn't have to commute down to her vineyard on weekends anymore to tend to the vines and inspect the damage from marauding deer—she lives in a house with a commanding view on the crest of the hill. (Lincoln still works in Seattle and comes down on weekends.) Today she not only tends the vineyard but supervises the harvest, makes the wine, tends the tasting room, and goes on the road to promote the wines—not to mention raising two young sons. She moves with the confidence of someone who doesn't have time to fool around—a tour of the vineyard becomes a kind of footrace, with Joan leading the way up and down rows, giving along the way a nonstop high-speed lecture on each variety and its vagaries. Every year at Salishan is a race against the weather—the harvest here is even later (by about a week or so) than in the Willamette area and often in the rain.

Inside the winery one has to wander through twisting canyons between case goods piled to the ceiling in order to get to the working winery. There are a couple of neighbor ladies methodically hand-corking and hand-labeling wines, sipping coffee and chatting quietly (the labels don't always get on quite straight—a hazard in a small winery). French oak barrels, notoriously expensive, have been slowly collected over the years—the trick is to get last year's wines out and bottled to make room for the new wines. There's an odd-sized collection of tanks and a minimum of equipment. The wines here are made not with money and technology but with sheer back-breaking labor.

Wolverton is not a complainer. If the weather is uncooperative, then the wines will be made to fit the fruit: With grapes of lower sugar, Salishan has pioneered the making of dry Washington Riesling and Chenin Blanc, both excellent ("I don't like sweeter wines," says Wolverton). The Pinot Noir is never a big wine, so the goal is delicacy and balance. The Chardonnays don't have the body of their counterparts from eastern Washington ("I don't like big, buttery wines") and the Cabernet Sauvignon, she admits freely, has been less than successful. But she never loses the smile that stretches broadly across her craggy face— whatever the grapes produce, she will deal with.

When Joel Klein dedicated his new winery, Snoqualmie, in 1985, he managed to get the Episcopal Bishop of Olympia, the Right Reverend Robert Cochrane, to turn out in full episcopal regalia on a windy ridge in the Cascade foothills to bless the place. Klein is not known for dreaming small. He arrived in Washington in 1974 with impeccable California credentials, having married the daughter of one of the enology profs at the University of California at Davis, the winemaker's Harvard, and he helped design and then put into operation the new premium wine operation called Chateau Ste. Michelle. Klein, in his eight years at Ste. Michelle, was among those who set a style for Washington wines and helped the state make its mark in the wine world with his consistently good and popular releases.

A man of restless energy, he decided to move on and start his own winery, confident of his ability to make it grow quickly. Although the plans have hit a number of snags, the dreams are still there. A conversation in the fall of 1987 found him excited about a new lodge to be built on the winery's property, with future plans for the site including not just one but several wineries, plus a microbrewery, restaurants, shops, and an amphitheater. But like many winemakers, he's caught between a capability to make large quantities of good wine and the increasing difficulty of selling it. When it's pointed out that his fine Saddle Mountain Chardonnay must compete against similarly priced wines from huge California wineries, he scoffs—his wine is much superior. But one wonders if the consumer looking for a $5 Chardonnay really cares. Is Klein concerned about the ever lower prices for Riesling, the state's staple wine? He reaches for his calculator and quickly works out the figures: "You could do a dollar-ninety-nine Riesling" and still make money. But doesn't the state's reputation for premium wines suffer in the process?

Klein is a huge man, with features that cartoonists dream of—wiry hair and bushy eyebrows—and he dominates most conversations he's a part of. A man always on the run (he has spent much of his career traveling back and forth between eastern and western Washington), he's perpetually late, and then makes up for it with huge charm and a genuine interest in others. Although the marketplace is sometimes a puzzle to him, the grapes and the wine don't hold any mysteries—there is a solution for every problem. He can expound at length on why a degree-day (a standard measurement of climatic heat) in Washington is different from one in California; he doesn't worry over what to do about vegetal flavors in Washington Cabernet ("The trick is not to get the characteristic in the fruit in the first place—it's a matter of mature fruit"). There is about him a missionary's fervor: He sees so many grapes in the vineyards and wants to convert them to wine. He knows how to do it. In the summer of 1987, with an immense harvest predicted and other winery owners worried about selling their wine, Klein was buying new tank capacity for the Saddle Mountain facility. He smiles: "The winery is full."

Visitors at Amity Vineyards tend to get a loud shout of welcome and a warm hug—Myron Redford knows everyone. Then it's scrounging through the cluttered lab for a clean glass and a wine thief and off to sample barrels. The winery is crammed with barrels, with many from the newer vintage still outside in a makeshift shed, and Redford climbs among them looking for what he wants. There is the air of the mad scientist about him, but he is meticulously rational about the differences among all the different lots of Pinot Noir he has aging. Try this one, from such and such a vineyard; now try this one—same vineyard, different vintage; now this one—different vineyard, same vintage. Do you see? It's the fervor of the tent-meeting preacher. The grapes are made in the vineyard, but the winemaker's art is in the selection and blending. The year 1984 was particularly difficult—how to make a decent wine out of awkward components? With friends, he kept mixing and tasting, mixing and tasting, until finally an exasperated friend told him to "blend the damn wine."

Amity has one of the prettiest sites in the Willamette Valley. From a steep hillside above the tiny town of Amity (where, as in most small Willamette towns, the lawns are all brown in the summer and the gas stations still just sell gas) the winery looks across the valley to the southwest, fields of grass and nut trees with small patches of Oregon oak fading into the blue haze among the green hills on the other side, leading on to the ocean. It's not a big vineyard, jammed in among the dark firs—it's a kind of beachhead that says this part of the world was meant not for lumber but for wine. As Oregon wineries have achieved a measure of prosperity (one sees winemakers now driving Jags and Mercedes) older wineries have spiffed themselves up; Amity is bigger now than ten years ago, but has exactly the same ramshackle look.

You might take Redford for the Last of the Hippies—hairy, disheveled, with wire-rimmed glasses and a benign smile (the last time he wore a coat and tie he drew startled looks and comments from everyone who knew him). His background is academe: He was a minor functionary at the University of Washington in Seattle when he overheard a conversation at the UW faculty club about Washington wine and was immediately intrigued. One of the conversers was Lloyd Woodburne, UW professor and winemaker at Associated Vintners. AV in the early years functioned almost entirely with volunteer labor, and Redford, a sizable man, lent his "strong back" to the winery's efforts for several years, believing that rolling barrels around a warehouse was highly romantic work.

He became convinced that Oregon was the place to be for his favorite wine, Pinot Noir. Oregon's climate was so marginal: "If you're picking the grapes and the leaves are turning yellow on the vines, you're growing grapes in the right place." His challenge was not just growing the grapes but fighting off deer and robins and struggling at the same time to scrape together the money to keep going. A relentless optimist, he can delight visitors with harrowing tales of beasts of prey (including creditors). Today his chief complaint is about wineries that release their Pinot Noir too young. Amity is notorious for late releases (the '83 Reserve wasn't put on sale until 1988), but Redford is unwavering in his insistence on releasing the wines when they're drinkable, and he worries about consumers' souring on too-young wine. His patience, for a man of so much energy, is surprising.

It's not often that lunch on a folding table on a cement floor in the utilitarian lobby of a warehouse turns into an elegant and relaxing affair, but host David Lake at Columbia Winery has a convivial nature that makes such an event (a private wine tasting in this case) a festive occasion. There is crab and pâté, each showing off a Columbia wine, and then a barbecued pheasant for the main course—Lake claims somewhat sheepishly that this is a chance dish, provided by the bird's unfortunate encounter with his pickup truck. The lunch is a leisurely affair, as Lake likes to talk—an initial diffidence, with shy smile, giving way to a more seriously thoughtful frown and an ability to analyze with confidence almost any aspect of the winemaking business.

Although he's Canadian, Lake fits most Americans' idea of what an Englishman should be like: very soft-spoken, with a refined air, modest to a fault, but with a sincere, precise way of talking about his wines. He spent ten years in the British wine trade (the only one in the world that requires an appreciation for and knowledge of wine), where he earned the title of Master of Wine, held by only a hundred or so people in the world, by virtue of his exhaustive understanding of international wines. Attracted by the potential of the Northwest (and having acquired the requisite enology degree from the University of California at Davis) he first worked in Oregon for David Lett before being lured to Bellevue, Washington, to take over wine-

American Wines of the Northwest

making chores for Associated Vintners (now Columbia Winery).

Many winemakers, with their wines at the mercy of the marketplace, have more in common with the door-to-door salesman than with the scientist, but Lake retains a scholarly distance and sense of caution about his wines, treating them like so many untested theories. He's a believer in what he calls the "predestination theory of wine," which says that you "make the wine as it comes"—the fruit from the vineyard, not the winemaker, determines the style of the final product. One senses in Lake a great deal of respect for the natural shape of wine, the need to let it do what it's going to do. It's remarkable to see what different wines can be made from the same grape grown under slightly different conditions in several different places, and Lake continues to experiment: with Chardonnay from southwest Washington, for example, not a region noted for the grape. In addition to its regular Cabernet Sauvignon, Columbia makes three different "David Lake Signature" Cabernets from the Sagemoor, Otis, and Red Willow vineyards, all good, all of different character. Other winemakers would see their task as producing the perfect blend; Lake is content to let each vineyard have its own forum.

There is an air of innocence about Philippe and Bonnie Girardet. It's easy to detect a childlike delight in the good press some of their wines have attracted recently—after all, they came to Roseburg, Oregon, from southern California precisely to escape big-city life, and they've been growing grapes for fifteen years without drawing much attention until the last year or so. There's little self-promotion. We taste the current release of Chardonnay, which is very good—but not so good as last year's, notes Girardet. The wines are light, deliberately so—they are meant to be approachable and popular. (The most popular is the soft, full-fruited Riesling, but Philippe scoffs: In Switzerland, only women drink Riesling; it's not a serious wine.) Philippe says modestly, "We've been extremely lucky—I don't attribute good wine to my great skill."

Perhaps not great skill, but hard work. Their vineyard has a lovely site, nestled in a small bowl, surrounded by pine-covered hills. The exposure is perfect—a gentle slope to the southwest. But the soil is terrible, clay with a layer of shale underneath. They've brought in tons of mulch, but the vines are obviously struggling, with straggly, light-colored foliage by the end of the season, and some sections that are completely bare. Yields have been tiny. But to hear the Girardets talk, you'd think it was Eden. Like so many Oregon winemakers, the Girardets came pursuing that elusive "quality of life," and they wanted to be someplace off the beaten path, where they could grow grapes in their own way and reap their reward of self-satisfaction.

Philippe Girardet is Swiss born and brings a Gallic skepticism about American wines to his business. Small and wiry, with an Arafat-like growth of white beard, he seems very relaxed and at home tending his small winery. He talks quietly. Wife Bonnie is American, thin and bespectacled, straightforward and unaffected—she could be a small-town schoolteacher. Various small towheaded children and large dogs come and go regularly. They are the sort of folk who used to be called the salt of the earth, except there is a watchful intelligence behind the aw-shucks openness.

Girardet is trying to do something different, to use hybrid grapes blended with vinifera to make fine, inexpensive table wines. This is the European way, he insists. In Burgundy, growers find a vine on the property of a neighbor whose wines they like, and take a cutting—they don't know what the variety is; they just like the wine. Vineyards are planted with many different varieties and clones, and no one really knows what's there, but the wine is good. Girardet knows he's bucking the trend—Americans are used to varietal wines—but he's undeterred.

The Girardet Chardonnay is lighter and more delicate than most American ones. "Americans don't know what Chardonnay tastes like." The Chardonnay clones developed at the Davis campus in California to suit the warmer climate are simply "not Chardonnay." What can be done? He sighs and shrugs his shoulders. "California has ruined the wine industry in this country by using bad grapes and making lousy wine"—it's not a bitter assessment, just an honest one in his judgment. The Girardets have found themselves outsiders in the wine fraternity and seem content with that.

In the middle of a conversation outside the winery, a dusty truck drives up and two burly men hop out. One is from a neighboring piece of property, eighty acres or so of hillside, with water and a trailer, which he would like to sell. Would the Girardets know of anyone who might be interested? There is some desultory talk about the value of the property as vineyard land, but it doesn't seem to take with the man. They drive off. The locals, says Philippe, "just don't know what they have."

Walla Walla doesn't share the boom-town atmosphere of much of eastern Washington—Walla Walla had a history when most of the Columbia Basin was still just high winds and empty hills, before irrigation arrived. The town was an important stop on the Oregon Trail in the mid-nineteenth century, a green respite after weeks coming across the parched lands to the east; today it's a quiet college town, full of old homes on tree-lined streets. The Small family has been around a while, too, raising wheat and cattle and running grain elevators out at Lowden, a tiny burg about ten miles to the west.

Walla Walla folk have been a bit slower than the rest of eastern Washington to take to grapes, whether because of their long-standing conservatism or an already well-diversified and prosperous farm economy. When Rick Small decided to plant grapes on a small parcel of family land unsuited for wheat and make wines right there in Lowden, he had few local supporters, even among his family. "I was called an outcast," he says, and recalls the four-letter descriptions as well. But the fact that he was a native helped a bit—he's not sure an outsider would have survived.

Small's success with the Woodward Canyon Winery is testimony to the American dream, winemaker version—a dream that a small-town lad (even if from a prosperous farming family), without the benefit of the academics at the University of California, can plant a tiny vineyard, raise a few grapes, open a small tin-roofed winery, and make world-class wines—and sell them without doing any marketing. But to meet Small is to know something of the reasons for his success: He's a compact, energy-charged man with bright eyes who, if he weren't making wine, ought to be selling something. After a few hours talking wine with him (or listening to him talk wine, really) it's difficult not to be caught up in his enthusiasm.

He claims to have caught that enthusiasm from his friend Gary Figgins of Leonetti Cellar down the road in Walla Walla. They got to know each other as fellow drill sergeants in the army reserve and spent many hours together talking wine. When Figgins turned his experiments and home winemaking into a commercial operation, Small was there to help, and finally decided to try it on his own.

Small's approach was very different from the cautious, corporate approach of most wineries, which dictates a multitude of grape varieties, cost-effective winemaking, "popular-style" wines, price points. Small's wines, principally Cabernet Sauvignon and Chardonnay, are made like jet fighters, without regard to cost or compromise on detail. Oak is an example. Small admits to "pretty strong feelings" about French oak (all his wines spend some time in new French oak) and shakes his head at those who claim American oak (which is much cheaper) can produce the same quality. "Look," he says, "the guys at Lafite and Latour are making the best wine they can make; if American oak were the best, they would be using it." Case closed.

Like that of most small producers, his approach is very hands-on. After trying to explain how much his Cabernet needs to punched down during fermentation, he gives up—"You have to feel the process; you just know." In the vineyard one wouldn't be surprised to hear him call each vine by name. Some grow more vigorously, some are more straggly; Small notes each of them. Other vineyards are crowded with weeds and grass—his is immaculate. "I work hard at this." Watching him tinker with an antique tractor, hand-cranking it repeatedly to get it started, one tends to believe him. For several years, before new water tanks were installed above the vineyard, Small had to haul water by truck to the top of the hill to irrigate his young vines.

There's probably no other winery in the state that does so consistently well with its two top wines, but Small claims to have no secrets. It's just a matter of buying grapes from vineyards with ridiculously low yields, using all new French oak for aging, making a severe selection of barrels for his best wines, and blending wines from different vineyards. Perhaps this last point is the secret: Aside from a paltry ten acres of Chardonnay, Small has no grapes of his own, so he must buy each harvest, sometimes from as many as five different vineyards for Cabernet Sauvignon. In every vintage, he says, one thing stands out: No matter how good a wine from an individual vineyard may turn out, "the finest wine is always a blend."

His almost instant success surprises and delights him (he's amazed at the rock star treatment he gets at some wine events—"crazy stuff"); he started out with a view to the long term. "I don't plan to make a success of this for myself—if it's a success, that will be something for my children to enjoy." That's the European approach, building from one generation to the next. At forty-two, Small is still a young man, still looking forward to seeing the local wine industry grow from its present infancy. He stands on a little ridge at the top of his vineyard (a small green patch on the broad brown shoulder of hill), pointing out all the potential sites for grapevines in this little valley. He grins broadly. "I love it, I just love it."

When the Wallaces began making wine in the early seventies in a small warehouse in Prosser, Washington, they *were* the Yakima Valley wine industry. Winemaker Mike Wallace grew up in the Seattle area, where his father was a police detective, but after his training in enology at California's Davis campus, he and his whole family migrated to eastern Washington (highly unusual for urban folk) to plant a new vineyard named Hinzerling near Prosser.

Prosser is a small, leafy town two thirds of the way down the Yakima Valley from Yakima to Richland, butted up against the rolling brown Horse Heaven Hills. Now home to five wineries, it still doesn't have much in the way of tourist amenities, and is even short on fast-food places. Outside of town, on the gently inclining slopes to the north, grow hops, wheat, and Concord grapes, with an occasional vinifera vineyard. The Wallaces planted their first vines in 1972, hand-watering to get them started, then suffered through a very tough winter (to which the valley is prone) that killed off about two thirds of the vines. Discouraged by this blow to their dream, they were told by a local expert to "go replant them—this is agriculture."

Everything was a struggle in the early years, but for a time it seemed the sky was the limit for these new premium Washington wines. Hinzerling tried to expand in the early eighties, just when a lot of new wineries were starting, but discovered the returns were meager. "We

American Wines of the Northwest

were making more money, or at least losing less, and having more fun making less wine," notes Mike. So the Wallaces cut back on production and went back to tried and true marketing—selling wine directly from the winery and driving truckloads themselves across the mountains to selected outlets. But the effort took its toll. "I spent sixteen years on the winery and did everything I wanted—and I spent a lot of time working real hard."

So did Mike's parents, Jerry and Dee. The Hinzerling winery, on a dusty road at the edge of town, was not designed to attract tourists, but visitors always got a cheery welcome from Dee, who held court in the tiny tasting room where, if she liked your looks, she might bring out something special from the "library." Jerry, lanky and fit looking in his rubber boots, did an amazing amount of labor both in the vineyard and the winery. But when the decision was made in 1988 to sell the winery, the older Wallaces were relieved. They hadn't planned to be working seven days a week for the rest of their lives—now there's more time to spend at their winter place in Arizona.

Mike has been actively involved in the Washington wine industry for fifteen years, has served as a spokesman for the wineries, and has provided guidance for many newer wineries, but he doesn't have the look of a mover and shaker. He sports a drooping mustache, hair that falls loosely over his forehead, and a perpetual squint, even when he's not in the sun, which gives him the look of a man sizing things up. Mostly what he has sized up is Cabernet Sauvignon, his first love. (Hinzerling has a purple sweatshirt with the slogan "Life is a Cabernet"). Like most wineries, Hinzerling started out making a little bit of everything, but other varietals gradually fell by the wayside, until it was pretty much Cabernet here (though Hinzerling has produced some spectacular dessert wines as well). Mike's palate favors blockbuster wines, and although he continued to turn out a more forward blend of Cabernet,

Merlot, and Malbec, it's the regular Cabernet Sauvignon that shows his style best. The wines tend to be so hard and tannic in their youth that they have been dismissed by some experts, and vintages are held back much longer here than at other wineries, but at ten years these wines have blossomed when their contemporaries are decrepit. The wines haven't changed much over the years—Mike's not the kind of guy to try to be fashionable.

If he were to do it over again (not a likely prospect in the near future, though he is doing some consulting), he would focus on one wine—probably a Cabernet blend. But the sweet wines continue to intrigue—perhaps a port, perhaps a fortified Orange Muscat.

Like Bill Preston, Mike Wallace was a pioneer, naïve perhaps, certainly undercapitalized. Today in both Washington and Oregon people keep looking over their shoulders, a little apprehensive about the "big money" that rumors keep saying is about to move in. Certainly wine folk are much more sophisticated about selling these days. Maybe, as some wine people say, making the wines is the easy part. Maybe so, but there's an awful lot of sweat and love in these wines.

2

A BRIEF HISTORY

hile it's true that the story of Northwest wine is a story of remarkable growth in a short thirty-year stretch, it's also true that grapes have been grown and made into wine over a much longer period in this region. California had Spanish missionaries who brought the grape-growing traditions of Europe to the new land; in the Northwest those same traditions arrived with French, German, and Italian immigrants who quickly saw that the fertile land and mild climate ought to be wonderful for vines and grapes. Unfortunately, the restrictions of Prohibition and changing consumer preferences choked off the early wine industry in the region, until it was revived by a new round of "pioneers" in the 1950s and 1960s.

WASHINGTON

The first grapes in the state were planted around 1825 at Fort Vancouver, on the Columbia River, by traders working for the Hudson's Bay Company, though it's not known whether or not they made wine from the grapes. But there were certainly vines planted at Fort Walla Walla by French settlers before the arrival of Marcus Whitman—

these vines may predate the first plantings in the Napa Valley. In any case, a commercial winery operated in the Walla Walla Valley in the 1860s and 1870s. Italian immigrants in the area are also known to have grown grapes, while in 1871 a family of German immigrants planted vinifera vines in the area of Yakima—some of which are still producing.

In the western part of the state, Lambert Evans, a Confederate Civil War veteran, planted labrusca grapes on Stretch Island, at the southern end of Puget Sound, around 1870, selling the grapes at market in the state capital, Olympia. Again, it's not clear whether he made wine or not. In the 1890s, this vineyard was bought by Adam Eckert, a settler from New York, who developed a strain of the Campbell Early grape that he named Island Belle, and that is still being used for commercial wine (see Hoodsport Winery in Part Two).

Grape growing in the arid Columbia and Yakima valleys had to wait for early irrigation efforts, but by the turn of the century there were small plantings of both European and American grapes in what is now the Tri-Cities area. In 1914 William Bridgman, who had been active in bringing irrigation to the Sunnyside area in the Yakima Valley, planted his first grapes. Having survived Prohibition by selling grapes for the table and for home winemakers, Bridgman opened Upland Winery (later called Santa Rosa) in 1934. The wines were, according to wine historian Leon Adams, not very good, and the winery closed in 1968, but it did use some European vinifera grapes, including Muscat, Riesling, and Semillon. The year 1934 also saw the beginnings of two other wineries, Pommerelle and Nawico, which would eventually be transformed into Chateau Ste. Michelle.

The truth is, the sizable wine industry that grew up in Washington following the end of Prohibition in 1933 is something most Washington wine lovers would like to forget. Cheap, sweet, fortified wines of the type favored on Skid Row, made from Concord grapes and other fruit, were produced by the millions of gallons by the Pommerelle and Nawico companies. In 1947, twenty-one Washington wineries sold a record total of almost 2.8 million gallons of wine; by contrast, annual sales forty years later (by then mostly of premium varietals) were 2.6 million gallons.

The Concord grapes are still there, their thick, unruly, dark green foliage much more noticeable in parts of the Yakima Valley than vinifera vines. Today they go mostly into grape juice (and sometimes fetch a better price than their vinifera cousins). And the loganberry farm (one of the largest of its kind in the world) that produced fruit for Hadassim kosher wines is still on Puget Sound's Whidbey Island—today it provides the fruit for Whidbeys Loganberry Liqueur.

Ironically, immediately after the repeal of Prohibition there began another legislative movement that probably did as much to hinder the development of a premium wine industry in the state—protectionism. In 1935 state wineries were permitted to sell directly to wholesalers and taverns while out-of-state wine had to go through the newly formed Liquor Control Board. This was the first of a series of restrictive measures designed to protect the small state industry against "foreign" (read "California") competition. As a result, outside wines were few and expensive for the state's consumers, who had little opportunity to improve their palates, and the Washington industry, increasingly committed to making cheap Concord wine, had little incentive to improve its product. These forgettable Concords gave the state a poor reputation for its wines, providing endless material for cartoonists' jokes and snide remarks about wines for down-and-outs.

Nevertheless, there were experimenters in vinifera wines. Julian Steenbergen, winemaker at Upland in the thirties and forties, made the first blends from vinifera grapes. In 1954 Pommerelle and Nawico merged to form American Wine Growers and the first acres of the vinifera grape Grenache were planted to produce a rosé. The first commercial plantings of vinifera had been in 1951, but these grapes were simply blended into fortified wines. By the sixties, the state's agricultural research station at Prosser was making experimental vinifera wines, there were two wineries preparing to make premium vinifera wines, and the legislature was beginning to remove some of the restrictions that had protected the old Concord industry.

The watershed year for Washington premium wines was probably 1967. That year saw both the first commercial crop for Associated Vintners and the first vintage for Ste. Michelle Vineyards to be directed by André Tchelistcheff, the California wine consultant who has had enormous influence on the development of Washington's wines.

Associated Vintners was founded by a group of scholarly professionals, mostly professors at the University of Washington in Seattle, who were enticed into forming a winery by their love of home winemaking. Dr. Lloyd Woodburne, one of the founders and a psychology professor at the University of Washington, had been making wines in his basement since 1951, a year's study in Germany having drawn him to the pleasures of wine. In 1962 Woodburne joined with Philip Church and some others to form the AV group. Church was a meteorologist who studied thirty years' worth of weather records in the Yakima Valley and decided that Sunnyside, in the heart of the valley, got just the same amount of sunshine and heat as Beaune, in France's Burgundy region. Based on this study, the grapes chosen for the new vineyard were the classic ones of the Burgundy and Alsace districts of France (areas noted for their cool, marginal climates). Chardonnay, Pinot Noir, Gewürztraminer, and Riesling, with Semillon and Cabernet Sauvignon thrown in for good measure, were the foundation of this new vinifera planting.

The vineyard prospered, and eventually the volume of production threatened to overwhelm the capacity of a small group of amateur winemakers. They decided to open a commercial winery and in 1967 produced their first commercial crop under the AV label. Setting the pattern for so many small Northwest wineries to come, they started off doing all the work themselves, hand-hauling grapes and must in a rented warehouse in a Seattle suburb filled with old equipment.

Leon Adams, the well-known writer on American wine, notes his own role in the "discovery" of Washington wines in his book *The Wines of America:* "In 1966, I visited the Yakima Valley and saw several vineyards of such pedigreed varieties as Cabernet Sauvignon and Pinot Noir. I was amazed to find the wineries were wasting these costly grapes, mixing them with Concord in nondescript port and burgundy blends. The only fine Vinifera wine I tasted on that trip was a Grenache rosé made by a home winemaker [Lloyd Woodburne] in Seattle." But Adams suggested to Victor Allison, manager of American Wine Growers, that a consultant like André Tchelistcheff might be of use to the state's industry.

Tchelistcheff is one of the graying gurus of California wine, a courtly gentleman of old-world charm and a razor-sharp palate. Born in Moscow and educated in Europe, he was largely responsible for fashioning the great Cabernets of Beaulieu Vineyard and has acted as a consultant to many a fledgling California winery. He admits that he was initially "very pessimistic" about the potential for Washington wines. Having been persuaded by Allison to visit the state, he tasted a number of the commercial wines then available and pronounced his negative judgment. However, a three-year-old homemade Gewürztraminer served to him (with salmon) by the Associated Vintners' Philip Church was all it took to incite enthusiasm. "It was such a delicate wine I went crazy about the quality," he later recalled. It was, he felt, one of the finest Gewürztraminers yet produced in this country. He signed on to help American Wine Growers produce its vinifera wines.

By 1967, under Tchelistcheff's direction, American Wine Growers made its first varietal wines under the Ste. Michelle label. At the same time many new varieties were planted as an experiment, and a huge vineyard at Cold Creek, north of Richland in the Columbia Basin, was established.

These early plantings were plagued by the one climatic negative in eastern Washington—deathly cold winters. The winter of 1978–79 was the worst, with months of temperatures in the teens and lower and a cold, dry wind. Ste. Michelle lost two thirds of its vines; other growers didn't fare so badly, but the lessons learned in that winter have been beneficial to all of them. The hard winters have been tamed, though late frosts still cause occasional heavy bud damage.

The early seventies saw the beginnings of a number of new vineyards and small wineries in various parts of the state: the Wallace family's Hinzerling Vineyards in the Yakima Valley, Preston Cellars and the huge Sagemoor and Bacchus vineyards near Pasco, Bingen Wine Cellars (now Mont Elise) in the Columbia Gorge, and Salishan Vineyards in southwestern Washington. In 1974 Ste. Michelle was sold to U.S. Tobacco, the chewing tobacco company, which began a massive building program that continues to this day and that has certainly done more than anything else to bring Washington wines to national attention.

By 1988 there were 11,000 acres of vinifera vineyards in the state, with almost 70 wineries producing close to 5 million gallons of wine—almost all of it in the premium varietal category. Compared to California, or even just to

Napa Valley, this is still small potatoes, so to speak, but a tremendous achievement over a stretch of thirty years.

OREGON

As noted above, traders of the Hudson's Bay Company at Fort Vancouver (across the Columbia from the greater Portland area) may have been the first to cultivate grapes in the Northwest—the diary of an early settler remarks on grapevines growing on a house at the fort. Grapes were also among the crops planted by settlers in the fertile Willamette Valley in the middle of the nineteenth century, although most of these were probably table grapes. The 1860 census reports 2,600 gallons of wine produced in the state. By the turn of the century, Frank Reuter, a German immigrant, was making prizewinning wines at his estate in the northern Willamette, near Forest Grove; his was one of a number of wineries in the area, with a total of about 300 acres of vines under cultivation. With Prohibition all the vines were pulled out, and at the end of Prohibition, Reuter's teetotaling daughters decided not to replant. (This property was eventually bought in 1966 by Charles Coury, a modern wine pioneer and one of the first to see the potential for vinifera grapes in the region. Coury's winery went out of business but the property recently re-emerged as Laurel Ridge Winery.)

There were also vineyards in southern Oregon, planted, again, by European immigrants with a tradition of home winemaking. Figures from 1880 show that Jackson County, the area around Medford and Ashland in the extreme south of the state, was producing 15,000 gallons of wine a year. By 1890 there was a commercial winery in the Umpqua Valley, near Roseburg, run by a German immigrant, Adam Doerner, which continued to make wine (interrupted only by Prohibition) until 1965.

Following Prohibition, there was a short-lived boomlet

in Oregon wineries (twenty-eight wineries by 1938, producing a million gallons of wine), most of them making fruit and berry wines, but only Honeywood and Henry Endres among all of those have survived to the present day—by 1960 the boom in California wine had dried up support for a local wine industry.

But in 1961 Richard Sommer planted his first grapevines at Hillcrest Vineyard, near Roseburg. "It was maybe foolhardy, or something like that, planting grapes out here," he says. "I don't know if I did it to prove a point, or what." Sommer's grandfather had planted a tiny three-acre vineyard years before, near Ashland in the Rogue Valley, but he never made any wine himself (the grapes were sold). When Sommer studied viticulture at the University of California at Davis, he says he was taught that wine grapes couldn't be grown in Oregon. "But I saw these big old grapevines, big and knotty and gnarly, but still producing, had survived. . . ." So he took a chance and planted his own grapes. Sommer's primary varietal was, and remains, Riesling, and despite the attention that Willamette Valley Pinot Noir has received in recent years, Riesling remains one of the most widely planted grapes in the state.

At about the same time, Charles Coury, another graduate of the enology program on the Davis campus, was planting his new vineyard in the Tualatin Valley west of Portland, determined to make great dry white wine, for which he thought the Roseburg area too warm. Other small growers began in the sixties and early seventies: the Bjellands near Roseburg, Richard Erath near Newberg in the Willamette, the Ponzis near Portland, and David Lett, of Eyrie Vineyards, in McMinnville.

Lett studied viticulture at the University of California at Davis, but he decided that his first love, Pinot Noir, would never do well in California's climate. Traveling to Europe, he studied firsthand which grapes were suited to which regional climates, and when he returned to the United

States he decided, against the advice of all the experts, that the Willamette Valley was the right place for the wines he wanted to make (though his specific location in the Dundee Hills on the west side of the valley was largely the result of happy accident). He started off small in 1970, and the winery really hasn't grown much in the intervening years. But the whole industry has grown, thanks in large part to Lett's example—he has helped a number of other winemakers get started and inspired them with the high quality of his wines.

The event that really put Oregon on the wine-producing map deserves a special note. Gault Millau, a heavyweight publisher in the French gastronomic world, sponsored a wine competition in 1979 that saw American entries do very well. Robert Drouhin, owner of one of the large and prestigious Burgundy houses, was displeased with the results and the way the competition was handled. In 1980 he offered a rematch on his home turf, against his own hand-picked selection of the best that Burgundy had. The French won the Pinot Noir category—with a twenty-one-year-old Chambolle-Musigny, one of the great red wines of the world. But in second place, ahead of ten other top French and foreign wines, was Eyrie Vineyards Pinot Noir 1975 South Block Reserve. The French had just discovered their first real competition for red Burgundy, and the publicity-shy Lett had just become the Northwest's first wine superstar.

This story has an interesting afterword. Drouhin has taken a strong interest in the Oregon industry, visiting several times and sending daughter Véronique to work the grape harvest one year. In 1987, with help from several Oregon winemakers, including David Lett and David Adelsheim, the Drouhin firm purchased a 100-acre parcel of land in the hills near Lett's own vineyard in order to begin a significant new wine venture focused on Pinot Noir. Said Drouhin at the time, "I live in an old world where we follow tradition. Tradition means a lot of laws, and it is sometimes difficult to experiment. And here I could be in your new world, new frontier, [where] everyone retains the pioneer's mind. And that would be really great. ... It seems a bit pretentious, but I know that the quality of Oregon wines will be recognized throughout the world. ..." Oregon has clearly arrived on the international scene.

As in Washington, the eighties have seen tremendous growth in the Oregon industry, though starting from a much smaller base. By 1988 acres planted totaled 4,500 (having doubled in just a few years) and the number of wineries had surpassed 60. The Oregon industry has always been much smaller than Washington's and continues so today. There has never been an Oregon winery on the scale of a Ste. Michelle. The long-settled Willamette Valley is a patchwork of small farms and orchards, whereas the Yakima and Columbia valleys, which have flourished only in the last seventy years due to irrigation, are home to a number of large agricultural concerns. Just so, Willamette wineries are mostly small, family operations, while there are a number of large vineyards and wineries in eastern Washington. Given local geography, this seems unlikely to change.

IDAHO

It will come as a surprise to many that grape growing and winemaking in Idaho have nearly as old a history as they do in Washington and Oregon. As they did elsewhere, European immigrants brought their traditions with them when they settled in the Snake River Valley in the late nineteenth century. Lewiston, about halfway down the state, just on the Washington border, was home to several commercial vineyards established by Frenchmen Louis Delsol and Robert Schleicher. Delsol built his winery about 1875 and Schleicher several years later; their wines were good enough to win a number of honors across the country.

By 1909 there were at least three wineries in the Lewiston area, and in 1911 a Portland entrepreneur, James Moore, bought the properties of German winemaker Jacob Schaefer with the intention of building a large winery. Unfortunately, these plans fell victim to increasing pressure for Prohibition, as more and more Idaho counties voted to go dry well in advance of passage of the Volstead Act.

Today there is just one tiny winery in the Lewiston area, Camas (though there are some small vineyards in the nearby Clearwater Valley), and the center of wine activities has shifted south to the Snake Valley between Boise and Twin Falls. The impetus this time came not from immigrants but from a large fruit concern looking for diversification and a very determined winemaker, Bill Broich. The result was Ste. Chapelle Winery, which began operations only in 1975 and was until the eighties the only winery in the state. Today, with only a half-dozen commercial wineries, the Idaho wine industry is still in its infancy—and antidrinking sentiment is still strong, while the state lacks a strong wine-consuming market. If the Idaho industry is going to prosper, it will have to come from the "export" market, in which Ste. Chapelle has proven very effective.

Northwest wines would not have experienced successful growth without the enthusiastic support of wine drinkers in their respective states—Washington and Oregon in particular have high per capita rates of wine consumption and have been quite loyal to the local product. But today the production capacity for Northwest wines has outstripped the demand in the local market, and continued success will depend on exporting more wine. The challenge of the late 1980s is not just to make world-class wines, but to sell them in a highly competitive world market. Thirty years ago, California wines had the similarly difficult task of breaking into a national market dominated by French, German, and Italian wines (especially on the East Coast). They succeeded, but today Northwest wines face not only the traditional European imports, but imports from new world wine powers like Australia and Spain, as well as the now solidly entrenched California wines. New markets in the Far East, especially Japan, may help, but the Northwest will have to fight hard to carve out a domestic consumer niche, in order to be truly the next great world wine region.

3

CLIMATE, REGIONS, AND GRAPES

The Case for Northwest Wine

rapes are peculiar. Grow them in an "ideal" climate, with plenty of sunshine and warmth, rich soil, and plenty of water, and you get so-so wine. Grow them in a climate where they must struggle, where ripening is an iffy matter, in poor soil, and with too little water—and you get excellent wine. Champagne and Chablis are really too cool to grow grapes, and have funny, chalky soils. Burgundy is beset with late frosts, hailstorms, and fall rains. The Rhine Valley is also too cool, and occasionally an entire harvest is lost to poor weather. But in the good years, these areas produce some of the greatest wines in the world.

California's Central Valley is just about ideal for growing almost anything under the sun, and grapevines thrive there—producing table grapes and raisins and undistinguished wine grapes. But in the foggy valleys of northern California, not in the fertile bottomland but on the rocky, soil-poor hillsides, the best wine grapes in the state are grown.

The truth is, grapes love adversity, and the *true* ideal climate for a premium grape variety is the marginal climate, where the grapes will ripen only at the very end of the growing season, causing growers to watch the skies and bite their nails just about every year. In such a climate the grapes ripen slowly, develop a complexity of flavors, and maintain the crucial balance of sugar and acid that is essential to fine wines. The risk, of course, is that there will be years when the grapes won't ripen. It used to be that as many as three or four of every ten vintages in regions like Burgundy and Bordeaux would produce mediocre wine; advanced winemaking techniques have improved the odds, but even so, not every vintage is a great one.

The case is much the same in the Northwest, particularly in Oregon. Here, cool cloudy summers and wet autumns are not uncommon, and the wines from such years, though they are perfectly drinkable, will not show the best flavors of the grape. The climate in eastern Washington is more reliable—here the problem is more usually late-spring frosts, which kill the new buds on the vines and reduce the crop. Nevertheless, when the weather cooperates, the grapes of Washington and Oregon (and, increasingly, Idaho) produce intensely varietal wines, precisely because of the long, relatively cool growing season. They may not have the degree of alcohol of California wines; they may not leap out of the glass with forward fruit. But neither do the great wines of Europe. The grape-growing climate of most of California is basically Mediterranean, and most of the great wines of Europe come not from the Mediterranean but from the more northerly limits of the grape-growing region. Europeans have long known that grapes with higher acids and lower sugar, grapes that are mature but not overly ripe, make the best, most balanced, and longest-lived wines. Grape growers in the Northwest are drawing on that long experience.

It is not surprising, then, that the grapes that do best in the Northwest are those which come from the cool growing areas of Europe: Johannisberg (or White) Riesling from the Rhine and Mosel valleys of Germany, Lemberger from central Germany, Gewürztraminer and Pinot Gris from France's Alsace, Pinot Noir and Chardonnay from Burgundy, Chenin Blanc from the Loire Valley of France, and Sauvignon Blanc, Semillon, Cabernet Sauvignon, and Merlot from Bordeaux. In fact, devotees of California wine will discover that several of these varieties, considered inferior because they produce dull or unbalanced wines in the heat of California, have totally different personalities in the Northwest. Pinot Noir is rich, delicately fruity, and velvety—not raisiny and harsh as so often in California. Chenin Blanc is racy, crisp, and honeyed—not bland and heavy. The only varieties that have not proven successful are those characteristic of the Mediterranean regions: hot-weather grapes like Zinfandel, Nebbiolo, Barbera—but even these may find a home here, in the proper locations, and experimental plots are proving very promising.

The premium grape industry in these Northwest states is still young, and the future may well bring new grapes and new wines, as well as new growing areas. Although grapes have been grown in the Northwest for over a century, it was not until thirty years ago that a serious premium wine industry based on European (vinifera) grape varieties began. The Northwest industry is still dwarfed by the California industry—but remember that thirty years ago, California premium wine was considered in its infancy, too. Intense experimentation with grape-growing and winemaking techniques and rapid developments in wine technology have led to spectacular changes in California. The same is happening in the Northwest, but even more quickly.

Oregon Wine

Although Oregon and Washington tend to get lumped together in the category of Northwest wine, the climate and thus the wines of the Willamette Valley (or the Ump-

Wine Grape Acreage: Washington and Oregon

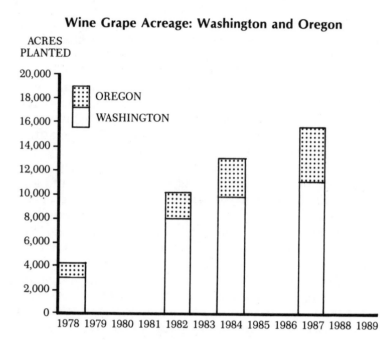

ACRES PLANTED

Legend: OREGON, WASHINGTON

Years shown: 1978, 1979, 1980, 1981, 1982, 1983, 1984, 1985, 1986, 1987, 1988, 1989

qua Valley) are quite different from those of the growing regions of eastern Washington. And quite different from California, too, of course. Although we may think of Oregon as being relatively northerly for grape growing, it lies at just about the same latitude (45 to 46 degrees north) as the Bordeaux region of France (though it has a different climate) and a good 100 miles or so south of the latitudes occupied by Burgundy, Alsace, or Champagne. By contrast, the Napa Valley of California, for example, at 38 to 38½ degrees of latitude, is no farther north than northern Sicily or southern Spain.

Latitude, however, is hardly the whole story, though it does mean relatively long hours of sunshine in the summer. To look at climate as a vineyardist does, one must compare degree-days, which measure total heat over a growing season. (The higher the number of degree-days, the warmer the growing season.) By this yardstick, the Willamette comes in between 1,600 and 2,300 degrees, a fairly wide range, which testifies to the variability of the climate from one year to the next (as well as to different "microclimates"—small areas of relative warmth or coolness). This is considerably cooler than Napa, at 2,700 to 3,400 degrees (though some subregions, Carneros, for example, drop as low as 2,500.) The average in the Willamette is about 2,100 degrees, just a bit cooler than the season in Burgundy, at about 2,400.

The Willamette River, running roughly north and south, lies to the west of the Cascade Mountains and therefore its valley ought to have a maritime climate—moderate temperatures and rain. But the low-lying Coast Range, which separates the valley from the Pacific, blocks out some of the cool flow of ocean air and allows the region more warmth and less rain than, say, western Washington—especially in the summer and fall seasons. Summer temperatures can easily get as high as California's. (In August 1987, French participants in the first International Pinot Noir Conference listened to Oregonians explain about their cool climate and then had to endure sipping wine in temperatures that hit 108 degrees.) Although the area gets considerably more rain than any grape-growing area in California, the rain comes mainly from November to April, and summers tend to be quite dry. (This also represents a contrast to the Continental growing regions of Burgundy and Alsace with which the Willamette is frequently compared, for they tend to get quite a bit of rain in spring and summer—not to mention hailstorms.)

The marginal climate requires careful vineyard management. The larger the grape crop, the more slowly it ripens, so growers may go through the vineyard in August cutting off as many as one third of the grape clusters, thus reducing the crop. Some growers also remove leaves during the summer (especially on vigorous varieties like Chardonnay), both to let more sunlight in and to guard against bunch rot in the event of fall rains—fewer leaves mean the grapes can dry more quickly. A few growers are experimenting with planting vines much closer together than in California, reducing the number of grapes per vine but allowing them to ripen earlier.

Indeed, the principal problems to bedevil growers in northern Oregon are the sometimes relentless early fall rains. Vineyard owners have learned to expect a week or so of rain in September or early October; with patience they can wait it out, as growers in France and Germany have had to do for centuries. (In 1986 growers who waited out two weeks of rain harvested healthy and mature fruit.) It may even have the salutory effect of reinvigorating the vines after a very dry summer. But there are those seasons (like 1984) when the rains arrive and settle in for weeks. In 1984, the summer was just about perfect, but rain came in mid-September, just as the grapes should have been finishing their ripening. It continued steadily through October and into November, finally forcing even the most patient growers to pick in the rain. Rot was endemic in the 1984 crop, and those grapes that escaped the rot were swollen with rainwater, which dilutes flavor. (With such a deluge to contend with, that vintage produced a surprising number of decent, lighter wines.)

A vineyard's site can make a considerable difference in how the grapes grow. Many Willamette vineyards take advantage of southern-facing slopes on the myriad of hills that run through the valley. Not only do these get the advantage of better exposure to the sun, but several hundred feet of elevation off the valley floor protects the grapes from spring and fall frosts (cold air settles). But individual vineyards are still so widely scattered among the 5,000 square miles of the region that it's difficult to compare microclimates of particular vineyards closely or to decide yet which subregions are best for which grapes.

Perhaps the most annoying headache for many growers in the Willamette is migratory birds, especially robins. Unfortunately, they tend to arrive in the area on their way south, just about the time the grapes ripen in the fall. They can easily strip a vineyard of ripe grapes in a day or so, and once established, they are difficult to get rid of. Rarely deterred by any technologically advanced scarecrows, they are also cooly indifferent to withering fire from shotgun-toting growers—there are numerous horror stories of hungry robins munching their way through the vines right next to hundreds of bodies of fallen comrades.

Total acreage in Oregon remains relatively tiny, but is growing quickly. A 1987 report from Oregon State University noted that the number of producing acres of wine grapes had doubled from 1984 to 1986. Tons of grapes crushed jumped from 4,300 to 7,200 from 1986 to 1987 alone. Total acres planted had reached 4,500 by 1987, with more than a quarter of that planted to Pinot Noir. The next two most widely planted varieties are Chardonnay and Riesling, with much smaller quantities of a number of other grape types. Moreover, a state survey in 1987 found that almost 600 more acres are planned for planting in 1988 and 1989, with almost two thirds of that committed to Pinot Noir. (Chardonnay and the newly popular Pinot Gris will also get significant additions; Riesling very little.)

Looking at the state county by county, one may be surprised that Morrow County in the hot and dry northern section of eastern Oregon has the highest number of acres—but very few of these are yet in production. It may be that eastern Oregon, which shares many of the climatic characteristics of Washington's Columbia Basin, will prove to be an equally fruitful home to wine grapes. Yamhill, Washington, and Polk are the next three most heavily planted counties; all of these are in the northern section of the Willamette Valley, to the west and south of Portland. The southern counties Douglas, Jackson, and Josephine also have significant plantings.

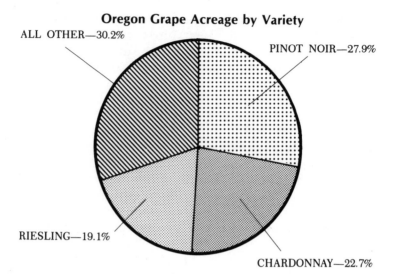

Oregon Grape Acreage by Variety

ALL OTHER—30.2%

PINOT NOIR—27.9%

RIESLING—19.1%

CHARDONNAY—22.7%

Grape Variety	Acreage, 1986	% of Total
Pinot Noir	1,074	28
Chardonnay	873	23
White Riesling	736	19
Gewürztraminer	274	7
Cabernet Sauvignon	208	5
Müller-Thurgau	164	4
Sauvignon Blanc	120	3
misc. white	116	3
Pinot Gris	102	3
Merlot	75	2
misc. red	50	1
Chenin Blanc	49	1
Zinfandel	4	0
total	3,845	100

Source: Oregon State University Department of Agriculture and Resource Economics, 1987

American Wines of the Northwest

Oregon was quite unprepared for the explosion of interest in its wines that hit after the 1983 vintage was released. For years the few pioneering wineries had been producing fine Pinot Noir, but all would agree that it was a tough sell. Riesling was the popular wine (almost all of it sold to Oregonians); Pinot went to scattered lovers of French Burgundy in various states, when it went at all. It wasn't so many vintages ago that a large Washington concern offered Knudsen Erath several dollars a gallon for its Pinot Noir juice—to blend into other wines. Owner Bill Blosser of Sokol Blosser Winery notes, with a sense of wonder, that when his '83 Pinots were released, the winery already had a ten-year supply of past vintages in the warehouse, calculated at the rate the wines had been selling up until then. Then came the national publicity, and all those wines sold out in eight months.

Oregon Grape Acreage by Region

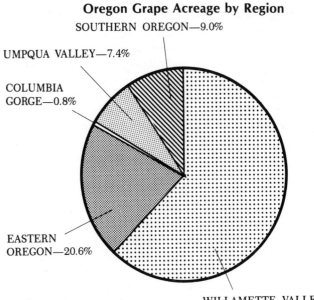

SOUTHERN OREGON—9.0%

UMPQUA VALLEY—7.4%

COLUMBIA GORGE—0.8%

EASTERN OREGON—20.6%

WILLAMETTE VALLEY—62.2%

Now the problem is meeting the demand. The fact that about two thirds of the wine produced in the state is sold in the state (much of it to thirsty Portlanders who can make quick wine-buying trips to nearby wineries) means not much is available for the rest of the country. Many of the acclaimed '85 Pinot Noirs from smaller producers sold out in a month after release. The wines are on allocation out of state, meaning that distributors don't get nearly as much as they want and have to ration the wines among their retail and restaurant customers. Indeed, some of these wines may be more readily available on the East Coast than closer to home, as the wineries try to maintain their national reputation. High prices have not deterred customers. Three years ago the best Oregon Pinots were available for around $10 a bottle; now most are in the $15 to $18 range and will probably go higher. The reason, of course, has to do with the extremely limited availability of the French Burgundies that these Pinots compete with. Prices for good Burgundy begin around $20 and zoom skyward.

Supply will get better. Although it's a good three years' time from planting a vine to its first few grapes, production of maturing vines planted in the early eighties will provide a lot more fruit in the next few vintages. For example, Knudsen Erath nearly doubled its production of Pinot Noir from 1985 to 1986, to more than 10,000 cases. In 1987 production jumped to 15,000 cases, making this winery one of the largest producers of varietal Pinot Noir in the country. Sokol Blosser, the second-largest producer of Pinot in the state, made 3,300 cases of Pinot in 1985 and increased that to 7,000 in 1987. But a number of small producers in Oregon (Eyrie is a good example) are content with their tiny production even though they could sell a lot more. Pinot will probably never be a wine for the mass market.

The relentless clamor for Oregon Pinot Noir has also caused many wineries to release their wines before they

American Wines of the Northwest

really wanted to. Pinot Noir as a wine has an unstable development in the bottle—showing well now, poorly a little later, and then bouncing back again. Although some Pinots show lovely fruit early on, it usually takes three or four years for them to develop their characteristic perfume and velvet texture. The '83 Oregon Pinots were very forward and attractive wines and have remained so, but the '85s, with deeper tannins and more reticent fruit, clearly need some more time. Most of the '85s were released two years after the vintage, probably a bit early, though a number of reserve wines, as well as regular bottlings from a few producers like Amity and Rex Hill, were held three years.

The same might be said about Chardonnay. American consumers are so used to California Chardonnay, which really needs to be drunk within the first few years of the vintage, that they may be reluctant to let Oregon Chardonnay develop. But develop it does—showing some of the butterscotch flavors that some French white Burgundies acquire with age. A few wines that seem excessively tart when young will soften perceptibly with several years under their belts, and most top-quality Chardonnays will mature well for at least five or six years.

Although Riesling is the third most popular grape in Oregon vineyards, there is a limited market for it outside the state. Wineries like it—it is easy to make a lovely, crisp, fruity Riesling from Oregon grapes, and it's popular among the local population. But nationwide, Riesling doesn't have a premium reputation, so as Oregon's national market increases in importance, it's likely that this varietal will lose importance, particularly given intense competition from the flood of Riesling produced in Washington.

So far Oregon has not developed a "jug wine" industry. Given the demand for its premium wines and the high prices its grapes now fetch, this may be an unlikely development, though newly planted vineyards in the hot and arid eastern part of the state could change that. In any case, Oregon has some of the strictest wine-labeling laws in the country. Generic names like Burgundy and Rhine wine are forbidden, varietal names are strictly controlled (there's no "Johannisberg," only "White" Riesling), labels must indicate where the grapes came from, and at least 90 percent of wines labeled with a varietal name must be composed of that grape (the federal standard is 75 percent)—an exception being made for Cabernet Sauvignon, which may be 75 percent.

Given Oregon's newfound wine fame, it seems inevitable that larger wine operations from outside the state will move in, perhaps dramatically changing its laid-back, family winery image. The new Drouhin estate is evidence of that, as is the Crochad sparkling wine operation. Rumors have had a number of large California producers interested in Oregon land, and the first concrete evidence of that was the purchase late in 1988 of a large parcel of potential vineyard land in the southern Willamette Valley by Steve Girard of Girard Winery and Carl Doumani of Stags' Leap Winery. Initial plans call for eighty acres of Pinot Noir to be planted in 1989, with a winery to be built eventually. If this commitment is the beginning of a rush by Californians to buy still-inexpensive Oregon land, it could mark a real transition in the state's wine industry.

Washington Wine

There are now three official regional appellations in the state: Columbia Valley, Yakima Valley, and Walla Walla Valley. By far the largest is the Columbia appellation, which takes in much of the southeastern quadrant of the state. Much of this area is arid semidesert, requiring irrigation from the Columbia River, which meanders through the region. The Yakima Valley is a subsection of this area, a broad, incredibly fertile valley that is home to many of the state's profitable fruit and vegetable crops and now, increasingly, grapes. Walla Walla, in the southeastern corner of the state, is a relatively small region and home to only 100 or so acres of wine grapes.

Chateau Ste. Michelle has long made the claim on its bottles' labels that the latitude of Washington's growing regions is the same as that of Bordeaux, but this is misleading. First, the eastern Washington growing region, extending from roughly 46 to 47 degrees north, lies 75 miles or so north of Bordeaux (though it's the same as the Mâconnais and Beaujolais in eastern France); second, latitude is not the real story, or else Mongolia, too, would be famed for its claret. The climate of eastern Washington resembles neither Bordeaux's nor Burgundy's—it is hot in summer, cold in winter, and dry year round. But it does happen to be just about perfect for growing grapes, particularly those varieties that do well in northern Europe. And the potential is just beginning to be tapped. Although 10,-000 acres are planted with European grapes, the limits of possible vineyard sites are really set only by the availability of water—there are vast tracts of inexpensive land that could be planted.

In contrast to Oregon, viticulture in eastern Washington is very straightforward. The growing season presents few problems, other than late-spring frosts; there is little trouble with predators or pests; soils are easy to work with. Indeed, the main long-term concern may be overcropping—the tendency to let the vines give too many grapes, delaying ripening and leaving the vines vulnerable to winter damage. Growers and winemakers are beginning to work more closely on this, with wineries providing incentives for growers to get the best grapes, not just the most, out of vines.

In many ways the story of Washington wine is the story of one company, Chateau Ste. Michelle. Consider the num-

Washington Wine Sales

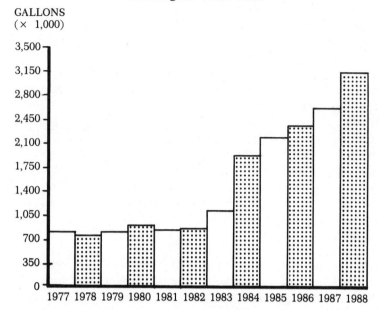

bers. In 1987 Washington's grape crop was 38,000 tons, which was a record and represented a substantial increase from previous years. Of that total, over 19,000 tons, or just about half, belonged to Stimson Lane, the holding company for both Chateau Ste. Michelle and Columbia Crest, its new sister winery. In many areas of the United States, Ste. Michelle, available in all fifty states, is the only Northwest wine on the shelves, and in 1986–87, when the new Columbia Crest line was launched on the national market, the winery spent millions of dollars on a glossy national TV campaign to make the name known. No other Northwest winery could spend anywhere near that amount of money on promotion, and yet every Washington winery acknowledges its debt to Ste. Michelle for letting the wine-drinking public know that the state is making premium

American Wines of the Northwest

table wines. The result: Out-of-state sales of many wineries have taken off.

But production has increased so quickly since 1983 that many wineries have been hard put to sell all the wine they have made. Oregon has been fortunate in that its "star" wine, Pinot Noir, arrived on the scene just as it was becoming increasingly popular nationwide. Washington's star wine is Johannisberg Riesling, and despite the quality of the Riesling produced here, the grape continues to be shunned by many upscale wine drinkers. Riesling is (temporarily) overplanted in Washington, prices are way down, and wineries are just about giving the stuff away. Unfortunately, it seems that many wineries, having decided that they couldn't make any money with top-quality Riesling, are producing Riesling that matches the public perception—a nice wine, but not of great interest. This reputation overshadows the efforts of winemakers producing excellent Riesling, and particularly those concentrating on the Late Harvest dessert style. As a class, these are without question the best white dessert wines, and dessert wine values, in the United States.

The last five years have also seen Chardonnay, Cabernet Sauvignon, and Merlot emerge as excellent varietals in eastern Washington, but here again Washington wineries face a challenge, as these are precisely the wines (with the possible exception of Merlot) with which California has established its reputation. Washington wineries have tried to make the case, and it's a strong one, that *their* wines are different, but the "California style" has a strong grip on America's palate. Nevertheless, the current Chardonnay fad, which has caused a shortage of that varietal in California, has proved a boon to Washington growers. In 1987 a few large California wineries bought Washington grapes, liked what they got, and in 1988 were back in force, buying up as much as they could find and inflating grape prices along the way.

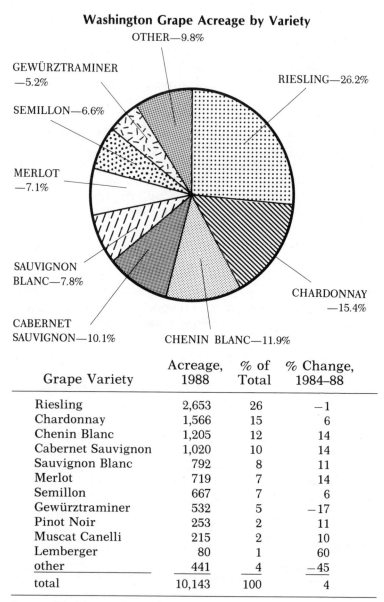

Washington Grape Acreage by Variety

OTHER—9.8%

GEWÜRZTRAMINER —5.2%

SEMILLON—6.6%

MERLOT —7.1%

SAUVIGNON BLANC—7.8%

CABERNET SAUVIGNON—10.1%

CHENIN BLANC—11.9%

RIESLING—26.2%

CHARDONNAY —15.4%

Grape Variety	Acreage, 1988	% of Total	% Change, 1984–88
Riesling	2,653	26	−1
Chardonnay	1,566	15	6
Chenin Blanc	1,205	12	14
Cabernet Sauvignon	1,020	10	14
Sauvignon Blanc	792	8	11
Merlot	719	7	14
Semillon	667	7	6
Gewürztraminer	532	5	−17
Pinot Noir	253	2	11
Muscat Canelli	215	2	10
Lemberger	80	1	60
other	441	4	−45
total	10,143	100	4

Source: Washington State University Agriculture Department Study, 1988.

American Wines of the Northwest

Figures from 1984 and 1988 indicate that while total acreage, which had gotten ahead of production capacity, has not grown much during this period, significant changes have taken place in the distribution of varieties. Red grapes (especially the unique Lemberger, growing from a tiny base) have increased their acreage substantially while white varieties have changed little. The figures show a trend away from Riesling and Gewürztraminer, though surprisingly Chenin Blanc, another grape in oversupply, has increased in acreage substantially over the four years.

Many of the state's winemakers are convinced that it is Cabernet Sauvignon that will make Washington famous. If you evaluate Washington Cabernet alongside California's you may miss the lush, plummy fruit and soft structure that many California Cabernets have. It may be, as André Tchelistcheff likes to point out, that Washington Cabernet grows differently from California's because it is grown on its own rootstock instead of being grafted onto American rootstock, as in California and Bordeaux.

But visitors from Bordeaux have been impressed: Peter Sichel, partner in Château Palmer, noted on a visit that Washington Cabernets "have a very similar structure to a ripe year in Bordeaux. Some of the complexities are fantastic. They're going to develop in the bottle for years." Like Bordeaux, these wines are often lean and hard in their youth, with subdued aromas. But they are deep wines that age slowly and gracefully.

In an attempt to crack the national market for Cabernet, Washington wineries took six of their best 1983 wines to New York in the spring of 1987 to challenge some of Bordeaux's best-known reds (also from the fine '83 vintage) in a blind tasting. The five judges were mostly writers, all from New York, and they came away impressed. The first six wines were all from Washington, led by Paul Thomas Cabernet; they finished ahead of Château Cos d'Estournel,

Château Lafite-Rothschild, and Château Langoa Barton, three of Bordeaux's classed growths. The French will surely scoff that of course the French wines were not nearly at their peak at such an early age. But neither, in all likelihood, are the Washington wines. In the near term, Merlot may be the wine that gives Washington a niche in the red wine market—the forward, fruity Merlots being produced can be very appealing and more drinkable early on than the Cabernets.

Sauvignon Blanc, Semillon, and some combination thereof are the other wines that should do the state proud, especially because they match the seafood theme of Northwest cuisine. Washington Sauvignon Blanc has begun to find a style, after much experimentation; and as Americans focus more on wine as food and wine with food, this light, crisp wine should attract more attention. Semillon, though currently out of favor, shows perhaps even greater potential.

Oregon is a state with innumerable tiny family wineries. Washington has two huge wineries and lots of small ones, but perhaps the strength of the state is in a half-dozen or so midsized wineries determined to make a national market for their wines. Most of them are offshoots of sophisticated large-scale farming operations; all are committed to a broad line of premium and superpremium wines; all have produced consistently excellent wines at very reasonable prices. The wines from these producers (e.g., Arbor Crest, Columbia, Covey Run, Hogue) are excellent examples of an emerging Washington style.

While, as in Oregon, there is no real jug wine industry in Washington (though Chateau Ste. Michelle offers a line of table wines called Farron Ridge), an increasing number of wineries are offering a second line of less expensive varietals. Marketing these "second-label" wines, a well-established practice in the California wine industry, offers wineries a chance to take wines they are less pleased with, or those made in a fairly simple fashion (with no oak aging, for example), and sell them at good prices without lowering the reputation of their premier lines. Often these wines are aimed specifically at the restaurant business, where they make an inexpensive "wine by the glass," and they tend to be fruity, simple, and slightly sweet. Such wines from top producers, though, are sometimes fine values and equal in quality to many "first-label" wines.

NORTHWEST GROWING REGIONS

Far from being one vast, soggy rain forest, the Northwest is a landscape of remarkable variety—there is rain forest and endless acres of Douglas fir, but also desert, arid high country, and fertile farmland. Two mountain ranges run north and south through Washington and Oregon, the Cascades and the Coast Range, and they divide the two states climatically. West of the Cascades, the weather is basically northern maritime—wet, mild winters and springs, dry but cool summers, variable autumns. But while the Cascades protect the western region from the extremes of continental weather, they also shield the inland region from rain. So the eastern parts of both Oregon and Washington as well as western Idaho are very dry, hot in the summer, cold in the winter, with autumn weather that sees wide temperature differences from day to night.

Columbia Valley (Washington)

Most of eastern Washington and Oregon, and part of Idaho, is a vast, relatively high (1,000 to 2,000 feet), and flat plateau, cut through by two massive river valleys, the Columbia and the Snake. Without the water from these rivers, the area would have remained what it had been from the days of the Oregon Trail—empty, dry rangeland. But federal hydroelectric projects in the thirties and forties brought irrigation to the land, and the natural fertility of the deep, loose soil has been brought to life. In the last fifty years the gently rolling hills have been covered with the velvety gold of ripening wheat; today, in addition to huge quantities of wheat, apples, and other crops, the Columbia Valley produces wine grapes.

Much of the Columbia Valley seems to have been designed perfectly for grape growing. From the Columbia River in the south, where it forms the border with Oregon, a series of roughly east-west ridges sweep north, like waves rolling onto a gentle beach. Each of these (from south to north, the Horse Heaven Hills, Toppenish Ridge, Ahtanum Ridge, Rattlesnake Hills, Yakima Ridge, Saddle Mountains) has a gradual slope on the southern side. Several of these areas, like Toppenish Ridge, have hardly been touched yet by vineyard development.

Although rainfall is light, less than ten inches per year, grapes don't need much water (though all the vineyards here require irrigation); low rainfall induces the vines to sink their roots deep, which increases the nutrients they take up from the soil. In all the great grape-growing areas of the world, the soil, whatever its makeup, is loose and light, and does not retain moisture. Eastern Washington is no exception—the soil is fine and sandy or loamy to a good depth.

Summers are hot, but because of the elevation, by the crucial ripening period in September and October, nights are cool even while days are warm—temperature differences of 40 degrees per day are not uncommon. Winters are cold, so the vines have to be carefully encouraged to go dormant well before the first frosts. Most of the Northwest's largest vineyards, including Columbia Crest's 2,000 acres at Paterson, are in the Columbia Valley, and the valley was awarded its own appellation in 1984. A wide range of grapes do well in this region, from Riesling and

Chenin Blanc to Chardonnay and Cabernet. Sites tend to be a little warmer than those in the Yakima Valley, but much depends on the particular location of the vineyard. Ripening conditions are highly reliable from year to year, since even very late harvests are rarely threatened by rain.

While heat unit measurements can be used to compare the Columbia Valley to, say, the Napa Valley or Bordeaux, they don't tell the whole story. What many local viticulturists remark on is the long daylight hours during the summer (due to the northerly latitude), which give the vines maximum photosynthesis—considerably more than Napa, for example. Experts feel this is a particular advantage with respect to crop yields: More sun allows the vines to ripen more grapes. While Europeans emphasize the link between low yield and high quality, eastern Washington growers claim not to have noted a direct relationship; here the limiting factor is the stress of high yields on the vines, making them prone to winter damage. But for growers this is grape paradise: large crops of high-quality grapes, year after year.

Yakima Valley (Washington)

The Yakima River runs through a broad, seventy-mile-long valley down to the Columbia, and this growing region shares much in common with the Columbia Valley, though it has its own appellation. From Yakima in the west, at about 1,000 feet in elevation, one drives through a patchwork of orchards—apples, cherries, peaches—through Zillah ("the apple of the valley's eye") to a small mound of hills at mid-valley, near Grandview and Sunnyside, where the valley seems wide open, and the gentle slope of the Roza stretches off to the north. From here the valley begins to narrow again, with the brown bulk of the Horse Heaven Hills closing in from the south, down to Prosser ("a pleasant town with pleasant people"). Just before the river empties into the Columbia near the Tri-Cities, Red Mountain (at about 400 feet) pokes into the valley from the north.

The Yakima Valley has long been a fruit basket for the state, producing much of the nation's mint and hops, as well as apples, peaches, apricots, cherries, asparagus, potatoes, and so on. The climate is somewhat more temperate than that of the Columbia Valley, particularly toward Yakima, at the western end of the valley, closer to the Cascades. Now home to twenty wineries and hundreds of acres of wine grapes, the Yakima Valley can be considered the heart of Washington wine country. Most of the vineyards are located between Prosser and Sunnyside, at mid-valley, but there are successful new vineyards at either end. Chenin Blanc, Semillon, Muscat, and Merlot all grow well here. Varieties like Cabernet that need a little more heat do particularly well toward the eastern end (with Red Mountain in particular beginning to garner a reputation), Chardonnay seems to do extremely well at mid-valley, while Riesling seems to do well almost anywhere. But specific sites defy geography: One of the most heralded Cabernet vineyards has been Red Willow, an isolated patch on the Ahtanum Ridge at the western end of the valley. Only as vineyardists experiment with different varieties at different sites will a true viticultural map of the valley emerge.

Walla Walla Valley (Washington and Oregon)

A historic area, the site of the Whitman Mission, Walla Walla was a welcome sight for the pioneers on the Oregon Trail—a sign that their long trek across the desert was over. It is a lush island in a sea of brown hills, the valley floor sitting at about 1,000 feet, slightly cooler than the surrounding area, and with significantly more rainfall than the Columbia Valley (the locals say that for every mile you go toward the eastern Blue Mountains, you get one more inch of rain per year). As in the Columbia Valley, soils are deep sandy loam. The appellation (the third official one in Washington) is small, stretching south slightly into Oregon, and so far little planted with grapes. Indeed, most of the prizewinning wines from Walla Walla wineries have been made from Columbia or Yakima Valley grapes.

The grapes that the Walla Walla Valley does produce, especially Chardonnay and Cabernet, have been excellent, but the scattered vineyards are almost all tiny. The largest holding, Seven Hills Vineyard in Milton-Freewater, is already acquiring a reputation for outstanding grapes. But wheat is still king here, and the prosperous wheat farmers (who get much higher yields than elsewhere in eastern Washington) don't seem much interested in developing alternative crops. Local grape enthusiasts keep looking wistfully across the valley and hoping for someone to plant some substantial vineyards.

Columbia Gorge (Washington and Oregon)

One of the most dramatically beautiful areas in the Northwest, this deep valley that the Columbia cuts through the Cascade Mountains bears a physical resemblance to the Rhine Valley in Germany. Vineyards rise high above the river, some on steep and terraced slopes. The weather is interesting: The heat of the semidesert Columbia Valley meets the cool, maritime air from the Pacific. Much of the time strong winds sweep down the valley from the east (Hood River is a wind-surfing mecca), and grapevines must be grown close to the ground to get maximum heat and to avoid wind damage.

There are a number of small vineyards planted on both the Oregon and Washington sides of the river. Riesling and Chardonnay both do well here, though there are plantings of warmer-climate varieties like Cabernet and even Zinfandel farther to the east, around The Dalles (which is at the far western edge of the Columbia Valley appellation). Some grape experts think the gorge ideally suited for Gewürztraminer, which so far has not been terribly successful in eastern Washington. There is also some Pinot Noir, though it's too early yet to judge whether winemakers will have the same success with the grape here that Willamette Valley growers have had. Most vineyards in this region are still young, so their potential is largely untapped.

Western Washington

Although the cool, damp climate of western Washington is better suited to berries and rhubarb (which can make very pleasant fruit wines), there are small vineyards dotted about. The problem is not summer temperatures, which can be quite hot, but the ripening season in the early fall, when the weather often turns wet and grapes can succumb quickly to rot. Western Washington growers are experimenting, therefore, with early-ripening grapes, many of them grape crosses developed recently by German viticulturists coping with the same kinds of problems. So far there are several little-known white varieties, with exotic names like Madeleine Angevine and Siegerrebe, as well as the better-known Müller-Thurgau, which have worked well, ripening in early September with low sugars but mature flavors. Wines made from these grapes tend to be low in alcohol, light in flavor, but with very flowery aromas somewhat reminiscent of Riesling (many of them have Riesling somewhere in their lineage).

Southwest Washington

A small section of southwestern Washington, in the Columbia Valley between Vancouver and Longview, deserves separate treatment, because it has a local climate significantly different from the rest of western Washington. Although it is on the west side of the mountains, practically in the shadow of Mount St. Helens, it gets more warmth than other areas and is almost an extension of the Willamette Valley, which begins on the south side of the Columbia. Here, in 100 or so acres of vineyard, Pinot Noir and Chardonnay, as well as several other cool-climate varieties, and even Chenin Blanc, have proven to do quite well. The harvest tends to be a week or so later than in the Willamette, which makes it that much riskier, but the wines of Salishan, the first commercial winery in the area, have shown that in good years the quality of the fruit can be very high.

Willamette Valley (Oregon)

Shaped like an elongated V, this valley stretches over 150 miles from the Columbia River in the north roughly to Eugene in the south and is the center of the state's young wine industry. It was the destination of many of the pioneers on the Oregon Trail and is long-established farming country, dotted with small towns that bear New England names and look as if they could be in New Hampshire. The valley is a patchwork of gently rolling hills covered with evergreens, fields of hay and seed-grasses, and orchards of nut trees (the Willamette is the filbert, or hazelnut, capital of the world). While the flatland is devoted to crops like seed-grass (the burning of grass fields lays a perpetual haze over the valley in the summer), many thousands of acres, on slopes that face south and west, are suitable for growing grapes, of which only a couple of thousand have been planted.

Vineyards in the Willamette tend to be small and are concentrated in the broad northern section, forty miles or so south and west of Portland. Two sets of hills, the Red Hills of Dundee and the Eola Hills, have several hundred acres of what have turned out to be excellent vineyards. Hillside slopes, especially those facing west and south, are preferred for several reasons: They receive sunlight more directly, especially from the low-lying autumn sun, and they are quicker to warm in the mornings and less subject to the harmful effects of cold air, which accumulates in valley bottoms. At the very northern end of the valley, west of Portland, lie more scattered vineyards, in the tributary Tualatin Valley. Farther south, there are clusters of vineyards near Corvallis and near Eugene, but there is clearly much land suitable for grape growing that has not been developed. The whole eastern side of the valley has very few vineyards, although it was this area that David Lett of Eyrie Vineyards first searched for a piece of acreage to buy. The problem is not microclimate—this section gets basically the same weather as the western side with, if anything, a bit less rain. But the parcels of land, much of it involved in seed farming, are much larger on average and not readily broken up—most grape growers are looking for 20 acres of land rather than 200, so the western side, with smaller parcels, has been more attractive economically.

Although there is considerable rain in the winter, summers can be hot (temperatures of 90 to 100 degrees are not uncommon), while autumns are usually cool but relatively dry. Those who suspected that this area would make a fine home for the varieties grown in Burgundy have proven to be correct: Both Pinot Noir and Chardonnay, the two principal grapes of the region, have done extremely well, as well as several other cool-climate whites, including Riesling, Gewürztraminer, and Pinot Gris. The growing season is long and the harvest is usually late, especially for Pinot Noir, but this only intensifies the varietal flavors of the grape. The one drawback is that in some years autumn rains come and stay, and the crop doesn't get completely ripe, or succumbs to rot. Nevertheless, doomsayers who predicted disastrous vintages one year out of three have turned out to be wrong, and even the early believers in Willamette Valley wine have been surprised at how successful they've been.

Umpqua Valley and Southern Oregon

The Umpqua and Rogue valleys are really two separate growing areas (only the Umpqua has its own appellation so far), though the small number of wineries in each makes it difficult to speak about general regional characteristics. Both rivers flow in a generally westerly direction, cutting their way through the low-lying Coast Range to the sea. The Umpqua looks like rangeland—grassy bottomland, hills spotted with pines, small ranches tucked here and there—and indeed, it's Oregon's sheep country. Not only has the Umpqua been settled for a long time, but it takes pride in being the "cradle of the Oregon wine industry," since the local Hillcrest Vineyard was the first premium grape winery established in the state, in 1961.

The climate is just slightly different from that of the Willamette Valley to the north—the Umpqua gets a couple of inches less rain and a little more sun. Harvest tends to be a week or so ahead of the Willamette, but the same grape varieties do well here—Chardonnay, Pinot Noir, Gewürztraminer, Riesling. The area is largely undeveloped for wine; there are only a half-dozen smaller wineries in operation, clustered around the town of Roseburg, with a few hundred acres of vineyards, and there doesn't appear to be any rush to plant more vines.

There are even fewer, well-scattered wineries in the far southern section of the state, in an area roughly bounded by the watershed of the Rogue River but which has markedly different growing conditions from one subregion to another. The whole area is more mountainous, rougher, and wilder than the Umpqua. The fruit-growing areas in the eastern section, in the Applegate Valley and around Ashland, are much warmer and drier than other areas in western Oregon (rainfall in the Applegate averages about half that in Portland). On the other hand, the higher elevation, around 1,500 feet, makes for colder winters and the danger of spring and fall frosts. Assuming that climatic problems can be dealt with (as they have in eastern Washington), the area seems particularly well suited to Cabernet Sauvignon and Merlot, as well as to Chardonnay. The red varieties ripen well here and can produce intensely flavored wines.

Meanwhile, the Illinois Valley, nearer to the ocean and just north of the California border, which is cooler and gets more rain (an average of forty inches per year), is already producing fine Müller-Thurgau and Gewürztraminer. Growers contend that Pinot Noir also does extremely well in this area, which gets about as much heat as the northern Willamette, but it's difficult to describe the wines of the region because the wineries are new and few—indeed, some area grapes have gone unpicked.

In addition, all of southern Oregon suffers, by contrast with the Willamette, in being relatively far from a population center that could stimulate interest in the wines. One trend that may change this: Grapes from southern vineyards, especially in the Rogue Valley, are finding their way into Willamette wines and even into California wines.

Eastern Oregon

It will surprise many familiar with Oregon's wine image to discover that about a fifth of the state's vineyard acres are east of the Cascades, most of them in one huge operation, Boardman Farms. Located on the Columbia River, almost directly across the river from the huge Columbia Crest vineyard at Paterson, this Oregon vineyard has more in common with those in eastern Washington than with the small vineyards of the Willamette. The landscape is sagebrush, cattle, wheat, and potato fields; the 500 acres of vines, producing high yields, are mostly intended for second-tier or bulk wines, with Hinman Vineyards near Eugene the principal customer. Varieties such as Cabernet Sauvignon and Sauvignon Blanc, which do not do well in the Willamette, may find a much more suitable Oregon home here, but the plantings will need to mature before the results can really be evaluated.

Snake River Valley (Idaho)

Most of the broad, high plain through which the Snake River runs near Boise is dry range country, but close by the river there is a gentle southwest-facing slope (called Sunny Slope) that has long been a fruit-growing area and that seems ideally suited to grapes as well. The whole valley is high altitude, averaging around 2,500 feet, so winters can be especially hard and autumn temperatures typically vary 30 to 40 degrees from daytime to nighttime. This turns out to be excellent for grapes, because they ripen more slowly and hold their acid levels better, which produces very balanced flavors in the wines. As in the Columbia Valley to the northwest, the region sees very little rainfall, and autumns are typically very dry, which allows the grapes to ripen under ideal conditions. The principal distinction between the two regions is probably the Snake's shorter growing season, which makes it unsuitable for late-ripening varieties (except the adaptable Riesling). Even more than in eastern Washington, growers must take extra precautions to see that the vines are "hardened off" before the early fall frosts.

Chardonnay is probably what will make this region's name—it ripens exceptionally well here—though Riesling and, to a lesser extent, Gewürztraminer do well also. (Sauvignon Blanc and Cabernet Sauvignon don't ripen well.)

Ste. Chapelle made some very ripe and lovely Chardonnays early on, and now other Idaho producers like Rose Creek and Weston are showing that this success was no fluke. Grapes were first planted only in the early seventies, so there is a long way to go in determining best locations and best varieties for the area, though a scattering of vineyards planted in the early eighties are now coming on line. There are several vineyards planted to Pinot Noir that are only now coming into production; local winemakers are enthusiastic about prospects for this grape, which has been so successful in cool growing areas in Oregon. But early efforts to turn the grapes into wine have not been impressive.

Other areas along the Snake are also being planted with small vineyards now—there is probably an extensive amount of potentially excellent wine-grape acreage in this part of the state.

THE GRAPES

Cabernet Sauvignon

This may well prove to be Washington's premier grape variety, if consumers can accept the fact that Washington Cabernet is not the same as California's. Though not as winter-hardy as some other varieties, Cabernet thrives in eastern Washington and ripens well in the long, dry autumn. But whereas Cabernet from California tends to be lush, plummy, or berrylike, with forward flavors when it's young, the best Washington Cabernet is often quite closed in and awkward in its youth. The berry flavors are hard, there is often a touch of herbaceousness, and the acid levels are high. Making up for this youthful hardness is depth, power, balance, and potential complexity; if the best Oregon pinots are "feminine" in style, then the best

Washington Cabernets are "masculine." More than one French wine professional has noted that Washington Cabernets are closer to classic Bordeaux than California Cabernets. While some winemakers have opted for the more aggressive oakiness of American oak, most of the top producers have found success with liberal doses of new French oak.

The one consistent difficulty winemakers have had is a vegetal quality in the grape, and there are a variety of theories on how to deal with this. Since it seems to be more of a problem in young vines, the long-range solution is to let the vineyards mature—meanwhile, careful vineyard management and a firm application of oak has worked well. The current craze of picking according to pH (acidity) levels has also resulted in some wines from less than mature grapes; winemakers are learning that it's not hard to add acid (routine in California) but ripe flavors are irreplaceable.

In reality, of course, there is a considerable range of styles, with many wines vinified to be more fruity and accessible early on, and winemakers are just beginning to experiment with blending wines—not only from different vineyards but using some of the other traditional Bordeaux grapes: Merlot, Malbec, and Cabernet Franc. However, so far 100 percent Cabernet or very close to it remains the norm. The success of Cabernet Sauvignon in eastern Washington has caught many grape growers by surprise—there is much less Cabernet planted than Riesling or Chardonnay. New vineyards in new sites should provide an even richer variation in the wines from this grape.

So far excellent Cabernets have come from the Walla Walla region in southeast Washington (and stretching into Oregon), from the Horse Heaven Hills on the south side of the Yakima Valley, and from the eastern end of the Yakima Valley and the Columbia Valley near the Tri-Cities, and some of the very best wines have been blends from several different vineyards (e.g., Woodward Canyon's wines). Vineyard designations to look for include Kiona, Otis, Seven Hills, Red Willow, Sagemoor, and Mercer Ranch.

The story in Oregon has two sides, because the Cabernets from the warmer southern region of the state are quite different from those of the Willamette Valley. Cabernet Sauvignon always has some herbal flavors lurking under the surface—it's one of the intriguing qualities of the grape. But the cool climate in the Willamette turns those flavors positively vegetal—all the northern wineries get pretty much the same results. That's just the way the grapes taste, but if you like that green pepper–olivey flavor (not unknown in Bordeaux), the wines can be attractive. On the other hand, Cabernets from the Umpqua and Rogue regions show deeper color and more berrylike Cabernet flavors—some of these are quite powerful. Cabernet from this area shows considerable promise, but additional experience is needed. It seems doubtful that Cabernet will ever be as important a red varietal in Oregon as Pinot Noir.

Excellent Examples—Oregon: Alpine, Valley View. Washington: Chateau Ste. Michelle, Columbia (Red Willow, Otis, Sagemoor), Hogue, Hinzerling, Kiona, Leonetti, Mercer Ranch, Neuharth, Quilceda Creek, Woodward Canyon.

Chardonnay

If Oregon is America's Burgundy, then one might expect the Chardonnays from the region to be on the same scale with the Pinot Noirs, since these two are the twin giants of Burgundy. But so far, at least, Oregon Chardonnay has not gotten the acclaim that Pinot has. This is due no doubt in part to the huge success California has had with Chardonnay, which has both set the style for American Chardonnay and provided less incentive for consumers to search out new sources of the wine, as well in part to the clumsiness with which winemakers have often handled the rather delicate flavors of the grape in Oregon.

There's no question that Chardonnay grows well in Oregon—perhaps too well. The clone most widely planted (about 85 percent of the total vines) is the 108, developed for California, which is extremely vigorous and a heavy bearer. French winemakers who walk through Oregon vineyards and see the huge clusters of large berries refuse to believe they're looking at Chardonnay. Their Chardonnay is a shier producer. It may be that Oregon growers will have to work to reduce their yields to produce more intensely flavored wines—so far the best wines have come from vineyards that carefully control tonnage per acre. The 108 is also relatively high in acid, which is great for California, where low acids are a problem, but not really necessary in Oregon's cooler climate, which already produces sufficient acids. Other clones in use are the Draper and Wente, also from California, which have lower yields and ripen earlier, producing wine a bit softer in acid.

Some winemakers attribute their lack of success to poor clonal selection and argue that until French clones arrive (another five to ten years in all probability), no great Chardonnay will be made. But successful Chardonnay producers think this too easy an excuse. Perhaps the clones are not ideal, perhaps having more clones available will allow more complex wines, but, as one maker of excellent Chardonnay says flatly, "If people are not making good Chardonnay with the clones they have, new clones won't help." Nevertheless, everyone seems agreed that making excellent Chardonnay is a much tougher task in Oregon than making excellent Pinot Noir, requiring considerable skill in several areas: grapes, yeasts, oak, primary and secondary fermentation, lees contact, blending.

Oregon Chardonnays are stylistically quite different from California's and, some would say, closer to those of

Burgundy. (As in Burgundy, variation from one vintage to another can be notable—in light years Oregon Chardonnay can be too lean, lacking fruit.) The wines are not as fat tasting, but have restrained fruit and solid structure (here the acid really helps). To compensate for the relative lightness of fruit in Oregon Chardonnay, most top wineries have gone to barrel fermentation, which adds a richness and "toastiness" of flavor without overwhelming the fruit with new-oak flavor. (But in cool years the oakiness can seem quite pronounced, as the fruit seems to disappear.) Almost all the wines are also put through malolactic fermentation, which reduces the acidity and introduces some additional complexity, though again sacrificing some of the fruit flavor. Many winemakers are also now experimenting with letting the wine sit on the lees (mostly dead yeast) in the barrel after fermentation, to add yet another dimension of richness. There's little question that the wines can age well, holding their flavors better than their California counterparts.

The value of Oregon Chardonnays comes out particularly strongly with food—their most subtle flavors, backed up with good acidity, match beautifuly with a wide range of rich foods. And, at least until they attract more attention, they are relatively fine values. Until the wines become more consistent, though, it's best to search out those from the best producers and the warmer vintages.

Although the best Oregon Chardonnays are quite similar to the best from Washington, there are some subtle differences. The Oregon wines seem a bit leaner, firmer, crisper, while the Washington wines are more forward, a little softer, more assertively fruity. The Chardonnay grape produces such excellent fruit in eastern Washington that it's been easy for winemakers to ferment it like other white wines, run it briefly through oak, and release it with lots of forward, tart, applelike flavors and reasonably good body. This has become such a predominant style in Washington that one might not realize the grape could be treated differently. For some reason—perhaps the larger size of Washington's wineries or the farming background of its winemakers—there has been a reluctance to move, as Oregon has, toward a more Burgundian treatment of the grape, which sacrifices some of the fruitiness in order to achieve richness and complexity (some farmer types think of these flavors as "dirty"). But in the most recent vintages, several top producers have moved in this direction, and the quality of Chardonnay (at the top end) is probably improving more rapidly now than that of any other grape in the state. (Meanwhile, California producers, faced with a short supply of grapes from their own state, have been scouring Washington vineyards for excess Chardonnay to use in their wines.)

Some early Washington Chardonnays were excessively ripe and had little staying power, but the grapes are now usually harvested with lower sugars and higher acids. As they accumulate oak barrels, many wineries are fermenting at least partially in French oak, which, as Oregon winemakers have shown, makes wines with toasty, buttery flavors instead of the harsh, woody flavors that often come from simply aging the wine in new oak. Lees contact and malolactic fermentation complete the techniques being used to achieve a richer style for this grape.

Forward, fruity versions of this grape are best enjoyed young, while the more complex, barrel-fermented ones have shown some aging potential. Because these Burgundian techniques have only been in use in the last half-dozen years, it will take time to know exactly how well these wines age, but several five- to six-year-old Chardonnays have maintained excellent flavors and developed fine, rounded qualities without succumbing to oxidation (as so often happens to their California counterparts of a similar age). But the best Washington Chardonnays are also very appealing when young, with round buttery flavors; they're often a bit plumper than their Oregon counterparts, with more of the tropical fruit character of California Chardonnay. Some winemakers note differences between Chardonnays from the Yakima Valley and those from the Columbia Basin, but it's too early to define those clearly. The Yakima is cooler, and these wines may have a little more finesse, with the Columbia wines richer and deeper—but, again, with Chardonnay so much depends on the winemaking. Although the "Washington style" is still in flux, this seems to be one of the grapes with greatest long-term potential for this region.

Most of the above comments about Chardonnay in eastern Washington would also apply to the Snake Valley, and several producers have made rich, ripe wines from this region.

Excellent Examples—Oregon: Adams, Adelsheim, Bethel Heights, Cameron, Eyrie, Girardet, Ponzi, Shafer, Sokol Blosser, Tualatin. Washington: Barnard Griffin, Bonair, Chinook, Covey Run, Hogue, Kiona, Stewart, Paul Thomas, Woodward Canyon. Idaho: Rose Creek, Ste. Chapelle.

Chenin Blanc

This grape grows easily in Washington, ripens well, produces huge crops, and makes a very nice white wine. So why hasn't it attracted more attention? Chenin Blanc is the grape of France's Vouvray, where it makes a wine with a characteristic rich, honeylike flavor in either off-dry or sweet style. With typically high acidity it can also age beautifully. In California it loses its distinctive flavors in the hot sun and makes dull blending wine, and perhaps California has ruined the Chenin Blanc market irretrievably.

Washington has a climate better suited to Chenin, and

the best Chenin Blanc here can be deliciously fruity, with wildflower scents and often a more robust character than Riesling. Whether it will ever match Vouvray's intriguing flavors remains to be seen (eastern Washington is somewhat warmer than Vouvray, but the cooler Willamette hasn't had great success with the grape), but in the meantime it makes a sturdy sipping wine that often is bursting with fresh flavor and is almost always a good value. Unfortunately, the wines are in a tailspin in the marketplace, prices for grapes have dropped precipitously, and few wineries are interested in treating the grape seriously. Several wineries are experimenting with a dry style of Chenin Blanc, which retains fine fruit but is lighter and crisper and turns out to be an excellent wine with lighter seafoods. This grape deserves better billing.

Several Oregon growers are convinced that Chenin Blanc, which grows well under cool conditions in the Loire Valley, can do well in the Willamette. But Chenin doesn't ripen terribly well in the Willamette, except in very warm sites and is far less widely planted than Riesling. So far, although there are some pleasant, light-flavored versions, there is nothing to suggest that a Vouvray-style wine is in the offing for Oregon, and those who enjoy the grape should probably look to Washington's fruity, flavorful wines.

Excellent Examples—Oregon: Eola Hills. Washington: Hogue, Latah Creek, Salishan (dry), Snoqualmie, Paul Thomas.

Gamay Beaujolais

Really a clone of Pinot Noir, this grape suffers from a severe identity crisis. It's not the true Gamay grape, which makes the great French Beaujolais, and in Washington its fate is to make a very light rosé-style wine, or even a blush. In such form it can be quite good, offering attractive strawberry fruit and light body—a nice picnic wine, not to be taken seriously. Several Oregon vineyards are cultivating Gamay Noir, the true Beaujolais grape, and wineries should be releasing these wines soon.

Excellent Examples—Washington: Mont Elise, Worden's.

Gewürztraminer

The butt of numerous insider jokes, Gewürztraminer has become a marketing nightmare. Consumers won't buy it, grape prices are scraping bottom—and it's a tricky grape to grow. Many wineries have simply written it off, but for some devotees it remains a world-class wine.

Along with Pinot Gris, Gewürztraminer is one of the top grapes of the Alsace region in France, where it makes powerful, spicy wines of enormous character. Unfortunately, American growers have simply not been able to achieve the same depth with the grape, though there are a number of pleasant, flowery wines with a slight bitterness produced in both California and the Northwest. Whereas the style in Washington tends toward the fruity and off-dry, the Oregon Gewürztraminers, in an attempt to reproduce the Alsatian style, have tended to be dry and fairly austere, so the Oregon wines will be more satisfying to those seeking a French-style wine. Most are light, though there are a few heavier examples, but even these lack the richness of their French counterparts. There is also a little Late Harvest wine being made, which is occasionally excellent.

A few dedicated souls in Oregon, committed to the grape for love and not money, are still working on it, experimenting with different sites (the coolest seem to be best) and letting the grapes hang on the vine as long as possible, as they do in Alsace. Warmer fermentation, to extract as much flavor as possible, may also help. One has a sense that Gewürztraminer, like Pinot Gris and Chardonnay, should be a stand-out wine in Oregon; there may yet be world-class wine here, but there's a long way to go.

One of the first Washington wineries, Associated Vintners, made its reputation with an austere, bone-dry Gewürztraminer, but more typically in the state it is made slightly sweet, with a very flowery nose and slight underlying bitterness. In eastern Washington's warm climate the grapes ripen early, which clearly does not contribute to excellence of flavors. So the search is on for cooler areas—the Columbia Gorge, some feel, is an ideal location for the variety, and some very nice wines have indeed come out of this region. But new plantings in the state are scarce.

Increasingly, because of its failure to sell, Gewürztraminer is being blended into other white wines to give them a little extra zip, and unless someone comes up with the right formula for both making and selling the wine, varietal Gewürztraminer may gradually fade out of the picture. It's really too bad, because great Gewürztraminer is fabulous.

Excellent Examples—Oregon: Airlie, Alpine, Amity, Callahan Ridge, Henry, Pellier, Shafer. Washington: Columbia (Woodburne), Mont Elise, Staton Hills. Late Harvest: Elk Cove, Hinzerling.

Lemberger (or Limburger)

A grape unique to Washington in this country, it came here from central Europe (probably Hungary originally), where it makes a light, rather dull red wine. Promoted by the state's agricultural research station at Prosser, as an experimental wine it proved to be more popular among the public than such varietals as Cabernet or Pinot Noir. It's easy to see why: It has a characteristic dark color, bright berrylike fruit, and a velvety feel on the palate. Whether made in a light, fruity style, without any oak contact, or in a more serious, oak-aged fashion, it is appealing in youth, because despite its dark color the tannins are very moderate. And its precocious qualities do not preclude it from aging well.

Lemberger has been called Washington's Zinfandel, but, unlike Zinfandel, it thrives in cool temperatures and ripens a couple weeks earlier than late varieties; winter-hardy, it grows very vigorously and can be a prolific producer as well. Now made commercially in small quantities by four state wineries, with several more planning to add it, it remains to be seen whether this grape's attractive qualities can overcome an unfortunate name and a lack of consumer awareness.

Excellent Examples—Washington: Covey Run, French Creek, Kiona, Mercer Ranch.

Merlot

Merlot grows quite prolifically in Washington, but local winemakers have fiddled considerably with the grape, as it presents some problems to them. It's an earlier ripener than Cabernet, and when allowed to ripen too much it produces flabby, high-alcohol wine that tends to flame out early on. There has also been a nagging weediness or vegetative quality in some Merlots. Successful producers have done much as many Zinfandel producers have done in California—moved toward a lighter, softer, more forward, and less tannic style. The result can be very pleasing—almost like Beaujolais in its strawberry-raspberry fruitiness and freshness. A few producers have managed to combine jammy flavors with good structure in the wine. Merlot is often blended with a little Cabernet to give it better structure (Merlot on its own lacks the characteristic complexity of Cabernet), and at least one producer is playing with a Merlot–Cabernet Franc blend to give the wine more interest and body but retain its innate plumpness. There is still considerable tinkering going on with this varietal, but the best Merlots in the state should be very appealing to most people for their lush, round flavors. How well they will age remains to be seen.

In contrast to eastern Washington, Oregon doesn't seem destined to make fine Merlot. The problem is simple. Except in the very warmest spots and finest springs, the vines simply will not set berries. Growers are understandably reluctant to grow vines that produce only every four or five years, so there's little inducement to plant more of this variety. The exception is a small patch of southern Oregon, in the Rogue Valley, with an unusually warm climate that has turned out some very ripe, rich Merlot.

Excellent Examples—Oregon: Valley View. Washington: Arbor Crest, Chateau Ste. Michelle, Chinook, Gordon Brothers, Hogue, Latah Creek, Leonetti, Paul Thomas, Waterbrook, Woodward Canyon.

Müller-Thurgau

A cross of Riesling and the undistinguished varietal Sylvaner, Müller-Thurgau (named for its German creator) is widely planted in Germany because of its early ripening ability. It's also a heavy bearer and usually makes a soft, floral wine without much character—it's the principal grape of Liebfraumilch of Blue Nun fame. Ideally suited for a cool climate, it has been widely planted in England, and there is a small but growing amount in Oregon. It will never make a great wine, but when the grape is not overcropped or overripened it can produce very attractive wine, with a flowery aroma similar to that of Muscat and a delicate fruitiness, with some earthy undertones. There are some nice examples of the wine in Oregon, made in a slightly sweet style—an ideal sipping wine—and although it's little known, when consumers get a chance to try the wine they almost always like it. A number of small wineries, therefore, use it as their "tourist wine."

Unknown in eastern Washington, which has too warm a climate, Müller is prized in western Washington vineyards for its ability to produce good yields of ripe grapes under cool conditions. As in Oregon, several producers have managed to make wines of considerable character and interest by keeping sufficient acid to give the wine some backbone.

Excellent Examples—Oregon: Airlie, Serendipity, Siskiyou, Tualatin. Washington: Bainbridge Island, Johnson Creek, Mount Baker.

Muscat (Morio-Muscat, Muscat of Alexandria, Muscat Blanc, Muscat Canelli, Muscat Ottonel)

A neglected grape (or, really, family of grapes), but one that can produce remarkably good wines in Washington. Muscat comes in several different varieties, but the one that is emerging as a favorite is Muscat Canelli (also called Muscat Blanc), now being produced by a number of wineries. The trademark of all Muscat is an extremely aromatic quality—it smells like a whole collection of tropical fruits and flowers. This pungency sets it apart from almost any other white grape, and indeed winemakers often add just a bit of Muscat to an otherwise rather dull white blend to put some zip into the nose.

Muscat grows well in eastern Washington, is a heavy producer, and is generally made into a fairly sweet, low-alcohol wine, emphasizing the fresh fruit qualities of the grape. Lighter and subtler than California Muscats, Washington Muscat works well as a light dessert wine—its open, obvious flavors are appealing to a broad range of wine lovers, and it has enough flavor to compensate for low alcohol.

It should be noted that Morio-Muscat is not a true Muscat but a cross of Pinot Blanc and Sylvaner that has the wonderful pungency of Muscat and so acquired the name. It's also sometimes spelled "Muskat."

Muscat Ottonel is grown in Oregon by Eyrie Vineyards

and made as a dry-finished, lightly aromatic wine.
Excellent Examples—Oregon: Eyrie. Washington: Covey Run, Latah Creek, Mercer Ranch, Snoqualmie, Stewart, Paul Thomas, Tucker.

Pinot Gris

This is the hot new white varietal in Oregon right now. Although there are only a few wineries making wine from this grape, and only about 100 acres planted, its potential seems enormous. Unknown in California, it is one of the principal grapes of Alsace in France, where it regularly makes excellent, full-bodied white wine (also called Tokay d'Alsace). A cousin of Pinot Noir, the grape does well under the same conditions and seems to produce excellent fruit more consistently than Chardonnay. What is remarkable about it is that fermented dry it has much of the richness and weight of Chardonnay without the benefit of any oak. In addition it has lots of enticing exotic fruit flavors.

David Lett at Eyrie pioneered this wine in Oregon (he prefers it to Chardonnay) and established its style here, but a couple of newer wineries have broken with the fifteen-year "tradition" and are using oak on the wine, feeling it merits such serious treatment. The favorable results (more roundness) suggest this approach may be imitated as more and more producers bring out their own versions. Significant increases in production await new plantings, but Pinot Gris may one day be *the* Oregon white wine.

In the Northwest, Pinot Gris has acquired a well-deserved reputation in restaurants as an excellent seafood wine, marrying well with all kind of rich dishes, especially salmon.
Excellent Examples—Oregon: Adelsheim, Eyrie, Lange, Ponzi, Rex Hill, Tyee.

Pinot Noir

This, of course, is the grape that put Oregon on the map, and it's not hard to see why. While Californians have fussed and struggled for decades with this difficult variety, Oregon wineries have been making lovely Pinot Noir literally from their first efforts (David Lett's early wines at Eyrie Vineyards did impressively in international competition). The number one factor is climate: Oregon's cooler growing season allows Pinot Noir to ripen slowly—in the Willamette Valley, the main growing area, it is harvested in mid- to late October and sometimes into November. Maturity is achieved with relatively low sugar and high acid, essential to bring out the fruit of the grape; in contrast, many California Pinots harvested at higher sugar levels taste pruney or raisiny when made into wine, and can be quite harsh. In fact, there are occasional vintages in which Oregon winemakers must "chaptalize" their Pinot Noir—that is, add sugar to the juice before fermentation. Chaptalization is not practiced in California (where it's really unnecessary), but rather common in Burgundy, where it can give the wines more body and slightly higher alcohol. Experience in Oregon has proven that this "artificial" technique can be very beneficial and has no adverse effect on flavor. (Even in 1987, a hot year, several wineries picked early to avoid overripeness and then chaptalized.)

Low yields are another factor in quality. In France's Burgundy district, home to the finest Pinot Noirs in the world, yields are severely restricted. In Oregon, the grape is naturally a shy bearer, but the flavors intensify the more the crop is controlled, which suggests the need for careful pruning. Average yields in the best Willamette vineyards are two to three tons per acre, considered very low by traditional California standards. At the same time, the vines need to be trained to maximize the sunlight that the leaves and berries receive, and growers are still experimenting with a number of different systems. To add to a grower's difficulties, Pinot Noir is really a whole variety of related clones, each with slightly different characteristics. The most prevalent is Pommard, which gives considerable backbone to the wine and sometimes a kind of black pepper quality, but Wadenswil, a lighter and fruitier clone characterized by fresh raspberry or cherry flavors, is also in use. Although the trend has been more in favor of Pommard in recent years (wineries like its greater body), a blend of several clones gives the wine greater complexity.

And complexity, plus texture, is what this wine is all about. Pinot Noir isn't meant to have the sheer power of Cabernet and is often surprisingly light in color. When young the wine can have an enticing fresh cherry or raspberry fruitiness, but it's with some aging that it develops a melding of fruit and spices and other flavors (cinnamon, cloves, tea, black pepper, leather, and so on). Most exciting is the texture, the feel of the wine—with age it becomes truly velvety and so delicate that its depth is surprising. Many critics, including this one, would agree that at its height Pinot Noir is unquestionably the greatest red wine in the world.

There's little debate over aging the wine in French oak—discussion turns more on what kind of French oak and how long. Some producers prefer the assertively spicy and caramely flavors that lots of oak contact can give; others prefer to let the fruit of the grape stand out, even at the risk of sacrificing some body. Consumers will find a variety of styles to choose from.

The aging of Pinot Noir raises another issue. Some Oregon Pinots have been justifiably criticized for their tendency to go "over the hill" after four or five years in bottle, often because of low acid levels. On the other hand, some experts argue that Pinot Noir, in contrast to, say, Cabernet, is a wine meant to be enjoyed young and that aging it brings no long-term flavor enhancement. A useful guideline for consumers is probably somewhere in between: Most Oregon Pinots seem to need several years to settle down and show their best, but most are probably at their peak by the time they are five or six years old.

Oregon Pinot Noir is already a world-class wine, and demand for it now regularly outstrips supply by two or three times at the best wineries. Prices have moved up smartly in response, although the wines are still a bargain when compared to their French counterparts. (It should be noted that there are also several wineries, especially Amity, Cameron, and Glen Creek, producing very attractive, inexpensive fruity Pinot in a grapy Beaujolais style, for early drinking.) There are a number of wineries producing consistently excellent wine—even in cool years the wines have been fine, though light. Pinot Noir is the classic wine for beef, but it goes readily with any number of full-flavored dishes, and there are those who enjoy it with salmon.

Although Pinot Noir was one of the first vinifera varieties to be planted in the Yakima Valley, it has not proved to be a popular grape for growers in eastern Washington and has gotten little attention from wineries. Part of the problem may have been that for years Ste. Michelle bought most of these grapes for its sparkling Blanc de Noir—leaving very little for anyone else. And Pinot is not an easy grape. A few wineries (Ste. Michelle, Columbia, Preston) have made occasional good varietal Pinot Noir, but these wines have tended to be Californian in style: dark, overripe, plummy and raisiny in flavor, rather hot. In their youth they can be flamboyantly impressive, but they can also get harsh in maturity. The success of Oregon wineries with the varietal has induced new plantings in Washington, with an ongoing search for appropriately cool sites, but these efforts have yet to bear fruit.

A footnote needs to be added for Pinot Noir from southwest Washington, in the Columbia Valley north of Portland and west of the Cascades. This region is sparsely planted with grapes, but the climate is very similar to that of the Willamette Valley to the south. One small winery (Salishan) has already demonstrated the fine potential for Pinot in this area, and it may be that more ventures will be added in the future.

Excellent Examples—Oregon: Adams, Adelsheim, Amity, Bethel Heights, Cameron, Elk Cove, Eyrie, Glen Creek, Knudsen Erath, Oak Knoll, Panther Creek, Ponzi, Rex Hill, Sokol Blosser, Tualatin, Veritas, Yamhill Valley. Washington: Salishan.

Riesling (Johannisberg Riesling, White Riesling)

There's no question—this is Washington's grape. The problem is, the grape has been so successful that it is now clearly overplanted; close to a third of the acreage of wine grapes in the state is planted with Riesling. The growth has been so spectacular that the market has broken down, and prices for Riesling in the bottle have hovered at the break-even point, while much wine sits in warehouses and some grapes hang unpicked on the vine. (Growers are now shipping Riesling fruit to wineries all over the United States and even to Japan.)

Growers in eastern Washington discovered early on that the grape liked the climate. Riesling is a late ripener but is extremely sturdy, suffers little from cold winters, and thrives in cool autumn weather. The greatest Rieslings in the world come from western Germany, in the Rhine and Mosel valleys, where the climate is so marginal that the grapes often don't ripen at all. The Yakima and Columbia valleys have a much more consistent environment, and there are rarely problems with the Riesling harvest. Washington Riesling typically has lots of fresh fruit flavor, ranging from applelike to more peachy or apricot in flavor. The usual style is an off-dry one, with 1 or 2 percent residual sugar, which gives a pleasing fullness to the wine.

But what distinguishes Riesling here from its counterpart in warmer regions in California is the very crisp acidity—the result of cooler weather—which gives the wine more backbone and a sense of freshness.

Yet Washington Riesling is not exactly like German Riesling either. So far at least it hasn't shown the earthy, minerally flavors that give the best German wines a feeling of depth and complexity. Nor does the market price encourage winemakers to concentrate on top quality. However, the most sought-after German Rieslings are the richer and sweeter Spätlese, Auslese, and so on, and Washington has an abundance of sweet Late Harvest–style wines of fine quality. The *Botrytis* infection that dries out the grapes and gives them more sweetness and richness develops readily and naturally in Washington vineyards, but even without *Botrytis,* there are nicely balanced sweet wines from ripe grapes every year. Here again, the acid levels are essential to maintain structure in the wine. Many of these Late Harvest wines, with sugar levels that vary from 4 to 15 percent at bottling, have rich, creamy, peachy flavors that will appeal to dessert wine lovers. For price and quality, these Late Harvest wines are clearly superior as a class to Rieslings from any other region in the world.

Unfortunately, although Riesling sells very well in the Northwest, it has been difficult to convince the American wine consumer elsewhere that Riesling is worth the money as a premium wine. Although it is traditionally regarded as one of the four or five classic premium vinifera varietals, American experience with dull and flabby California Riesling, grown in a climate that is simply too hot, has lowered our perception of what the grape can do. The quality of Washington Riesling is consistently good—it's easy to make a very good one—and consumers are well served with almost any of the wines on the market. At the low prices that it currently fetches, Riesling represents one of the best bargains in the American market for those who like fruity white wine. (A few wineries are now turning to dry Riesling as a possible way to entice consumers, but there seems to be little pressing demand for this wine either.)

In an attempt to stimulate interest in Riesling, the Washington Wine Commission will sponsor a World Vinifera Conference in July of 1989 in Seattle to bring together experts from all parts of the wine industry to focus on Riesling. Says noted wine author Hugh Johnson, "I am sure that next July will witness the start of an unstoppable Riesling Renaissance." One can hope.

Riesling (called White Riesling in Oregon) is also a popular grape to grow in Oregon (third in acreage after Pinot Noir and Chardonnay), and it does grow well, although its late ripening makes it susceptible to poor autumn weather. Oregon Riesling is lighter and more delicate than Washington, and several wineries make it in a dry style, as a food wine. The problem is, as Washington has found, that even excellent Riesling is a tough sell outside Oregon. The few excellent dry Rieslings, with more restrained aromas and steely flavors than their more flowery, sweet Washington cousins, are well worth trying, and there are even some fine, crisp late-harvest-type wines.
Excellent Examples—Oregon: Alpine, Girardet, Hillcrest, Knudsen Erath, Ponzi (dry). Washington: Barnard Griffin, Bookwalter, Chateau Ste. Michelle, Kiona, Oakwood, Salishan (dry), Stewart, Paul Thomas, Worden's. Late Harvest: Arbor Crest, Blackwood Canyon, Cameron, Covey Run, Chateau Ste. Michelle, Elk Cove, Hogue, Langguth, Mount Baker, Stewart, Yakima River.

Sauvignon Blanc (or Fumé Blanc, Washington Only)

In eastern Washington, Sauvignon Blanc has been made in a variety of styles, from aggressively herbaceous to austere and steely, but one style seems to be emerging as the leader. Under this approach, the naturally vegetative flavors of the grape (it can be made to taste almost exactly like bell peppers) is toned down by short-term oak aging and by leaving a small amount of residual sugar in the wine to soften and round it out. The wine doesn't end up tasting sweet because of the high natural acidity of the grape, but it does acquire a little more body and drinkability. Arbor Crest is the acknowledged model for this style, which has been remarkably successful.

Various vineyard techniques are also being used to manage the flavors of this grape, which requires a fairly lengthy growing season but is a vigorous grower and can be a very heavy bearer. Many growers have reduced the amount of water the vines receive from irrigation to control vine growth. Making sure that the grapes get sufficient sun and not picking them before they are totally mature also help avoid the more annoying qualities of Sauvignon Blanc. Many wineries are also blending in varying quantities of Semillon, which is usually a little softer and fruitier—the blend of Semillon and Sauvignon Blanc is the traditional Bordeaux technique for making that region's fine, dry white wines. Often described as "the poor man's Chardonnay," Sauvignon Blanc in Washington bears little resemblance to soft and fruity Chardonnay, with a tartness and often an austerity of flavor that make it in most cases far preferable to Chardonnay as a wine to match with seafood. Definitely not intended for sipping, the flavors of Sauvignon Blanc are drawn out with food, and often improve with several years of age.

This grape is little planted in Oregon. The problem is that it requires more heat to ripen than the Willamette generally provides and is a very late ripener. In California and Washington it can make distinguished, full-flavored dry white wine with a typically "grassy" aroma. In Oregon's cooler climate, the vegetal qualities of the grape are exaggerated, and the wine can reek of bell pepper, asparagus, and so on. There are a few who enjoy this strongly herbaceous flavor of the grape, but its appeal is limited.

The potential for the grape in warmer areas in southern Oregon seems much better, though it is still undeveloped. Excellent Examples—Oregon: Chateau Benoit, Hood River, Shafer. Washington: Arbor Crest, Chateau Ste. Michelle, Chinook, Covey Run, Hogue, Preston, Staton Hills, Paul Thomas.

Semillon

With Sauvignon Blanc, this grape is one of the two classic grapes that make the dry white wines of Bordeaux. The Bordelais consider it the classier of the two grapes, and the best dry white Bordeaux are predominantly Semillon. Nevertheless, California has devoted far more attention to Sauvignon, because it stands up better to California's heat, and Washington growers have followed suit. The unfortunate result is that Washington Sauvignon Blanc, an awkward and not always attractive wine, has outshone Semillon, which grows extremely well and makes consistently delicious dry wine.

Semillon is not quite as vigorous or heavy bearing as Sauvignon Blanc and typically has flavors that are not quite as aggressively vegetal. Washington Semillon can produce intensely flavorful wines, fruitier and softer than Sauvignon, with a flavor that has been described as fresh figs but is really a more complicated combination of fresh herbs and citrus.

Most Semillons in the state are made in a fresh, fruity, but dry style with plenty of crispness, which makes them excellent companions for many lighter seafood dishes. Although wineries have been favoring a fairly light approach to the grape, a few wineries are making a barrel-aged or barrel-fermented Semillon that has less fruit but more weight, but with a weak market there's little encouragement for winemakers to expend effort on the varietal. Though it was one of the first vinifera grapes planted in the Yakima Valley, Semillon continues to see its enormous potential go untapped (which may be the case as long as California rules the wine market). Savvy consumers, who appreciate not only the fine qualities of the grape but its excellent value in the marketplace, will search it out.

Several wineries, notably Chinook and Covey Run, are making fine blends of Semillon and Sauvignon Blanc, using proprietary names.

Excellent Examples—Washington: Blackwood Canyon, Chateau Ste. Michelle, Columbia, Columbia Crest, Latah Creek, Snoqualmie.

Others (Aligoté, Island Belle, Madeleine Angevine, Nebbiolo, Okanogan Riesling, Siegerrebe)

Two acres of Aligoté, a second-string variety from Burgundy, are planted in the Yakima Valley; Covey Run is the sole producer. Typically it makes a wine lighter than Chardonnay, with a little higher acidity and almost hay-like aroma—a very pleasant dry white that works well with lighter seafoods.

The desire to grow grapes in western Washington's cool climate has stimulated interest in new varieties (crosses between traditional vinifera varieties) that ripen well in cool temperatures. Among a number of experimental varieties, several have emerged commercially and are producing wine. Madeleine Angevine is one of the most important—an old French cross that produces a reliable crop and makes a soft wine with an exotic fruit nose. Another variety with considerable potential is Siegerrebe, a cross of Madeleine Angevine and Gewürztraminer, which has an even more flowery nose than either of its parents and can make an excellent dessert wine. One could also add Okanogan Riesling, which is not a true Riesling at all but a grape, probably hybrid, of unknown origin. Although it grows and ripens well, it has coarse and bitter qualities that limit its potential. One native American grape, Island Belle, has a long history in the Puget Sound region, where it is still grown (see Hoodsport Winery in Part Two).

Another oddity, grown on an acre and a half at the Red Willow Vineyard, is Nebbiolo, the great red wine grape of northern Italy (used in Barolo, Barbaresco, and so on), which Peter Dow at Cavatappi is using to make fruity, light-style wine. The early results look promising.

4

TOURING THE WINE COUNTRY

s the number of wineries in both Oregon and Washington has quickly grown, so has the number of visitors to wineries. Currently more than five hundred thousand people a year visit wineries in Washington alone, with Oregon reporting another three hundred thousand. Even for visitors from the Far East, a winery has become an obligatory stop, and some have taken home a newly acquired taste for the wines. For many wineries, tourists are a big business. It's not just a matter of selling T-shirts and other paraphernalia: Direct bottle sales from wineries represent 10 to 30 percent of all sales for many smaller wineries, and wine sold at the door earns a higher profit than wine sold to a distributor. With very few exceptions, wineries are eager to welcome the public—most will let you taste any and all of their current releases.

The most significant difference between states for wine tourists is that Oregon allows wineries to open separate tasting rooms along major highways, allowing visitors to sample wines without driving all over; Washington allows tasting only at an actual winery, though a few establishments have adapted to this rule by opening mini-wineries with tasting rooms attached (e.g., Covey Run and Staton Hills in the Seattle area).

When to Visit

Fall is an ideal time for touring Northwest wine country. The intense summer heat (which can be especially bad in eastern Washington) is over, but the weather in both eastern Washington and western Oregon is fairly dry through October. This is also the busiest time for the wineries, so be prepared for the "Closed to Visitors" signs at the tiniest places, where the staff consists of a couple and their kids. Winter in eastern Washington can be brutally cold and bleak, and in Oregon it's wet; many wineries run a skeleton operation through January and February and are not open for visitors at all, so it's best to call ahead. (In fact, calling ahead is a good idea anytime if you're going out of your way to visit someplace—it's not unusual to find a locked door even during regular hours at small wineries.)

Even at the height of the tourist season, in the summer months, it's unusual to find terrible crowds at the wineries—this is not yet the Napa Valley. Although a few places right off the highway (e.g., Staton Hills in the Yakima Valley and Sokol Blosser in the Willamette Valley) get a lot of traffic, many wineries have few enough visitors even on weekends that it's possible to stop and chat a while.

Before You Go

Unlike those in Napa, Northwest wineries are not all cheek by jowl on the same road. Many are off the beaten track and signing is not always good (it's much better in Oregon than in Washington), so you are well advised to travel with some kind of map and guidebook. The Oregon Winegrowers Association publishes an annual guide called *Discover Oregon Wineries,* available for $1.00 at almost any winery or by writing to P.O. Box 6590, Portland,

OR 97228. This little brochure has dandy maps, suggested routes, and hours of operation.

Washington has no equivalent yet (though one is planned), so you'll need to turn to one of the several excellent guidebooks available. First choice, since it's being updated annually, is Chuck Hill's *The Northwest Winery Guide* ($11.95 from Speed Graphics). The maps here are also excellent, plus there are suggestions on where to stay, where to eat, and what to do with kids. Also recommended is Ronald and Glenda Holden's *Northwest Wine Country* ($12.95 from Holden Pacific), which provides more background information on wineries and wines, plus ratings of the wineries. The chief drawback here is that there are directions but no maps.

If you're traveling by car, be sure to take several other essentials. First is a corkscrew. There's nothing worse than being out in the country getting set to enjoy a bottle of wine under a shady tree and discovering that you've no way to open the bottle. A corkscrew should be part of every auto first-aid kit. The second essential is glasses. You'll need the glasses if you want to enjoy that bottle properly, and some wineries without washing facilities serve tasting samples in pathetic little plastic cups, like the ones at the dentist's office. Far better to be able to provide your own. The third essential is water. Especially in hot weather, wine tasting can make one very thirsty, and fresh water does a lot to refresh the palate along the way (as does some bread or plain crackers).

Tasting and Driving

If you're doing some serious tasting, visiting several wineries during the day (three is a good limit) and sampling a number of wines, you need to take some precautions. A designated nondrinking driver is great. A taste-and-spit discipline is equally good. Take it from a veteran: It is absolutely OK to taste a wine and spit it out without swallowing. Wineries that do not make this a ready option by providing accessible spittoons should be ashamed. But you can always ask for an extra glass to spit into, or you can let fly outside (and in any case, be sure to dump the extra wine when you've had your sip—you're by no means compelled to savor the last drop). Honestly, there's nothing uncouth about doing this, and it leaves you in much better shape to enjoy and evaluate the wines.

The Winery Tour

When you've seen one stainless-steel fermenting tank . . . Nevertheless, at some large wineries like Chateau Ste. Michelle, a tour of the facility is your only way in. (Ste. Michelle, or Columbia Crest, is worth seeing anyway, for its sheer size.) At smaller wineries, if they ask whether you want a tour, don't feel obliged to say yes—giving tours all day is not terribly exciting for a winery owner, either.

On the other hand, if you're genuinely interested in a small winery's operations, and express it, you will usually get a thorough introduction. If you show some knowledge you may even get a barrel sample or something not generally available to taste. When visiting during the grape crush, you might ask to observe unobtrusively—if you don't make demands on the winemaker, you'll get to see what really goes on. But, as one veteran winemaker warns, "We tend to get tired, cranky, and sometimes rude during crush; please ignore us."

The Tasting Room

Often it's the visitors who are cranky and rude. Most wineries will let you try their entire line of wines, though often you will need to ask if you don't see something open. However, some special wines are simply in too short supply to be available for daily tasting; others, like sparkling wine, don't keep well after opening—it's boorish to abuse the tasting room host or hostess in hopes of sampling these. It helps to know ahead of time which wines you would particularly like to try and politely to decline the rest.

Unfortunately, the trend toward a tasting room fee is building, especially in some of Oregon's busy wineries. The wineries claim it keeps out the boozers looking for a quick snort, but it's a turn-off for those with a real interest in wines, especially when wineries profit handsomely from tasting room sales. One would hope this will not become a general pattern.

Buying Wine

Do not feel obliged to buy wine at every winery you visit. In contrast to Europe, American wineries have traditionally welcomed casual visitors and given samples of their wine as part of their promotional efforts. On the other hand, don't expect to get a bargain at the winery; prices are generally the same as at local retail establishments in the state. But many wineries do offer substantial case discounts, discounts on wines they are closing out—and some have rare wines available only at the winery. (Oregon offers an additional retail bonus: no sales tax.) Many wineries will ship wine home for you at a price, though currently this cannot be done across state borders. If you're carting a lot of wine around in hot weather, take some precautions, as extreme temperatures can be very damaging to wine. The trunk may be the worst place for it; if you have room in the backseat, it's probably less likely to cook there. A cooler will also provide some shelter from the heat.

A last note about traveling with fine wine. It sounds silly, but when you get the wine home, let it rest for a week or so. Travel, with all the vibration and temperature changes, tends to make wine go "dumb"—it loses its most subtle flavors and bouquet. Give it a chance to recover.

Touring Routes: Oregon

As many ocean lovers have discovered, many of the Willamette Valley's wineries are right off Highway 99W and Highway 18, which run down to the beaches from Portland. Even if you're not on the way to the ocean, there are enough wineries within an hour's drive of Portland (including Ponzi and Oak Knoll practically in the suburbs) to keep the casual visitor occupied for several days. Once you get off the main routes in the wine country, you may easily get lost in a maze of small country roads, but the territory is so beautiful, it's difficult to feel concerned when this happens.

A thorough tour would go in a triangle, southwest down Highway 99W as far as McMinnville (perhaps with a side trip down 99W to the wineries in the Eola Hills), then north along Oregon Highway 47 to Forest Grove to visit the wineries near this college town, and then back to Portland on Highway 26.

A trip down I-5 from Portland to the California border brings one within easy reach of almost all the rest of the state's wineries. There is a string of lonesome wineries between Salem and Eugene, then another cluster around Roseburg, three quarters of the way down the state, and another couple between Grants Pass and Ashland in the far southern stretch (a good way to while away some daytime hours during the Oregon Shakespeare Festival in Ashland).

Although there are no grapes along the Oregon coast, there are lots of tourists, which is why a number of wine-tasting rooms are located there, as well as two wineries. From north to south along Highway 101, visitors can choose from Shallon Winery in Astoria, Nehalem Bay Winery in Nehalem, the Knudsen Erath tasting room in Tillamook, the Oak Knoll and Honeywood tasting rooms in Lincoln City, and the Alpine tasting room in Newport. Consult a guidebook for precise locations.

Touring Routes: Washington

There's a good concentration of wineries in the Seattle area (the standard one for tourists is the lovely Chateau Ste. Michelle, a great place for picnicking with the brand-new Columbia facility just across the street), as well as several in the Spokane environs, though neither of these is a vineyard area. If you want to see the wine country, you'll need to hop over the mountains to eastern Washington. The easiest route is down the Yakima Valley as far as the Tri-Cities—it's an easy drive on I-82, and there are more than twenty wineries to choose from, of all different sizes and styles. To extend this tour, you might turn south (don't miss the huge Columbia Crest winery near Paterson) and then back west down the spectacularly beautiful Columbia Gorge along I-84 or Washington Highway 14, visiting the half-dozen gorge wineries. Or you could head down to Walla Walla, an hour's drive or so from the Tri-Cities on Highway 12, to visit the five wineries down there.

In western Washington, other than isolated wineries like Mount Baker just south of the Canadian border or Salishan just north of Portland, the most scenic tour is out on Highway 101 to the Olympic Peninsula, to visit four small, scattered wineries—it's mostly Douglas fir rather than *Vitis vinifera,* but the wines are interesting.

Touring Routes: Idaho

Wine touring in Idaho is for those who really like a lot of driving and a little wine tasting. Actually, four of

Idaho's wineries are within an hour's drive of Boise, but the rest are very spread out—it's a two-hour drive just to get from Boise down to Rose Creek in Hagerman (and there's nothing on the way). Until the Idaho industry grows up a little, this will not be prime touring territory, though you'll get a royal welcome if you make the effort.

5

SHORT ESSAYS ON NORTHWEST WINE

THE HARVEST

he grape harvest. The romance of it is stirring. The age-old traditions: happy peasants with their carts of grapes, stomping grapes by foot in open vats, the harvest bacchanalia of feasting and dancing. The Yakima Valley provides a perfect setting: dry brown hills that look soft and fuzzy from a distance, warmed by the low-angled October sun and swept by the endless winds of that open land. The hills are a backdrop for the gold of the vineyard, with its half-hidden splotches of purple and yellow-green grape clusters.

The reality of harvest is backbreaking. You arrive early in the vineyard, it's cold yet, and you don't want to surrender your plastic cup of coffee. But the foreman hands you a pair of sharp cutters that look like small pruning shears, and a bucket. "We're picking Riesling today," and you are sent off down a particular row. The dry, sandy soil is full of burrs that cling to boots and socks—and if you try to pick them off, to skin as well. You dodge spider webs, stoop and poke beneath the vine tendrils to get at the grapes; the stems are tough and often wrapped around the wires that support the vines, and the grapes don't come without a fight. At first it's fun: The grapes come quickly, the sweet fruit (much sweeter than table grapes) is great for snacking, and there is much camaraderie, joking and gossiping with friends. The bucket must be emptied into a larger container, so back and forth you go, while the grapes seem to get heavier and heavier, and the vines seem more tangled. By noon city dwellers feel they have done a good day's work. Lunch in the vineyard, with cheese and sausage and lots of last year's wine, restores good cheer, but it's awfully hard to haul your carcass back to the grapes (which row was I on? where are my shears?). The afternoon is very quiet, except for the occasional low expletive.

For the vineyard owner and winemaker, the harvest is not just a long weekend's work but a round-the-clock operation that requires the planning of a military campaign and the fortitude of a long-distance runner. The work of the harvest really begins at least a month before the grapes are to be picked—an estimate has to made of when each variety will be picked, so pickers can be hired—and, of course, the weather may not cooperate. In the Yakima Valley, a major fruit region, there are usually pickers available, Mexican migrant laborers, but picking hops and apples is easier work and rounding up the necessary skilled workers is not always easy. Yeast cultures for the fermentation must be started several weeks before harvest to make sure they will be ready when the grapes arrive.

The harvest begins in the valley around the fifteenth of September and runs roughly to the end of October, but some years, like 1987, it may begin as much as three weeks early, and the winery may still be trying to empty tanks and finish bottling as the new grapes arrive. Day by day the sugar and acid levels are checked until the right levels are reached. Some growers rely more on sugar, some more on acid—the best growers know the final verdict is a matter of putting grape into mouth. There is a pattern to the harvest. Gewürztraminer is an early ripener and usually the first to be picked; Riesling ripens slowly and matures best as the weather cools, so it tends to get picked last. Cabernet and Chardonnay are somewhere in between.

At the winery, the day's activity typically starts around 6 A.M. Crushing the grapes takes place in the morning, when they are cooler, though Cabernet, which needs a warm fermentation, is crushed later in the day. Before crushing starts, the equipment is checked; cleanliness for the winemaker is probably even a little before godliness, and rubber-booted workers wash and rewash every piece every time it's used. The grapes go first through a stemmer-crusher, which magically mashes the fruit and simultaneously spits out the unwanted stems, then into a mechanical press, which gently squeezes out the juice, leaving the pulp, skins, and seeds behind. From here the juice is pumped into large stainless-steel fermenting tanks where the yeast is added and fermentation starts. (But for red wine, grapes, skin, and seeds all go in together.)

Modern equipment has made it all easier and faster than it used to be (Columbia Crest crushed nearly 1.5 million pounds of grapes in one record *day* during the '87 harvest), but problems still arise. The grape "must" (the stew of juice and skins) gets too thick and clogs hoses and pumps; the winery runs short on tank space; grapes back up on the crush pad or in trucks; fermentation gets "stuck" and won't continue. Every day the winemaker must check the fermenting grapes, fiddle with tank temperature to control the rate of fermentation. Red wines, fermenting on grape skins which float to the surface, must be punched down or pumped over, sometimes several times each day, in order to extract more color and flavor from the skins.

The winemaker's day ends around midnight, allowing him a few hours' sleep before the next day's routine, while the grapes bubble and undergo their mysterious transformation.

WINE AND FOOD

Northwest Cuisine?

Many of the great wine areas of the world are also famous for their local cooking (Burgundy and Tuscany come
to mind, though Bordeaux is an exception), but if there is
a distinctive "Northwest cuisine," it hasn't left its mark on
ordinary dining tables yet. Perhaps it's because there's
little ethnic base for great cooking—there are small Asian
communities in Northwest cities, but Italians, French, and
other Europeans with strong traditions of the table are in
short supply. The Scandinavian influence is fairly strong
in coastal areas, part of the fishing and lumbering heritage, but this has had little impact in the culinary field.
Excellent cooking does exist in restaurants all over the
Northwest, but until very lately these establishments have
taken their cues from New York and San Francisco rather
than developing a unique style.

That said, there have been some encouraging developments in the food field, the most important of which is the
blossoming of local food products. Ocean waters, coastal
beaches, and inland streams have always produced an
abundance of fresh seafood, which has been very much
taken for granted by the locals. (During the Depression,
some of the poor in Seattle were "reduced" to eating crab
nearly every day—one can still find survivors of this period who won't touch the stuff today.) Salmon, halibut,
clams, and oysters are standards, and interest (perhaps
under Japanese influence) has grown in more exotic
items—mussels, sea urchins, geoduck. But again, Northwesterners have never been terribly creative about how to
cook these; the simpler the better has been the rule, except
for the minority following French, Italian, or Japanese
rules.

It's only in the last ten years that there has been an interest in drawing on the abundance of other fresh local products, and an attempt to bring all of them together into a unique approach to cooking. High-quality game, lamb, and beef are now popular. There are lots of locally produced cheeses (but, surprisingly for country with so many dairy goods, local cooking doesn't use much butter or cream). Fresh vegetables and herbs are readily available, and the Northwest is a tremendous source of fresh fruit—apples, pears, peaches, cherries, berries—and nuts. Unfortunately, the supermarkets are still overflowing with "foreign" foodstuffs, mostly from California and Mexico, cheaper because they are produced in bulk, so locally produced food doesn't find as wide an audience as it should. Local strawberries, for example, are hard to find in stores all but a few weeks of the year—they don't travel as well as tough California berries.

If there is a new Northwest cooking style, it's eclectic—borrowed a bit from California, a bit from Japan, a bit from France, and, as up and down the West Coast, a bit from Mexico. But mass culture (the benefits of cooking shows like *The Frugal Gourmet* notwithstanding) has an even more powerful influence. Northwesterners would like to think that they eat as well as the native Indians ate, but pizza, spaghetti, hamburgers, and tacos have the same appeal here as they do elsewhere in the country.

Whether winemakers in various parts of Europe have deliberately shaped their wines to match the local food, or whether cooks have adapted to the wine, or whether such matches, when they work well, are just happy accidents, is a matter for debate. In the Northwest, there are very few winemakers who claim to have set out to make wines that would go well with Northwest food (most were trained in California, so if they betray any food influence, it is probably from there). Nevertheless, there have been some accidents that turned out very happily indeed, and, at least as concerns seafood, wineries are increasingly conscious of food and wine matchups, especially at the marketing end of the business.

Unfortunately, although a good argument can be made for Riesling as a food wine, it is not generally considered such in this country, so the relatively huge role that Riesling plays among Northwest wines has probably detracted from their image as food wines. (Most Riesling made here is intended as "cocktail" or "sipping" wine.) Nevertheless, many wines from Oregon and Washington are eminently suited for the table (more so than California wines), very much in the French or Italian tradition.

What makes a wine a "food wine"? First, let's admit that not all wines are great married with food. Some wines are just naturally like maiden aunts—chaste and unapproachable. Why worry about what goes well with port—port is fine all by itself. Ditto most dessert wines (the wine *is* dessert). Second, one can also forget the absurd claims for wines that go well with everything from halibut to huckleberry pie. A good food wine will match nicely with a broad range of foods, but there are limits. On the other hand, one can apply some broad criteria to wines that are meant for the table. We often talk about "dry" dinner wines, meaning wines without any sugar in them, but more important is the presence of a good backbone of acidity in the wine. A little sweetness is actually OK, as long as there is balancing tartness. Acid does two things: It stimulates the palate so that even when competing with the flavors of food, the flavor of the wine will continue to come through. And for rich foods (and most of what Americans eat is fairly rich), it provides a counterpoint of flavor and keeps us from being exhausted by the flavors of the dish.

Along with crisp acidity, a good food wine needs fruit and body, but not too much. Too much flavor in the wine, and you overwhelm the dish you're supposed to be complementing—the English call Bordeaux, one of the great food wines of the world, claret, which means "light." Delicate, rounded flavors usually work best with food—heavy wines, and those high in alcohol, may taste wonderful on their own but don't seem to work as well at mealtime.

By these criteria, many Northwest wines are model food wines. Acid levels, because of the growing conditions in both Oregon and Washington, tend to be fairly high, alcohol levels are rarely excessive, and the fruit is rarely overripe. Without needing to be conscious of it, Northwest winemakers find that they are producing balanced, dry, tart, medium-bodied table wines that complement food without overwhelming it. Even those Chenin Blancs and Rieslings that are finished with a degree or two of residual sweetness can be fine dinner wines; their surprisingly high acid levels provide a counterpoint to sugar and allow the wines to stand up nicely to full-flavored foods (something the Germans have known for several generations).

One needs to follow only a few basic rules to enjoy wine with food. First, the most basic: Drink the wines you enjoy with the foods you enjoy, whatever they are, and you will be pleased. Second, experiment; don't be afraid to try new combinations—even a failure will be stimulating and informative. Third, match wine and food for similarity or contrast—a buttery Chardonnay with a rich, buttery sauce, or, conversely, a crisp, lean white with a fat, oily fish. You either find flavors that complement one another or flavors that tone each other down and provide counterpoint. Fourth, match strength to strength: light-flavored wines with delicate foods, full-flavored wines with heavy, spicy foods. But remember that in many dishes, the secret is the sauce—don't match for the main ingredient but for how you're dressing it, especially if you're cooking with wine (recall the old rule: a bottle for the pot and one for the table).

The difficulties of making rigid, unique recommendations about this wine for that food are nicely demonstrated with respect to salmon, which is ubiquitous in Northwest restaurants. The fish itself is unlike many other seafoods— rich, with lots of flavors, quite fatty. By itself it's already too much for most light, dry "seafood wines" (like a steely Sauvignon Blanc). It needs a wine with some guts. Then there's the issue of how you prepare it: Salmon with creamy dill sauce is different from salmon with raspberry sauce or salmon with plain lemon. Cabernet Sauvignon with salmon? Well, if you cook the salmon with a reduced Cabernet sauce, you might be surprised. Salmon with a rich, creamy sauce, or with nuts, may want a fairly rich Chardonnay; with a fruitier, sweeter sauce a dry Riesling or Gewürztraminer may work nicely. And there are plenty of locals who swear by Pinot Noir for their barbecued salmon.

Some Suggestions

Some standard wine-and-food matches are well worth trying. Washington Sauvignon Blanc (or Fumé Blanc) has become for many the wine of choice with a whole host of seafoods, but a light Semillon is also an excellent choice. There are an increasing number of dry Rieslings and Chenin Blancs that also do beautifully with sweet-flavored shellfish. Oregon Pinot Noir is exquisite with beef in almost any form, or with almost anything that's barbecued. Washington Cabernet Sauvignon (or Lemberger) and lamb. Sweet Riesling or Muscat with fresh fruit. Rich, oaky Chardonnay with roast fowl or light casseroles. Dry, spicy, full-flavored Gewürztraminer or Pinot Gris with sausage, quiche, flavorful fish dishes. Soft, fruity Merlot with pork. With very spicy East Indian– or Asian-influenced cuisine, Gewürztraminer is the traditional recommendation, but slightly sweet Chenin Blanc or Muscat is often better.

Cabernet Sauvignon: Beef, lamb, pork, game, duck
Chardonnay: Chicken, turkey, veal, salmon
Chenin Blanc: Dishes with sweet or spicy sauces, ham
Gewürztraminer (dry):   Sausage, fish, quiche
Lemberger: Lamb, light meat, stews
Merlot: Pork, other light meats, cheese soufflé, turkey
Müller-Thurgau: Fruit
Muscat: Fruit, light cakes
Pinot Gris: Salmon, other full-flavored fish, sausage, quiche
Pinot Noir: Beef, barbecued or smoked meat or fish, light stews
Riesling (dry):   Crab, clams, light fish
Riesling (off-dry):   Fruit, full-flavored chicken, light casseroles, quiche
Riesling (sweet):   Fruit, custards, light cakes
Rosé or blush: Ham, picnic meats, sandwiches
Sauvignon Blanc: Oysters, chicken, strongly sauced fish
Semillon: Pasta, fish, chicken

DESSERT WINE CLASSIFICATION

It may well be that Washington produces the best white dessert wines in the country—those luscious, sweet wines made from Riesling (and occasionally Gewürztraminer). But how sweet is sweet? Consumers have been faced with a confusing proliferation of designations: "Late Harvest," "Select Harvest," *"Botrytis* Affected," "Select Cluster," and the modernistic "Ultra Late Harvest," any of which could mean anything the winemaker wanted it to mean, and none of which necessarily told you whether the wine was just a bit sweet or really supersweet.

Now consumers can make more informed choices. The members of the Yakima Valley Wine Growers Association, who collectively make most of the state's dessert wines, have agreed on standard designations for labels, which will guide sweet-wine lovers instantly to just the degree of sweetness they desire.

Such a system is not a new idea—the Germans have had strict label designations for several decades. "Spätlese," "Auslese," and other terms in the German system refer to the ripeness of the berries when picked, but the problem with this system is that it still doesn't necessarily tell you how sweet the wine is when it's vinted (it's possible to ferment sweet grapes to complete dryness). Those who buy an Auslese expecting a semisweet wine may be disappointed.

According to growers' association spokesman John Rauner of the Yakima River Winery, who has been a strong proponent of such a system, the Yakima system is a pioneering effort, and growers hope it may set the standard for the whole country. It specifies not only the ripeness of the berries, but also the "residual sugar"—the sweetness of the finished wine. (Wineries will be expected to put the residual sugar figure on the label as well.) Wines with less than 4 percent residual sugar (already a medium-sweet wine for most drinkers) will not be entitled to any designation. Above that level, in ascending order of sweetness, the designations will be: "Late Harvest" (at least 4 percent residual sugar), "Select Cluster" or "Select Late Harvest" (at least 10 percent residual), "Individual Bunch Selected" (at least 15 percent residual), and "Dry Berry Selection" (at least 20 percent). The last will be very sweet wine indeed, equivalent to the incredibly expensive German Trockenbeerenauslese (which happens to mean "Dry Berry Selection"). A standard has also been set for the very rare "Ice Wine" (made from berries frozen on the vine), which will have to have at least 18 percent residual sugar.

The new system took formal effect with the 1987 vintage. One can hope that uniform labeling will encourage more consistent pricing policies, since consumers will be able to compare more closely wines of the same level of sweetness. Sweet Rieslings are of necessity much more expensive than regular Rieslings, because the conditions that produce them are relatively rare, because it takes many more grapes to produce the same amount of wine, and because picking selected clusters or berries is a more laborious process. But consumers should note that high prices are offset by the fact that half bottles (375 milliliters) are appropriate for most occasions—a little dessert wine goes a long way.

SPARKLING WINE

With the national wine market stagnating and with Northwest vineyards facing a huge increase in grape production, wineries are scrambling for new markets. But there's one segment of the market that's literally popping: Champagne. And Northwest wineries plan to have a piece of the action.

Nationwide, sparkling wine sales, even for expensive lines, continue to bubble. "It's wild," says Mark Newton, proprietor of the Northwest's first all-sparkling-wine facility, Oregon Méthode Champenoise in Seattle. "Growth has been phenomenal—and projections show it will continue to be." So far, no French Champagne houses have stepped into the Northwest, as they have in California, but it may be only a matter of time before they do. Meanwhile, local wineries are increasing production sharply. Oregon Méthode Champenoise, for example, which began several years ago under the Newton and Newton label with 300 cases, is up to 1,500 for 1987, under a new label, Whittlesey-Mark. Plans call for an eventual production of 10,000 cases per year.

And Northwest sparklers may get a big boost in 1989

with the first release of wines from a Dundee, Oregon producer with the working name of Crochad. A partnership between Australian sparkling wine producer Brian Croser and American wine importer Robert Chadderdon, Crochad may make a large splash with the reputed 20,000 cases of bubbly it will have for the market.

Most of the energy is going into *méthode champenoise* wines that can compete with the best from California, and surprisingly, many wineries are turning to Riesling—a variety that does extremely well in the region—for their fruit. The Germans have long made sparkling wine, called *Sekt,* from Riesling; faced with a glut of the grape, it makes sense for Washington wineries to find new uses for it. Sparkling Riesling is usually made in a soft, fruity style with a bit of sweetness—a wine to be enjoyed young.

One of the best of the Riesling-based sparkling wines from Washington is the Hogue Brut—the new Hogue label drops the word "Riesling." Winemaker Rob Griffin argues that the type of grape is not that important. "We're trying to make sparkling wine with a classic character—and release it within the time frame we want," i.e., about a year after the vintage. In fact, the Hogue sparkler has a bit of Chardonnay in it (how much is Griffin's secret) to tone down the fruitiness of the Riesling and give the wine a bit more body. The flavors are dry, fresh, and crisp, with just a hint of the Riesling grape, and fine bubbles. Clearly this blend is a success and may encourage other producers to follow suit. At around $12 a bottle, it is priced very reasonably for "Champagne method" wine, and it has sold well—attention to packaging, with elegant labels, doesn't hurt. Other producers like Covey Run in Kirkland and Coventry Vale, the large custom winery in Grandview, are also making stylish sparklers from Riesling in that same price range.

The more traditional approach to Northwest Champagne uses the classic French grapes—Pinot Noir, Chardonnay, and (in tiny amounts) Pinot Meunier, varieties that do well in the Northwest as they do in the cool-weather Champagne district. Champagne is, not accidentally, the most northerly grape-growing region in France: Cool weather allows the grapes to ripen with low sugars and high acids—the still wine actually is tart, green stuff. But such wine is necessary to have a successful second fermentation in the bottle (to make the bubbles) without making the wine flabby and overly alcoholic.

One of the first and most successful of the Northwest sparklers is Chateau Benoit Brut, made in Oregon's Willamette Valley, newly famous for its outstanding Pinot Noir. Fred Benoit made his first vintage in 1981 after harvesting some barely ripe Chardonnay and wondering what he could do with it. Now, the use of Pinot Noir (about 70 percent in this blend) works out very happily for the winery: In good years for Pinot Noir, most of the grapes go into a still, red table wine. But in poor years, like 1984, when other producers lowered prices drastically on their regular Pinot Noirs, Chateau Benoit can produce more Brut. In 1984 it made 7,000 cases of Brut, while in 1986, a good year for Pinot, it made only 1,000. Doesn't this affect the quality of the Brut? No, the beauty of this system is that barely ripe grapes are perfect for French-style sparkling wine.

French Champagne typically has a "yeasty" character, reminiscent of the aroma of freshly baked bread, which comes from leaving the dead yeast in the wine after fermentation for as long as three or four years. To allow this aging "on the lees," French Champagne houses have huge storage cellars with massive inventories of wine, but most Northwest wineries don't have the financial leeway to build up that kind of reserve. So local wineries have opted for a younger, fresher, fruitier approach to sparkling wine. (The notable exception is Chateau Ste. Michelle—its current Blanc de Noir is a well-aged 1980.) Nevertheless, winemaker Newton, who uses Oregon fruit exclusively, feels that with eighteen months of lees contact his wine can pick up sufficient yeasty richness. Like others in the Northwest, it makes up in delicacy and elegance what it gives away in weight.

The champion sparkling wine producer in the Northwest in terms of volume has to be Ste. Chapelle, the large Idaho winery that is the only one in the region set up to make Charmat, or "bulk process," wines, considered not quite as classy as Champagne-method wines. Ste. Chapelle now has three Charmat sparklers: a light-style Riesling, a fuller and richer Chardonnay, and a "Blush." These wines have been enormously successful, and Ste. Chapelle's annual sparkling production of over 25,000 cases easily outstrips any other Northwest producer's. The process may be the same used by cheap Champagne giants like Cooks, but use of premium varieties brings finer fruit flavors to the wines. One reason for their popularity: They are very competitively priced. (Champs de Brionne and Staton Hills are having Charmat wines made for them in California.)

Can small premium Northwest producers compete with large California wineries like Domaine Chandon? "We can beat them," says winemaker Newton confidently. He argues that California's climate is actually too hot for classic sparkling wine—the grapes often must be picked before they're mature in order to have a low-sugar high-acid balance. Newton, who thinks his wine is "pretty damn similar" to French Champagne, prices it in the $15-to-$16 range (about the same as most premium California sparklers), in which he can make money and beat French prices. The Australian Croser has ventured into Oregon for the same reason: He feels that the state probably has the right climate for the kind of fruit he wants—mature grapes at low sugars. (Croser, incidentally, does not have the same high regard for Oregon Chardonnay and Pinot Noir as still wines.)

What about quality? There's no question that wines like the Hogue Brut demonstrate considerable potential for elegant and appealing wine, while Newton and Newton Brut (to be renamed Whittlesey-Mark), Chateau Benoit Brut, and Chateau Ste. Michelle Blanc de Noir are some of the nicest Champagne look-alikes to be found in the United States.

Producers of Champagne-method Sparkling Wines

Champagne grapes
Arterberry (Oregon)
Chateau Benoit (Oregon)
Chateau Ste. Michelle
    (Washington)
Ellendale (Oregon)
Horizon's Edge
    (Washington)
Knudson Erath (Oregon)
Mont Elise (Washington)
Newton and Newton
    (Washington)

Riesling
Arterberry (Oregon)
Chinook (Washington)
Coventry Vale
    (Washington)
Covey Run (Washington)
Hogue (Washington)
Laurel Ridge (Oregon)
Preston (Washington)

Producers of Charmat (Bulk Process) Sparkling Wines

Champs de Brionne (Washington)
Ste. Chapelle (Idaho)
Staton Hills (Washington)

6

A GUIDE TO VINTAGES

Lovers of French and German wines learn to pay attention to differences from vintage to vintage—the weather is variable enough to make a considerable difference in the quality of the wines. California fans are much less concerned about this, since the weather presents fewer problems in most parts of the state. In different ways, Oregon and Washington mirror these two "foreign" areas. Oregon's climate can be pretty dicey—1984 was horrible for the grape growers, even though some decent wines ended up being made. Winemakers say they reckon on as many as three in ten vintages being really subpar, but the last six years have given the lie to statistics: '83, '85, '86, '87, and '88 were all good growing years.

Eastern Washington is more like California in presenting mostly stable climatic conditions, so vintages are probably of less significance than in Oregon (though one veteran grower remarks that in thirty years he has yet to see a "normal" year). Here the main problem for vines is late-spring frosts, but while these reduce the crop (a drawback for growers), they often intensify flavors (a boon for winemakers and consumers). In recent years the odd-numbered vintages have been the better ones, so '83, '85, and '87 are years to look for in red wine. Idaho's vintages should closely parallel those of eastern Washington.

OREGON (WILLAMETTE VALLEY)

1988: Although initial reports indicate very good to excellent quality in the grapes, the crop in many vineyards was reduced by a combination of factors. Spring and early summer were cool, and the fruit set was poor, but late-summer warmth and a near-perfect October saved the day. For Pinot Noir, the low yields may mean concentrated wines. Chardonnay and other varieties were also good quality.

1987: Warm spring weather encouraged a large fruit set, and a warm, dry summer and one of the driest autumns on record brought the harvest in three to four weeks ahead of normal in most parts of the state. The grapes were very ripe, though acids were low in some cases, and the crop was large. Early samplings indicate that the wines will be more like the '85s (bigger and tougher) than the '86s, with the Pinot Noir showing more tannin than fruit in barrel. The Chardonnay looks excellent, ripe and rich.

1986: A year that equaled 1985 for warmth, though there was some rain in September. Fine October weather produced a moderately large crop of ripe grapes. For those who waited out the rain, the wines show excellent fruit and balance and are more supple than the '85s. Chardonnay was variable and often quite lean.

1985: An excellent year, though the Pinot Noir will require time. The weather was ideal, as in 1983, but the Pinot came in with more tannin; these wines are not as forward as the '83s, and some are rather unbalanced. An outstanding year for Chardonnay.

1984: A fair to good year. It was panned by many, but there are some fine, lighter-styled wines. Persistent autumn rains were the culprit—some vineyards finished the harvest after Thanksgiving. Careful selection made the difference this year.

1983: Excellent wines from an outstanding growing year. The Pinot Noirs are quite forward, with plenty of fruit, and seem to be developing quickly (some, indeed, are already past their prime).

1982: A good year, overshadowed by '83, but fairly typical of Oregon. A large crop. The wines are not as full-flavored as the '83s but have fine balance. Many of the Pinot Noirs have matured very nicely.

1981: A difficult year—not really enough warmth. A reduced crop of barely ripe grapes made wines that, with few exceptions, are light and lean.

1980: A good year, with pleasant if unremarkable wines. A cool spring caused late blooming, and autumn rains delayed the harvest into November. Lighter wines on the whole, though the best were very nice indeed.

1979: A ripe year, though like the '78s, many of the wines have not aged terribly well.

1978: A very good year, especially for Pinot Noir, but many winemakers, delighted with hot weather, let the grapes get too ripe. The Pinots were lush when young but have tended to crack up.

1977: A mediocre year.

1976: An excellent vintage.

WASHINGTON (YAKIMA VALLEY, COLUMBIA VALLEY)

1988: A normal growing season and a crop slightly reduced in size should allow for good, balanced wines. Reds have deep color and lots of fruit, and whites have better acidity than in 1987.

1987: An unusually warm spring led to a huge harvest, which created problems for vineyards and wineries alike in selling and processing grapes. The season was early and hot, and the wines from vineyards that don't overcrop or let grapes over-ripen should be fine. Many wineries had to add acid—unusual for the Northwest—but the fruit looked extremely good. The harvest began very early, in August. Initial releases of whites showed lots of fruit but not always good structure.

1986: A fair vintage—perhaps the least successful of the last five, although it was the largest. There was rain in the middle, but the grapes came in early, with low acids, and many lack varietal intensity. Probably won't be long-lived. Look for some nice late-harvest wines, though.

1985: An excellent year, though with a reduced crop, especially for reds. A late frost reduced the fruit set, and a very hot, dry summer produced small, intensely flavored grapes. Probably the best vintage of the eighties, so far.

1984: A good year—excellent for some reds. Another hard winter damaged the vines. Crop size was down, especially for reds, but harvest weather was good, and the small berries produced intensely flavored wines, with some particularly intense and age-worthy reds.

1983: Very good. Warm weather produced a very large crop of good quality, except where growers over-cropped. The Cabernet is fine and deep-flavored, and there were some excellent late-harvest wines made.

1982: Very good. A warm September produced good to excellent quality—especially for reds.

1981: A good year—cool weather produced another vintage of good but light wines.

1980: A good, if fairly light, vintage for both reds and whites. The year of the Mount St. Helens blast—but the ash didn't have much effect on the grapes (though it did kill a lot of vineyard pests). The vines were recovering from the 1979 winter kill. The season was cool and late, but there was a good crop of moderately ripe grapes.

1979: A most unusual vintage. A winter freeze killed a lot of vines—as many as two thirds in some vineyards—and the surviving vines produced little fruit. But an almost ideal growing season produced grapes of intense flavor and ripeness. Some reds have so much hard tannin that they are only just now becoming drinkable.

1978: An excellent vintage, though the reds haven't turned out quite as nicely as the '77s.

1977: An excellent year—both whites and reds (but especially the latter) have developed very beautifully in bottle.

1976: Very good.

Part Two

THE WINES AND THEIR PRODUCERS

7

INTRODUCTION TO LISTINGS AND RATINGS

The wineries are listed alphabetically for each state; the order of states is Oregon, Washington, Idaho. Some wineries use several different label names; all these wines are listed under the winery. The location listed is the closest town, which sometimes is a distance away. The year is that of the first vintage, or crush, though typically vineyards have been planted somewhat earlier. Production figures, unless otherwise noted, are based not on winery capacity but on how much wine a winery actually made in the 1987 vintage.

Not every wine produced by each winery is listed. Particularly for those wineries with ten to twenty different bottlings, I have chosen representative wines, or those that are most unusual and noteworthy (or those that are most available). It is possible I have overlooked a few gems—I hope not. Increasingly, especially in Washington, bulk wines are appearing under restaurant or special-event labels; I have not attempted to keep up with this profusion of (mostly lower-quality) wines. Names in parentheses after variety name usually designate particular vineyards or other geographical sources.

RATING SYSTEM

★   OK—not very interesting
★★   Well made, some interest
★★★   Very good quality, with some distinction
★★★★   Excellent, among the best in its class
★★★★★   Outstanding, world-class, unique qualities

The ratings and descriptions of wines are based on almost ten years of tasting Northwest wines in a variety of settings—at judgings, trade tastings, blind comparison tastings, the wineries, and (most important) at my own table and those of my friends. Many wines have been tried numerous times, though some, especially from new wineries, I have sampled only once. In those instances where my impression was highly negative, I have tried to give the wine the benefit of the doubt and taste it once again. Generally, the ratings apply to wines of the last several vintages, up to and including 1987. With just a couple of exceptions, only wines bottled and released to the market have been rated. Because consistency is clearly one of the marks of great wine, the highest ratings (with only a few notable exceptions) have been given only to wines that have demonstrated outstanding quality over at least a couple of vintages.

The limitations of this system are many. Wine is a living, growing thing, but a tasting can capture it only at a particular point in time. Many wines go through awkward stages only to blossom later on in wonderful, unforeseen ways. Moreover, a tasting samples just one bottle. Jug wines are heavily treated to achieve a uniform consistency of flavor, but many small premium wineries deliberately keep their filtering and other treatment to a minimum, which is good for the wine but makes the product a little less consistent. Nor does this book take into account variations among vintages—wines from poor vintages may not be as good as the ratings indicate. (The vintage evaluations found on pages 128–131 will be helpful in this respect.)

And then, of course, all of these notes are the impressions of my own palate. There is no way to judge wine on an absolute, objective scale—the evaluation of wine is largely personal and aesthetic. I make no apologies for my opinions, but you may find there are individual judgments with which you disagree. That, I think, is one of the pleasures of wine.

The vast majority of grapes grown in the Northwest fall into the premium category—there is little jug wine and few lower-end blends. I have tried to judge the wines not just against other Northwest wines, but against similar varietals from California and Europe. The wines of highest rating will hold their own, I believe, when tasted against great wines from anywhere in the world.

PRICES

$	$7 or less
$$	$7 to $12
$$$	$12 to $20
$$$$	more than $20

Prices vary widely from state to state and even within states, depending on how competitive the market is. These general price guides are based on prices for 750-milliliter bottles of current vintages at the wineries, or standard retail prices in Oregon and Washington. Prices may be lower in some large, urban markets. Restaurant prices, of course, will be 50 to 150 percent higher.

Introduction to Listings and Ratings   137

NOTE ON VARIETAL WINES

If a wine is labeled with the name of a grape, current federal law requires that at least 75 percent of the wine be from that grape. However, Oregon requires that at least 90 percent come from a single grape, except for Cabernet Sauvignon, which can have up to 25 percent of a related Bordeaux grape (e.g., Merlot). Some blended wines have a name that specifies the varieties (e.g., "Cabernet-Merlot"); others do not.

There are two varieties that can cause particular confusion. The first is Riesling, a grape known variously as Johannisberg Riesling and White Riesling. Both names are currently allowed (but only White Riesling in Oregon), and wineries can use whichever they prefer. To add to the confusion, some Washington wineries use one name for a drier version and the other for a sweeter—but there is no consistency in usage. Here they are simply called Riesling unless a winery uses the two names to distinguish separate bottlings.

The second potential source of confusion is Sauvignon Blanc, which some wineries call Fumé Blanc (but not in Oregon); two names, one grape.

8

OREGON WINES AND WINERIES

ADAMS VINEYARD WINERY
Portland   (1981)
4,000 cases

eter and Carol Adams are typical of the young urban professionals who have begun wineries in Oregon (Peter has a consulting business and Carol is an artist and food columnist)—but, atypically, they have not abandoned urban life to do it. Their thirteen-acre vineyard, first planted in 1976, is in the Willamette near Newberg, next door to Adelsheim Vineyard, which has provided assistance and where the first vintages were crushed. But the winery is in downtown Portland.

The Adamses fell in love with French Burgundy while running a wine shop in the early seventies, and they are convinced that Oregon can make consistently better wines than Burgundy. Pinot Noir is their first love, but both Pinot and Chardonnay have been excellent here—especially impressive given their newcomer status. Like most of the best producers, they stick close to Burgundian techniques and have not been afraid to pick their grapes early and then chaptalize (add sugar) in order to preserve good acid levels.

The results have been impressive. Both the Chardonnay and the Pinot Noir are more solid and full-bodied than many of their local counterparts, with as much flavor extract as possible. The buttery-oaky flavors of the Chardonnay are assertive without being deadening to the fruit; this wine will appeal to those who like lush, round Chardonnay. The Pinot is very firm and "meaty"—a big wine, with lots of flavor and excellent structure, needing several years to show its best. Not the most delicate and perfumy of Oregon Pinots, but fine stuff.

There is also an interesting Sauvignon Blanc, made from some of the few grapes of that variety grown in Oregon (it's not clear what the future of Oregon Sauvignon Blanc will be). And Portland's House Wine, a fruity young Pinot Noir, is very tasty as well and a fine value. The main problem for this winery is satisfying the growing demand for its small production (in spite of which, prices remain reasonable).

CHARDONNAY ($$) ★★★½ Rich buttery-oaky flavors, lots of weight but nice balance. Solid body, crisp, with fine length on the palate. Perfect wine for roast fowl.

CHARDONNAY, RESERVE ($$$) ★★★★ As good as the regular Chardonnay is, this is a bit better. Lots of very rich, butterscotch flavors with a thick feel on the tongue and long finish.

PINOT NOIR ($$$) ★★★★ One of the bigger styles of Pinot in the state. Full red color, ripe cherry nose, lots of body and tannin mark it as a wine to age well. Plump but not flabby.

PINOT NOIR, RESERVE ($$$) ★★★★ Intense cherry nose, good structure, rather closed in. A bit soft?

PORTLAND'S HOUSE WINE ($) ★★★ A delightful table wine made from 100 percent Pinot Noir. Light-colored, grapy, dry, lively. A fine barbecue wine.

SAUVIGNON BLANC ($$) ★★ Very intense oaky-peppery-weedy nose with full body and tart acid. Aggressive

Sauvignon Blanc like this is rarely seen in Oregon. Love it or hate it.

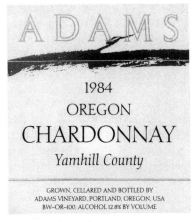

1984
OREGON
CHARDONNAY
Yamhill County

GROWN, CELLARED AND BOTTLED BY
ADAMS VINEYARD, PORTLAND, OREGON, USA
BW–OR–100, ALCOHOL 12.8% BY VOLUME

ADELSHEIM VINEYARD
Newberg (1978)
13,000 cases

David Adelsheim is one of the scholarly leaders of the Oregon wine industry—a discussion with him about the wines of Oregon becomes a seminar on planting, trellising, pruning, fermenting, grape clones, oak, and so on. Although Adelsheim is grateful for what he learned from Eyrie Vineyards' David Lett when first starting out, many newer vineyard and winery owners owe much to the experimentation and writing Adelsheim himself has done on the subject of grapes and wines. Much of his work has grown out of a conviction that many of the techniques of California vine tending and winemaking don't work in Oregon, and that Oregon must go its own way with help, when it is needed, from the French (Adelsheim has had hands-on experience in Burgundy and maintains good connections with several Burgundy producers).

In fact, Adelsheim has probably done more than anyone else to encourage Burgundy producers to get involved in Oregon, and he was instrumental in the deal that set up the large Burgundy firm of Drouhin with a 100-acre estate in the middle of vineyard country in 1987. Adelsheim is hopeful that the French will bring with them different grape clones and techniques to help the locals continue to perfect their own wines.

In addition to grapes from Adelsheim's own eighteen acres, planted in 1972 in the hills northwest of Newberg, the winery purchases a variety of grapes: Pinot Noir and Chardonnay from area vineyards and Merlot from both eastern Washington and southern Oregon. The winery also has a patch of Gamay Noir, the true Gamay grape of Beaujolais, an early ripener and large producer (there's no wine from it yet). Although Adelsheim's original intention was to blend his lots of Pinot Noir into one bottling, he has decided that the wines from the Eola Hills are sufficiently different (more fruity than elegant) from those of the Dundee Hills that beginning with the 1986 vintage he has released separate regional labels. The Polk County bottling from the Eola Hills is extremely pleasing, but the Yamhill County wine, called Elizabeth's Reserve in the 1986 vintage, is a knock out—one of the state's best wines.

Adelsheim believes the trend in the United States is toward "lighter, more delicate wines that fit in and don't compete with food," and his own wines, principally Chardonnay and Pinot Noir, demonstrate that approach with elegance. Although he strives to achieve as much ripeness as possible from Chardonnay, harvesting late and giving good skin contact, the wine doesn't have the forward fruit of many Chardonnays—it is a solid, taut, spicy wine with solid structure. The Pinot Noir, by contrast, is relatively delicate and rounded at a young age, a more subtle wine than many others. The other particularly pleasing wine here is Pinot Gris, which, like those of Eyrie and Ponzi, shows the excellent potential for this as a dry dinner wine—Adelsheim can't produce nearly enough of the stuff.

CHARDONNAY (OREGON) ($$) ★★★ Forward, melony nose, with nice spice and good acid.

CHARDONNAY (YAMHILL) ($$) ★★★★ A tart, taut, lean wine, with very firm fruit and spicy oak. With lots of depth, it needs time to open up. Excellent food wine.

MERLOT ($$) ★★ Dark and woody, with some berry in the nose, somewhat vegetal.

PINOT GRIS ($$) ★★★★ Takes a moment to open up, then rich apple-spice flavors, medium body, and a slight underlying bite. Seafood wine.

PINOT NOIR (POLK) ($$$) ★★★★½ Formerly blended with the Yamhill wine, with the '86 vintage this robust, fruity, tart wine has its own label. Loads of fruit.

PINOT NOIR, ELIZABETH'S RESERVE (YAMHILL) ($$$) ★★★★★ Outstanding release from the '86 vintage: like all Adelsheim Pinots, not weighty, but layers of fruit, oak, and leathery-earthy flavors. Great depth and balance, should be excellent long-term.

RED TABLE ($) ★★ Quite dark, with hints of Pinot Noir in the nose, but rather rough, plummy flavors.

SAUVIGNON BLANC ($$) ★★ Dark color, melony nose—quite biting, with a hint of caramel.

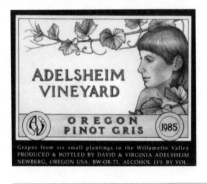

AIRLIE WINERY
Monmouth   (1986)
3,500 cases

Larry and Alice Preedy figure their friends back in Kansas farm country must be surprised that they're making wine, but for the Preedys, it's just a logical extension of growing the grapes. They harvested Christmas trees to plant vines in a fifteen-acre plot in forested hills well off the beaten track, southwest of Salem, inspired by their winemaking neighbors at Serendipity Cellars. But their farming experience and instincts have stood them in good stead, as they are clearly producing very nice fruit (they are also buying grapes from other nearby producers).

The initial focus here is on fruity whites, and what distinguishes them from so many others is that all are absolutely fresh and very crisp, with balancing acid for the slight sweetness. Most notable is the Müller-Thurgau, which can be too soft and rather dull elsewhere but here has delightful flavors and shows the potential for this grape in Oregon's cool growing areas. The Gewürztraminer is in the same class—not a big wine but lovely fruit. On the other hand, Preedy hasn't quite found the touch with Pinot Noir (as he himself will admit); though he made some prizewinning Pinots as an amateur, this wine has simple fruit and a bit too much ripeness. (But there's a very pleasant Pinot Noir blush.)

CERES ($) ★★   Pinot Noir made in Beaujolais style—but it's not as grapy as one might like. Tart, cherry-rhubarb flavors.

CRIMSON ($) ★★★   A blush from Pinot Noir with tart, fresh flavors and a nice balance. Not fancy, but tasty.

GEWÜRZTRAMINER ($) ★★★½ A lovely, clean, fresh nose with light spice—dry and balanced. An impressive first effort.

GEWÜRZTRAMINER, LATE HARVEST ($$) ★★★ Thick, rich, sweet, but rather bitter in the finish.

MÜLLER-THURGAU ($) ★★★½ One of the best in the state. Lovely wildflower nose, soft peachy flavors, just slightly sweet.

RIESLING ($) ★★½ A simple wine that features a bready nose and good tart fruit.

ALPINE VINEYARDS
Monroe   (1980)
6,000 cases

Alpine is an exception to the Oregon rule of wineries known for Pinot Noir and Chardonnay—Cabernet Sauvignon and Riesling are the bread and butter here. The difference is mostly location: The vineyards, twenty acres in size, are in rolling hills at the far southern end of the Willamette Valley, not far from Eugene, where it's clearly warmer and drier than farther north.

Owner Dan Jepsen, a physician, really came here from California to make Riesling, convinced that no decent Riesling was going to be made in California's warm climate. His winemaking began at home, but this small tidy operation impresses one for its thorough professionalism now. The winery first attracted attention for its excellent Riesling (which seems to have gotten more austere in recent years), but the most interesting wine is the Cabernet Sauvignon (blended with small amounts of Merlot and Cabernet Franc), which, while it doesn't have the weight of those from California or Washington, has considerable in common with medium-weight Bordeaux. Although Cabernet is not supposed to ripen consistently in the Willamette, Jepsen has had only one vintage when this was a problem. So far, at least, this is really the only good Cabernet from Willamette Valley grapes.

The Pinot Noir, while good, hasn't had the finesse of many others from the Willamette and sometimes seems overripe, while the Chardonnay, without the softening effects of malolactic fermentation, is firm and tart and needs time to develop. Despite the stylistic differences that set the wines apart from many of their counterparts, the overall quality has been quite impressive.

CABERNET SAUVIGNON, VINTAGE SELECT ($$$) ★★★★
A fine Cabernet from a state not noted for them. Soft, forward fruit, with a balance of berries and herbs in the nose, and a fair amount of spicy oak.
CHARDONNAY ($$$) ★★★ A firm and straightforward wine, with light fruit and solid oak—very crisp.
GEWÜRZTRAMINER ($$) ★★★½ A full-bodied version that can be positively fat in ripe years. Dry, soft lychee-nut flavors.

PINOT NOIR ($$$) ★★½ Very ripe flavors with some plumminess and lots of spicy fruit in the best years. Can be slightly harsh and hot.

RIESLING ($$) ★★★½ Always well made, it has varied from tart, grapefruity flavors to a ripe, soft peachiness. Always crisp and just off-dry.

AMITY VINEYARDS
Amity (1976)
9,500 cases

Myron Redford is one of the gurus of the Oregon wine industry. He abandoned academia for the opportunity to make world-class Pinot Noir and has clearly succeeded. Some of Redford's earliest efforts won national recognition, and the wines have only gotten better, establishing him as one of the best producers in the state. The production of Amity's own small fifteen-acre vineyard is augmented by grapes purchased from other local vineyards.

The Amity style is bone dry, even for the white wines, and the emphasis is on finesse and balance rather than weight. This is one winery that takes the idea of making "food wines" perfectly seriously. Amity was also the first to make a Pinot Noir "Nouveau"—a light, simple, fruity Pinot made using the Beaujolais method of carbonic maceration, for drinking right after the vintage (though Amity Nouveau typically lasts for a couple of years). And 1989 will see the first release in the state of a small amount of Gamay Noir—the true Gamay grape of Beaujolais.

Redford is unusual in holding back his Pinot Noir a good year or two after most Oregon wineries have released theirs (the '83 Reserve was released only in 1988); he winces at the thought that people should be drinking his Pinot Noir too early. Different releases include a regular "Oregon" Pinot Noir for earlier drinking, a blended Reserve, and an occasional Estate bottling for unusually fine individual batches.

The fruit is never overwhelming in these wines, and the color often seems quite light, but the appearances are deceiving. They have surprising depth, particularly the Reserves, and great staying power and are fine drinking even from off vintages, like '84. The whites show the same tendency to rein in the fruit. The Chardonnay may not appeal to those who like a fat, voluptuous Chard—the lean, oaky style takes some time to develop. Perhaps most successful is the Gewürztraminer, which avoids the flabby, overripe character of so much Gewürz and really does go beautifully with foods, particularly spicy but light dishes.

CHARDONNAY ($$) ★★★ Intense, rather citrusy flavors, some oak in the nose, tart. A fairly lean wine.

CHARDONNAY, RESERVE ($$$) ★★★½ Lots of buttery-oaky flavors characterize this wine, which has austere fruit. A lean, tart style that needs some bottle age.

GEWÜRZTRAMINER ($$) ★★★½ Light, dry, some flowery-apple aromas. More delicate than most, with pleasant spice but no bitterness.

OREGON BLUSH ($) ★★★ This is one of the nicer blushes around, with lots of earthy Pinot fruit. It may be a little dry for some blush fanciers.

PINOT NOIR ($$) ★★★½ The regular bottling, which is always reasonably priced, shows fresh, true, cherrylike Pinot flavors, in a light and lean style.

PINOT NOIR (ESTATE) ($$$) ★★★★½ Very dark, with cherry and oak flavors in good balance. Lovely, rich wine with solid tannin.

PINOT NOIR, RESERVE ($$$$) ★★★★★ This Reserve bottling is consistently one of the very best in the state. Deep, rich, velvety flavors develop in the glass. It doesn't seem as full-bodied as some, but there is plenty of spiciness and a long finish—and it has demonstrated ageability. Fine stuff (though the long-awaited '83 wasn't quite all-star quality at its release).

PINOT NOIR NOUVEAU ($) ★★★ The first Nouveau from Oregon and still probably the best, with surprisingly deep flavor and zingy tartness. It drinks well for at least a year or so. Fine value.

RIESLING, DRY ($$) ★★½ Light, tart, grapefruity. This uncomplicated wine is one Riesling that does fine with (light) food.

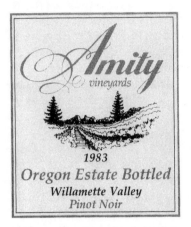

ANKENY VINEYARDS WINERY
Salem   (1985)
2,500 cases

The focus at Ankeny, by preference of partner-winemaker Joe Olexa, is on Chardonnay. Half of his vineyard (one of five in the partnership) is planted to the grape. He has balanced his plantings between the 108 and Draper clones, hoping that the higher sugars of the latter will balance the higher acids of the former. The vineyard, southwest of Salem, right on the valley floor, appears to have a warm microclimate, which suits Olexa's purpose: to produce a relatively ripe, higher-alcohol style of Chardonnay. His goal is to capture the fruitiness of ripe grapes: "Fresh grape juice with alcohol—that's my ideal," he says. The first vintages were interesting—warmer and more assertive than most Willamette Chardonnays, but with some off flavors.

Olexa's background is academic, and he claims still to be feeling his way along with wine. One experiment involves Cabernet Sauvignon, which he is hopeful will ripen reasonably well in his warm location. So far the wine shows the same herbaceous character as other northern Oregon Cabernets. The other white wines are not remarkable (though there's an interesting white blend), but the Pinot Noir shows good possibilities, and there will also be Pinot gris.

CABERNET SAUVIGNON ($$) ★★ Typically (for Oregon) very herbal–bell pepper on the nose, with light, clean fruit. Nicely made.

CHARDONNAY ($$) ★★ A big, hot wine with a woody oak nose and lots of ripe fruit. An aggressive style.

GEWÜRZTRAMINER ($) ★★ Interesting nose of apples and hay. Dry, soft, just a bit thin.

PINOT NOIR ($$) ★★½ Light color, cherry nose, tart, tannic. It shows promise, though it seems a bit hard and unyielding when young.

RIESLING ($) ★ Hot, overly ripe flavors, lacks varietal character.

WHITE TABLE ($) ★★ An interesting blend of four varieties. Slightly sweet, nice green-apple fruit.

ARTERBERRY CELLARS
McMinnville   (1979)
6,000 cases

Arterberry was the first winery in Oregon to experiment with Champagne-style sparkling wine, and although it now has a diversified line of varietals, it is still best known for its sparklers. Fred Arterberry, Jr., University of California at Davis trained, actually started out making sparkling apple cider from local fruit before turning to the demanding Champagne-method wines, which include a Pinot Noir–Chardonnay blend (the Brut) and a sparkling Riesling. Grapes come from the Red Hills Vineyard, in the hills above Dundee, not far from Knudsen Erath's vineyard.

Like other sparkling wine makers in the Willamette, Arterberry finds the grapes of lower sugar levels and high acidity ideal for sparkling wine production, but so far, at least, these wines don't have the richness one associates with French Champagne. In contrast, the still Reserve Pinot Noir produced by the winery is one of the riper, plummier versions in the area, with lots of fruit. Other wines are well made in a forward, fruity fashion and represent reasonable value. The Blush in particular will appeal to those who like a very soft style, while the Riesling has plenty of flavor.

BRUT (RED HILLS) ($$$) ★★½ Pretty color, pungent, somewhat woody nose, crisp fruit but a bit heavy in the mouth.
CHARDONNAY ($) ★★ Warm oaky-appley nose, fruity, medium-bodied.
PINOT NOIR, RESERVE (RED HILLS) ($$$) ★★★½ Ripe, plummy, almost raspberry fruit, spicy and soft. More berrylike and forward than many. Not an ager, one suspects.

RED HILLS BLUSH ($) ★★½   Very soft, strawberry flavors—quite nice.

RIESLING, VINTAGE SELECT ($) ★★★   Ripe, peachy fruit—very fresh—with good tartness.

ASHLAND HILLS WINERY
Ashland   (1988)
1,500 cases

The Oregon Shakespeare Festival town of Ashland, on the warm eastern side of the Rogue River growing area, is home to this tiny new winery, owned by Bill Knowles. An initial four acres of vineyard has been planted, with more planned; the initial crush of purchased grapes included Pinot Noir, Chardonnay, and Müller-Thurgau. The winemaker is John Eagle, formerly with Valley View Vineyard. Wines not tasted.

AUTUMN WIND VINEYARD
Newberg   (1987)
1,200 cases

An interest in the outdoors and a love for home winemaking brought Tom and Wendy Kreutner from Los Angeles to Portland and finally to a small vineyard northwest of Newberg, behind the famous Dundee Hills. Planting the vineyard (still just seven acres) was a struggle—"a little different from a desk job," notes Tom, a financial officer for a Portland bank. They have now given over the task of planting, as many local wineries have, to professional vineyard developers.

In addition to the standard Pinot Noir and Chardonnay, the Kreutners are also interested in Müller-Thurgau: They made some in their first crush for the Viento label (owned by Laurel Ridge winemaker Rich Cushman) and liked the wine. Now they're contemplating their own release. Although the youth of their vineyard dictates buying grapes, they plan to continue this anyway, liking the complexity in the wine that different vineyards can give.

The very young wines are hard to evaluate, but the Chardonnay has good body, and the Pinot Noir in barrel looks to have plenty of weight. The Kreutners like Pinot Noir Blanc as a "fallback wine," in case of a bad vintage.

CHARDONNAY ($$) ★★★ Some toasty character, tart fruit, medium weight. Needs some time.

VIENTO MÜLLER-THURGAU ($) ★★ Slightly flowery nose, light earthy flavors.

VIENTO PINOT NOIR BLANC ($) ★★ Nice strawberry nose, good fruit, quite soft.

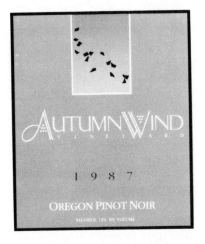

BETHEL HEIGHTS VINEYARD
Salem   (1984)
6,500 cases

The vineyard site was first picked out and established in the seventies by Vic Winquist, whom the present owners describe as a visionary. Many of the best-known vineyards in the Willamette Valley are in the Red Hills of Dundee, on the west side of the valley. Bethel Heights was one of the first vineyards in the Eola Hills, which rise in the middle of the valley; the weather is ever so slightly warmer here, the winery sits on the crest of a hill, and the sun exposure on south-facing slopes is excellent. A number of new vineyards have now been planted in the Eola Hills, and it is on its way to becoming a prime growing subregion.

The winemaking here is very serious, the product of a joint effort between two families who came here to fulfill "a 1960s dream" of living and working together on the land. When they planted the sizable fifty-acre vineyard in 1977, they "gambled" on the Burgundian varieties, Pinot Noir and Chardonnay, though these were not yet popular. One of the interesting features of the vineyard is the Wente clone of Chardonnay, not found in many Northwest vineyards; the Wente is an earlier ripener and can produce lusher flavors to add complexity to the final blend.

Vineyard manager Ted and winemaker Terry Casteel are both restless experimenters—with different grapes, growing techniques, blends—so it seems likely the wines will continue to evolve. But quality is already high. The Pinot Noir established its reputation from the first vintage, 1984 (the Casteels feel their grapes do better than most in cool years), though in earlier vintages Bethel Heights grapes had gone into some well-received California Pinots. Not one of the most complex wines, it is characterized by delicious fruit and lovely texture. The Chardonnay has not been consistent but has improved with each vintage, and the large assortment of other wines are all well made in a fruity style, and often quite interesting.

CABERNET SAUVIGNON ($$) ★★   Available only at the winery, this wine has a definite herbal, dill quality (the grapes don't ripen easily) with some oak.

CHARDONNAY ($$) ★★★½   Newer vintages have a big toasty oak nose, lots of spicy, fruity flavors. An open and appealing wine.

CHENIN BLANC ($) ★★   This will not seem typical to most people—an interesting nose of clover and citrus, light, tart.

GEWÜRZTRAMINER ($$) ★★   This used to be quite dry and subtle and has gotten sweeter and more floral. Nose of apples and nutmeg, balanced.

PINOT NOIR ($$$) ★★★★   Lovely black cherry nose. Tart, delicate, spicy—a very charming wine.

PINOT NOIR, RESERVE ($$$) ★★★★½   Very closed in its youth—some cherry and black pepper flavors. Quite rich and tannic. Time will tell.

PINOT NOIR BLANC ($) ★★★½   Very pretty color with lots of good Pinot fruit and a fine balance of sweetness and tartness. A great picnic wine.

RIESLING ($$) ★★★   Light, flowery, almost Muscaty nose. Fresh and crisp and slightly sweet—a popular style.

BETHEL HEIGHTS VINEYARD

OREGON PINOT NOIR

WILLAMETTE VALLEY

1984

GROWN, PRODUCED AND BOTTLED BY
BETHEL HEIGHTS VINEYARD, INC., SALEM, OREGON BW-OR-98
ALCOHOL 11.5% BY VOLUME

BJELLAND VINEYARDS
Roseburg   (1969)
500 cases

The fate of this tiny winery, one of the oldest in the state, is currently unclear. Owners Paul and Mary Bjelland are no longer able to manage the work and reportedly have been trying to sell the winery, including a farm and twenty-one acres of vineyard.

Although the winery has a full line of varietal wines, it is perhaps best known for its fresh, full-flavored wild blackberry wine, a consistent award winner. The other unusual offering is a woodruff-flavored May Wine. Paul Bjelland was the founder of the Oregon Winegrowers Association and has done much over the years to promote the wine industry in the state.

WILD BLACKBERRY ($) ★★★ Deep color, wonderful blackberry nose and flavors, dry.

American Wines of the Northwest

BRIDGEVIEW VINEYARD
Cave Junction   (1986)
25,000 cases

The theme here is clearly German. Owners Robert and Lilo Kerican and Ernie Brodie found winemaker Dieter Hemberger, who has had long experience in the German wine industry, while they were in Europe on an equipment-buying expedition, and much of the paraphernalia of the winery is of German origin. Hemberger has brought with him a German style—the wines are quite light, carefully made, fresh, and simple.

The German influence extends to the vineyard as well, where vines are planted much closer together than is usual in the United States. The theory is that more vines per acre will produce fewer, but higher-quality, berries per vine while still yielding the same tonnage. At least as important is that lower yields per vine allow the grapes to ripen more readily, which may prove important in this location, the Illinois Valley in southwestern Oregon, 1,200 feet high in the mountains just 30 miles or so from the ocean. It seems a curiously isolated place for a good-sized winery, surrounded by mountains and forest, but 75 acres of vines are planted and production is slated to increase rapidly.

The wines are aimed at the lower end of premium market—all reasonably priced, all straightforward and uncomplicated in their flavors. Assuming that its marketing is successful, Bridgeview could provide a good source of relatively inexpensive wines in good supply. The Müller-Thurgau may prove of most interest: It shows very nicely the softness and earthiness of this grape. The first release of Pinot Noir was grapy and boisterous and a super value. Drink it up.

For the 1988 vintage, the winery hired French-trained winemaker Laurent Montalieu to replace Hemberger, who returned to Germany.

CHARDONNAY ($) ★½ Restrained fruit, crisp, light, OK.

GEWÜRZTRAMINER ($) ★★½ Fresh, light Gewürz nose, some soft spice, slightly bitter finish.

MÜLLER-THURGAU ($) ★★½ Very soft and delicate, with earthy flavors.

PINOT NOIR ($) ★★½ Very ripe and fruity, tangy, not elegant, but lots of flavor. It would be tough to find a better bargain on the market.

PINOT NOIR BLANC ($) ★★ Rosé color, with fresh strawberry flavors.

RIESLING, DRY ($) ★★ Peachy nose, crisp, fresh, pleasant.

RIESLING, MEDIUM DRY ($) ★★ A more candylike nose, with a bit more body and medium sweetness.

BROADLEY VINEYARDS
Monroe   (1986)
2,700 cases

Producer of perhaps the first really exciting Pinot Noir from the south end of the Willamette Valley, this small winery has made an impressive debut. The fifteen-acre vineyard (Pinot Noir and Chardonnay only), located in the hills about twenty miles northwest of Eugene, occupies a site probably a bit warmer than those of the northern Willamette. Owner Craig Broadley believes the high ridges surrounding his vineyard provide protection from poor fall weather, enabling him to achieve the fully ripe qualities he wants in his grapes.

The Broadleys came to Oregon from the Bay Area; like many others in Oregon they dreamed of moving to the country. After taking winemaking classes at the University of California's Davis campus, and searching unsuccessfully for land in the Napa Valley, they decided to come north, settling close to Eugene as a compromise between rural and urban environments.

Expert opinion warned them off their chosen site for grapes, but the vines were planted anyway in 1981 and 1982. Broadley's goal is to make "old-fashioned wines, with lots of stems and tannin and oak." The first reserve Pinot, in a full, ripe, flavory style, has considerable flair, if not the elegance that marks northern Willamette Pinots. The regular Pinot, which Broadley calls a "prerain" wine (harvested before the rains in 1986), doesn't have quite the fruit but is equally well made. (The winery also produces a light, inexpensive nonvintage Pinot.) Broadley thinks Oregon Chardonnay tends to be "swamped" by new oak: He is using mostly old oak and hoping for ripe fruit flavors in the wine. The newest vintage is not a big wine but has a round feel to it. "I don't play around with it a lot," he says, and is unconcerned about aging potential.

CHARDONNAY ($$) ★★★   A subtle balance of fruit and oak, good crispness—forward and appealing.

PINOT NOIR ($$) ★★★   The fruit's a shade lean, but the structure is good. Well made.

PINOT NOIR, RESERVE ($$) ★★★★   Ripe cherry nose with black pepper accents; rich. May need a little time. Quite impressive.

BROADLEY
VINEYARDS
1986
RESERVE
OREGON PINOT NOIR
RED TABLE WINE
PRODUCED AND BOTTLED BY BROADLEY VINEYARDS
MONROE, OREGON
BW-OR-112
CONTAINS SULFITES

CALLAHAN RIDGE WINERY
Roseburg   (1987)
5,000 cases

When the original Garden Valley Winery partnership
split up, the wines went to Sweet Home. Meanwhile, former Garden Valley winemaker Richard Mansfield, in
partnership with Frank Guido, former Garden Valley
partner, is attempting to carry on with a new winery,
called Callahan Ridge, near the old location. Mansfield is
an Oregon native but his wine training is German, and the
light, fruity style of the old Garden Valley wines, even for
Pinot Noir, clearly showed this background. The new Callahan wines have been made in a fuller, riper style that
will probably appeal more to an American palate. In particular, Mansfield is making a serious effort with Gewürztraminer in a dry Alsatian style as well as with sweeter
dessert wines. Mansfield's winemaking has always been
careful, and this may be a place to watch.

CHARDONNAY (DOERNER RANCH) ($$) ★★½ Nose
and flavors of apple and oak, good fruit, slight harsh-
ness.

GEWÜRZTRAMINER (ELKTON) ($) ★★★½ Full-bodied, rich, with ripe apple flavors, fermented dry.

CAMERON WINERY
Dundee   (1984)
2,500 cases

Cameron made a splash with its first vintage of Pinot Noir, the '84, which turned out to be one of the better ones from a difficult year, but it's the Chardonnays that have really gained the winery a reputation. Winemaker John Paul, trained as a marine biologist, is another refugee from California, where he worked for several wineries, including Carneros Creek. He traveled as far afield as New Zealand looking for a climate approximating Burgundy's before he finally settled on Oregon, where he formed a partnership with Bill Wayne, owner of Abbey Ridge Vineyards. A seventeen-acre vineyard in the Dundee Hills will grow Pinot Noir and Chardonnay exclusively; grapes are also purchased from another Dundee vineyard. Production is tiny and will still be small even if Paul doubles it, as he hopes to. It would appear that Cameron may end up one of the area's top-quality producers.

Paul has worked hard on his Chardonnay, a wine he thinks requires much more effort than Pinot Noir. Blending fruit from different clones and different vineyards, and using a variety of yeasts including some he brought from Australia, he is striving to build richness and complexity into the wine, and his Chardonnay even from lighter vintages seems to have more body to it than others in Oregon.

The Pinots are silky and elegant, with plenty of fruit in a rather forward style. There are really three levels of Pinot quality here, providing something for a variety of consumers; the "press juice" from the Pinot Noir (the juice that comes off when the grapes are pressed hard) goes into the Red Table Wine, one of the nicest examples of young, fruity Pinot Noir in the state, and very reasonably priced. Keeping the press wine separate also helps keep the regular Pinot from being too rough or tannic.

Also notable is a Late Harvest Riesling, one of the few in the state, which is unusually full-bodied and alcoholic, as it was allowed to finish natural fermentation. An excellent wine.

CHARDONNAY ($$) ★★★★   Firm wine with a sweet butterscotch nose, round flavors, and good tartness.

CHARDONNAY, RESERVE ($$) ★★★★½   Very buttery nose, with very rich, tart, spicy fruit and excellent body. Not a bashful wine.

PINOT NOIR ($$$) ★★★★½   Delicious raspberry-cherry fruit, with good perfume and rounded flavors. Not fat, but soft and almost delicate.

PINOT NOIR, RESERVE ($$$) ★★★★½   Quite similar to the regular bottling, with solid cherry flavor, a little more depth, and a little more spice.

RED TABLE ($) ★★★   Quite pink in color, it has wonderful grapy flavors, good peppery qualities, and plenty of zip. Best young, but lasts well.

RIESLING, BOTRYTIS *"EUGENIA"* ($$$) ★★★★   Very ripe, heavy apricot nose and full, rich flavors, with excellent balance and a long finish.

CHATEAU BENOIT
Carlton   (1979)
17,000 cases

A substantial proportion of the production at this winery is in sparkling wine—a Champagne-method blend of mostly Pinot Noir, with smaller amounts of Chardonnay and Pinot Blanc. The Brut, which is well priced and well made, has proven to be popular, and it helps balance out the winery's production. In warm vintages, Pinot Noir can be made into varietal table wine, while in poorer vintages it goes into the nonvintage Brut—a nice insurance policy. More recently the winery has released a vintage Sparkling Blanc de Blancs, a 100 percent Chardonnay-based wine that spent three and a half years aging on the lees.

Chateau Benoit has twenty-five acres of vineyards, half of which are near Eugene, at the southern end of the Willamette Valley, and half of which are near McMinnville in the center of the valley. Unlike most of their neighbors, the Benoits have put less focus on Pinot Noir and Chardonnay and relatively more on varietals like Sauvignon Blanc and Müller-Thurgau. There have been several winemakers who worked well with the whites, and new winemaker Gerard Rottiers, from Chablis (where he used to have his own *domaine*), is determined to make a Chablis-styled Chardonnay. (But like some other Burgundy veterans, he is convinced that Oregon doesn't have the same Chardonnay grape grown in France.)

The Brut, although it spends a year on the lees, doesn't have the rich, yeasty character of French Champagne, but it has lively, delicate fruit and good bubbles. The Blanc de Blancs has more of the toasty quality of French Champagne but still lots of acidity—very much a food wine, it will probably benefit from some more age. The Benoits are also committed to Müller-Thurgau, which has the advantage of ripening early and being a heavy producer; the wine it produces can be attractive and floral, though not often substantial. The Sauvignon Blanc, by contrast, is one of Oregon's more assertive examples and is always well made. Pinot Noir, surprisingly, hasn't been as good here, though recent vintages have shown more fruit and depth.

The winery also produces a line of wines from Washington grapes under the Nisqually Ridge label.

BLANC DE BLANCS ($$$) ★★★½ Some toastiness, with tart, rhubarby flavors, more rounded than the Brut. Ageable?

BRUT ($$$) ★★★ Subtle Pinot nose with hints of rhubarb—tart and delicate, with excellent bubbles. A fine, light-styled sparkling wine well suited to food, but with no great complexity. It does round out with age.

CHARDONNAY ($$) ★★½ Light nose and flavors, some oak—not terribly varietal.

MÜLLER-THURGAU ($) ★★½ Very perfumey, light, soft, not much to it, but pleasant.

PINOT NOIR ($$) ★★★ Light color, ripe cherry nose with forward fruit and considerable bite. Newer vintages are showing more Pinot character.

RAINBOW RUN ($) ★½ Light, fruity flavors with a bit of bite. A blush made from hard-press juice from the sparkling wine.

SAUVIGNON BLANC ($$) ★★★ A warm, grassy nose with lots of tart fruit—can be a little sharp, but fresh and lively.

1983
CHÂTEAU BENOIT

OREGON
PINOT NOIR

Produced and bottled by Château Benoit, Carlton, Oregon (BW-OR 80)
Alcohol 12.5% by volume

CHEHALEM MOUNTAIN WINERY *See* MULHAUSEN VINEYARDS

COOPER MOUNTAIN VINEYARDS WINERY
Beaverton   (1987)
1,500 cases

Owner Robert Gross, a Portland psychiatrist, was part of a group of Seattle home winemakers, several of whom went on to found French Creek Cellars in Woodinville, Washington. Gross moved south and bought a seventy-two-acre estate just outside suburban Beaverton, Oregon (not far from Ponzi Vineyards), and planted thirty-five acres with grapes. For several years he has sold the grapes (mostly Pinot Noir, with some Chardonnay and Pinot Gris) to a number of local wineries; 1987 marked the first crush for his own small production. Although he has a solid background in winemaking, he has hired Rich Cushman of Laurel Ridge as a consultant. Production will remain small, and most of the grapes from what will eventually be eighty acres of vines will continue to be sold—but Gross wants to be able to showcase his own grapes, especially Pinot Noir.

CHARDONNAY ($$) ★★★   Very buttery nose opens into light fruit with good acidity. Long finish seems slightly off.

CÔTE DES COLOMBES

This winery, founded in 1977, is no longer producing its own wines, though in 1987 the facility was used by another winery for its crush. A few wines are still on the market.

CHARLES COURY VINEYARD   *See* LAUREL RIDGE WINERY

CROCHAD
Dundee

A partnership between Australian sparkling wine producer Brian Croser and American wine importer Robert Chadderdon, this low-profile operation in Dundee may make quite a mark when its first Champagne-method wines debut in 1989. The wines, a traditional blend of Chardonnay, Pinot Noir, and Pinot Meunier, are in bottle, getting eighteen months of lees contact, but Croser is aiming for a delicately fruity style. Most impressive is the scale of this winery—a reputed 20,000 cases, easily making it the largest producer of Champagne-like sparkling wine in the Northwest. The winemaker is Rollin Soles, who has worked in Australia as well as the Northwest. ("Crochad" is a working name only.)

DOMAINE DROUHIN
Dundee   (1988)

   The French parent company is Maison Joseph Drouhin
of Beaune, one of the larger and more prestigious of Burgundy growers and *négociants.* Intrigued by the quality of
Oregon Pinot Noir ever since his own wines were bested
in international competition by an Eyrie Pinot (see page
175), Robert Drouhin has bought 140 acres of prime land
in the Dundee Hills, though just eight have been planted
so far. Daughter Véronique, who has worked the Oregon
harvest before, will supervise the vintage; Domaine Drouhin is temporarily sharing the Veritas Vineyard facility
until its new winery is built. The first crush was in 1988;
it will be intriguing to see what influence this new French
enterprise, backed with tremendous experience, will
bring to Oregon wine. Wines not tasted.

ELK COVE VINEYARDS
Gaston   (1977)
14,000 cases

   Pat and Joe Campbell are not wine professionals by
background (Joe is a doctor), and while Pat has taken the
obligatory enology short courses at California's Davis
campus, they feel they have learned more from what they
have picked up informally from European winemakers.
Unlike most winemaking families that started off as amateurs, the Campbells have shown a consistent ability to
make top-quality wine. They have thirty-six acres of their
own vineyards on a picturesque hillside well off the beaten
track, on the western edge of the Willamette Valley, but
they also buy grapes from two other nearby vineyards,

Wind Hills and Dundee Hills, and often release separate vineyard-designated wines (which unfortunately can get a bit confusing).

Elk Cove made some excellent Rieslings early on, which helped make its name—wines with lots of fruit in a very crisp, fresh style—and it still makes fine Late Harvest Riesling and even Late Harvest Gewürztraminer, fairly unusual wines in Oregon. Chardonnay has been spotty: There is an excellent Reserve, barrel-fermented, with rich toasty flavors, but the regular bottling lacks depth, and there is also an "Oregon"-designated Chardonnay that has little character (though it's popular with restaurants for its low price).

Elk Cove Pinots have always been impressive—riper and fuller-bodied than most others from Oregon—though this has occasionally meant they haven't aged quite as well. They definitely show best in the warmer vintages, when several different versions are produced. The Wind Hills Pinot, from a warm vineyard site, is the most complex—a big, smoky wine with some tealike flavors. The Estate Pinot is also big and ripe and more straightforward, while the Dundee Hills can be a fairly hard and herbal wine that is not as forthcoming. All of them should appeal to those who like their Pinot full-flavored and spicy.

CHARDONNAY ($$) ★★½ Rich, fat, soft apple flavors—loose knit and slightly awkward. Can be lemony in cooler years.

CHARDONNAY, RESERVE ($$$) ★★★½ Restrained, almost Chablis-like style, with pineapple and oaky toastiness in the nose, and lovely fruit and balance.

GEWÜRZTRAMINER ($) ★★★ Dry, spicy, a strong lychee-nut nose, with good body.

GEWÜRZTRAMINER, LATE HARVEST ($$$) ★★★½ Definite Gewürz nose, with strong fruit and spice. An interesting wine.

PINOT NOIR (DUNDEE HILLS) ($$$) ★★★ Less fruity and more herbal than the other two—can be a bit harsh in youth, though there's good depth.

PINOT NOIR (ESTATE) ($$$) ★★★½ Big smoky nose, intense fruit, lots of flavor—a fairly straightforward style.

PINOT NOIR (WIND HILL) ($$$) ★★★★½ Most complex and interesting of the Pinots, with a spicy, smoky nose, solid fruit with some tealike accents, and a long finish. An excellent wine.

PINOT NOIR, WHITE ($) ★★½ Intense varietal flavors in a slightly sweet style—a very pleasant blush-type wine.

RIESLING ($) ★★ Pleasant apple nose and bright flavors, good tartness, but nothing special.

RIESLING, LATE HARVEST ($$$) ★★★ Straightforward nose, tart apple flavor with fine balance. Fairly lean for a late harvest.

ELLENDALE VINEYARDS
Dallas   (1981)
2,500 cases

It's hard to know how seriously to take this small operation in the middle of the Willamette Valley, run by retired Air Force officer and landscape artist Robert Hudson. This is, after all, the place with a blended berry wine called Woolly Booger. The array of fruit and berry wines was apparently a stopgap while the Hudsons waited for their fifteen-acre vineyard, planted in 1980, to produce grapes. The speciality is mead, wine made from honey, which comes in several versions here (including one aged in French oak). It's unquestionably an acquired taste.

The fruit wines seem rather ordinary—good enough, but without capturing real freshness as some Northwest fruit wine producers have. The grape wines, which the winery claims will increase in importance, also seem fairly ordinary and quite variable (there are a number of wines made from Washington grapes as well as those made from locally purchased grapes). The Pinot Noir is probably the best, with plenty of ripe flavor, but it doesn't have the balance and structure that one would like.

The newest effort for the winery is a sparkling wine, made by the Champagne method, from a blend of 70 percent Pinot Noir and 30 percent Chardonnay. The wine, called Crystal Mist, comes in both Brut and Demi-Sec styles and has full, fruity, if not elegant flavors.

BEAVER GOLD ($) ★★ From the American Niagara grape and surprisingly decent. Definite but not aggressive "foxy" nose, sweet, clean, tart.

CHARDONNAY ($) ★ Several different bottlings range from decent appley fruit to heavier, woody, viscous flavors. Not too interesting.

CRYSTAL MIST BRUT ($$$) ★★½   A big, grapy nose, lots of fine bubbles, and plenty of flavor.

PINOT NOIR ($$$) ★★   Loose-knit, plummy flavors— tends toward overripeness. Earthy, good fruit, but lacks finesse.

PINOT NOIR, WHITE ($) ★½   Some Pinot and berrylike flavors, light, good crispness.

LOGANBERRY ($) ★★½   Good, fresh berry nose and flavor. Not overly sweet.

MEAD, SEMIDRY ($) ½   Rather dirty, barnyardy aromas, strong honey aftertaste. Not for the faint of heart.

HENRY ENDRES WINERY
Oregon City   (1935)
4,000 cases (capacity)

The Endres family is still running this small fruit and berry winery, which was established after the demise of Prohibition, in Portland's suburbs. The wines are very traditional (there are none from vinifera), and they are mostly sold directly out of the winery. Wines not tasted.

EOLA HILLS WINE CELLARS
Rickreall   (1986)
2,000 cases

While everyone else in the Willamette has been planting Pinot Noir and Chardonnay, Tom Huggins decided to plant in addition Chenin Blanc, Sauvignon Blanc, and Cabernet Sauvignon. Why? "I didn't know any better." But he feels the decision was good: He has little competition in Oregon for any of these varietals, and he feels that if the wines succeed, it will put his winery on the map.

Huggins may have the right vineyard for these varieties. The seventy-acre Oak Grove Vineyard, which he owns, is right on the southwest edge of the Eola Hills and apparently soaks up a lot of heat—essential for the late-ripening grapes he has planted. Eola Hills has started small but will be growing; a large inventory of French oak barrels testifies to the winery's commitment to expansion as well as to serious winemaking.

Huggins got into grape growing as a hobbyist, found he had too many grapes for that, and developed a friendship with winemaker Ken Wright, of Panther Creek, which led to the latter's being hired as the Eola Hills winemaker. Wright's philosophy for reds is lots of extract and full body: The Cabernet Sauvignon, which is still in barrel, is very dark and rich and shows none of the green unripe character that plagues Willamette Cabernet. (Nor does the Sauvignon Blanc suffer from the common bell-peppery flavors.) Of the other wines, the Chenin may be of most interest—not a heavy wine but with considerable flavor.

CHENIN BLANC ($) ★★★ Light clover nose, some richness, with light sweetness and lingering flavors. Fine effort.

PINOT NOIR ($$$) ★★★ Restrained cherry nose with a bit of dill, good Pinot fruit, and some tannin—may age well.

SAUVIGNON BLANC ($$) ★★ Steely nose, with light varietal character, sweet oakiness in flavors. Doesn't quite come together.

EOLA HILLS
WINE CELLARS
OREGON
CHENIN BLANC
1987

Produced and bottled by
Eola Hills Wine Cellars, Rickreall, Oregon
Alcohol 11.8% by volume   Contains Sulfites

EVESHAM WOOD VINEYARD
Salem   (1986)
1,000 cases

In 1988 Evesham Wood moved from a rented garage in Newberg to its permanent home in the Eola Hills, where an eight-acre vineyard is planted near Bethel Heights. Owner-winemaker Russ Rainey studied enology in Germany and then apprenticed at the Adams Winery before striking off on his own. He is convinced the Eola Hills, just south and east of the better-known vineyards of the Dundee Hills, are the place for Pinot Noir: "If Dundee is Oregon's Côte de Beaune, then Eola should be our Côte de Nuit," he says, claiming title to the heartiest and most prestigious of Burgundy's red wines. Admitting the elegance of the Dundee wines, he is looking for more strength and structure in his Pinot.

The aim here is to make Chardonnay and Pinot Noir in as traditional and natural a way as possible, with a minimum of treatment. Wines from the 1986 vintage, from purchased grapes, indicate mixed results. The Pinot Noir looks to have the structure and solidity that Rainey wants, with intense fruit and oak and a good hit of tannin. But Rainey indicates he is less pleased with his first effort on Chardonnay—it's fairly hard-edged and has some peculiar flavors, which he attributes to difficulties in handling the grapes in an inadequate facility. Nevertheless, this appears to be a serious effort at making first-class wines.

With a view to the future, part of the vineyard has been set aside for the day when French (rather than Californian) clones of Chardonnay can be planted.

The winery is also producing wines for neighboring Redhawk Vineyard, to be released under a separate label.

CHARDONNAY ($$) ★★ This first effort has some nice toasty oak flavors, but the fruit's rather lean and the finish is awkward.

PINOT NOIR ($$) ★★★½ Ripe cherry-raspberry fruit with a bit of a "matchstick" nose; concentrated, oaky, tannic. Should be one to age.

THE EYRIE VINEYARDS
McMinnville (1970)
8,000 cases

This is where the modern Willamette Valley wine phenomenon started—inside a dilapidated warehouse in the middle of filbert country. David Lett, Eyrie's owner and winemaker and now a revered statesman of Oregon wine, was, as he says, "young and stupid" when he decided in the sixties that Oregon would be the next great wine region of the world. After extensive research on climate, he decided that the Willamette was the perfect place in the United States to grow Pinot Noir. Against the advice of all the experts at California's Davis campus, where he trained, he planted his thirty-acre vineyard in 1966, in the Red Hills of Dundee (where many grape growers have since followed), made his wines, and waited. In the process of developing his wines, he discovered he had to throw away much of what he had learned about making wine in California. But techniques that Lett pioneered in Oregon—fermenting Pinot Noir in small open tanks, barrel-fermenting Chardonnay, leaving the Pinot unfiltered—have been adopted by most other Oregon producers.

Fame arrived in 1979, when Eyrie's '75 Pinot Noir bested some of the great wines of Burgundy in two French tastings. The warehouse still stands, production remains small and is virtually by hand, and the wines are in enormous demand. The Lett style of elegance and balance instead of power and flamboyance has been emulated by a number of other Oregon wineries, but no one does it better than Lett. The wines show considerable flavor even in the off years, like '84, and they always age well—in fact, in their youth they often don't show as well as others.

Pinot Noir grabs most of the attention, but the Chardonnay is also topnotch. Lett dismisses most other white grapes as unsuitable for Oregon ("Riesling has no place here," he says) and his original Riesling vines have long since been switched to Pinot Gris. He makes an exception for this grape—a white cousin of Pinot Noir that Lett introduced to Oregon and continues to extol—and the little-grown Muscat Ottonel, which makes a flowery dry white. The Eyrie Pinot Gris is a very rich example, with considerable complexity and weight despite the fact that it sees no oak. The winery also produces a minute amount of varietal Pinot Meunier, a red cousin of Pinot Noir.

Prices for Eyrie's wines have never been cheap, but they compete in an international market in which they are still (comparatively) reasonably priced.

CHARDONNAY ($$$) ★★★★★ Lett is not sure that Oregon is the best place for Chardonnay, but you wouldn't know it from this wine. Barrel-fermented, it has the richness and butteriness of a fine Burgundy, with plenty of beautifully balanced fruit, though it's not as showy as others. The finish is very long and the wine ages wonderfully.

MUSCAT OTTONEL ($$) ★★★½ Not your average Muscat. Made in a totally dry style, it has an aroma of dried herbs with perhaps a bit of melon. Works well with moderately spicy foods.

PINOT GRIS ($$) ★★★★ The standard for Oregon Pinot Gris, with the dryness and body of Chardonnay but a rush of applelike fruit that is immediately appealing (it sees no oak). Excellent with salmon.

PINOT NOIR ($$$) ★★★★½ Fairly lean, understated style, with cherry fruit, excellent spice, and surprising length.

PINOT NOIR, RESERVE ($$$$) ★★★★★ Reserve bottlings are not heavy or tannic—fruit, spice, and oak are neatly balanced—but the depth is amazing, and the flavors linger on the palate. Very elegant, truly Oregonian.

FLYNN VINEYARDS
Rickreall   (1985)
3,000 cases

The long-range goal of owner Wayne Flynn is apparently to focus on Champagne-style sparkling wine. In the meantime, grapes from this large vineyard (including fifty acres of Pinot Noir) have been sold to other wineries; but a small amount of wine, produced at Yamhill Valley Winery, is being released under the Flynn label. The vineyard lies at the southern end of the Eola Hills, not far from Salem.

CHARDONNAY ($$) ★★★   Butter and vanilla in the nose, with light fruit, and a soft feel on the palate.
PINOT NOIR ($$) ★★★½   An emphasis on the fruit, with lots of cherry aromas in the nose. Good body but not tannic; quite forward.

FORGERON VINEYARDS
Elmira   (1978)
10,000 cases

Lee Smith claims to have the best-researched vineyard site in America—the government compiled hundred of pages of data on soil and climate when it was planning to build a nuclear reactor in this area near Eugene. The reactor plan died and the grapes—twenty-five acres planted, with another forty planned—have taken over. The overall climate is similar to that in the northern part of the valley, though Smith believes daytime temperatures are warmer and nighttime ones cooler. The results in the wines would suggest a somewhat warmer effect on the grapes.

Although Smith describes his own style as "light, high acid, delicate," in fact the wines seem a bit softer and fleshier than many in Oregon. Smith, who has worked in Burgundy, did his enological training in Germany, and a very floral Riesling has been one of the leading wines here. The Pinot Noir is stylistically quite different from most in Oregon—riper, with jammy qualities and a tendency toward harshness. But the warmer conditions are better suited for Cabernet, which has soft, fruity, olivey flavors. None of the wines is terribly complex, but they do seem to benefit from a little bottle age.

CABERNET SAUVIGNON ($$) ★★½ Soft, straightforward wine with enough of a Bordeaux character to make it interesting. Slight herbaceousness.

CHARDONNAY ($$) ★★ Heavy, oaky, soft.

PINOT NOIR ($$$) ★★½ Big, ripe, plummy nose with lots of fruit and spice. Some smoky qualities and occasional harshness.

RIESLING ($) ★★½ Very floral, apricot nose. Ripe (slightly stewed?) flavors, off-dry.

FORIS VINEYARD
Cave Junction   (1986)
4,000 cases

One of the older vineyards in southern Oregon, first planted in 1975, Foris has provided grapes for successful wines at several other Oregon and Washington wineries, including Amity, Bridgeview, and Staton Hills. Now vineyard owner Ted Gerber has decided to sell wine under his own label, though until 1988 the wines were still being made at neighboring facilities. Gerber has twenty acres in Muscat (a specialty), Gewürztraminer, Müller-Thurgau, Chardonnay, and Pinot Noir, all of which do well in the 1,500-foot-high vineyard in the Illinois Valley, though frost control presents some problems. Frosts aside, he likes the area because the cool autumn nights help the grapes retain good acid levels. Eventually he would like to have up to sixty acres in production.

A home winemaker for twenty years, Gerber has slowly moved into the commercial side, "reading every book and going to every wine seminar." While the lighter whites are already on the market, the oak-aged Pinot Noir will not be released for three years. The Muscat is made in a fairly dry style, designed as a dinner wine.

GEWÜRZTRAMINER ($$) ★★ Almost dry, with soft apple fruit—but some off flavors are distracting.
MUSCAT, EARLY ($) ★★½ Ripe Muscat nose with apple fruit, fresh, soft, just lightly sweet. Pleasant, not intense.

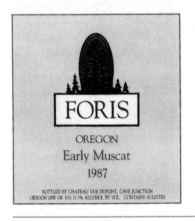

GARDEN VALLEY WINERY
Sweet Home   (1984)

A falling-out among the former partners has split the original Garden Valley Winery of Roseburg in two. One set of partners took the Garden Valley name and the original wines, picked up, and moved to Sweet Home (twenty-five miles northeast of Eugene), the site of one of the vineyards, with thirty-five acres in production, from which the grapes were coming. No wine was made in 1987, but plans call for a new winery in Sweet Home; meanwhile the old wines are still being sold under the Garden Valley name. For the rest of the story, see Callaghan Ridge Winery.

Although the future of this half of the enterprise is very uncertain, some of the original Garden Valley wines, reviewed below, are still on the market (though getting on in years).

CHARDONNAY ($) ★★½ Green apple flavors predominate; a fresh style, light and tart.

PINOT NOIR, WHITE ($) ★★½ Not really a blush, because it has no color to speak of, but a fresh Pinot nose and crisp fruit.

PINOT NOIR NOUVELLE ($) ★½ Pinot in the German style: very light, fruity, but without much interest.

GIRARDET WINE CELLARS
Roseburg (1983)
7,500 cases

It's refreshing and exciting to see a new winery doing something out of the ordinary. Although Girardet has made a splash with its very nice Chardonnay and Riesling, winemaker Philippe Girardet is most interested in his project of blending vinifera grapes with little-used hybrids of French and American grapes (which Americans call French hybrids and the French call American hybrids). The hybrids have several advantages over vinifera grapes, including higher yield and greater hardiness in poor weather and soil conditions.

The goal of the Swiss-born Girardet is to produce lighter,

"more approachable" wines at a reasonable cost, wines for everyday drinking in the European tradition. He deplores both the influence of the "California style" of heavy wine and the reluctance of Americans to try any but varietal wines. Although the first vintage was in 1983, the Girardets have been growing grapes in their eighteen-acre vineyard, on a warm slope just shy of the coastal hills near Roseburg, since 1972.

Girardet's Chardonnay, only lightly oaked, bucks the trend in Oregon toward bigger, more solid Chardonnay—his is delicate and very appealing. Both the Vin Blanc and Vin Rouge are interesting blends, emphasizing fresh fruit, but with some spicy backbone from the hybrids. But the Vin Rouge Reserve, oak aged, is a genuinely serious wine, with some of the rounded fruit and tarry flavors of a southern Rhône. A nice break from those endless Pinot Noirs.

CHARDONNAY ($$) ★★★½ A most appealing haylike nose, with fairly light fruit and delicate oak. Very like a good French Mâcon; all is in balance and it slides down smoothly.

RIESLING ($) ★★★ Ripe, soft fruitiness, good depth, and fine balance.

VIN BLANC ($) ★★ Some Chardonnay fruit on the nose (it's about 50 percent Chardonnay), but with an underlying bite and strength from the hybrids.

VIN ROUGE ($) ★★★ About 50 percent Pinot Noir. The nose is reminiscent of Beaujolais, with fresh, tart, grapy flavors. Simple and flavorful.

VIN ROUGE, RESERVE ($$) ★★★½ More flavor, tannin, and complexity than the regular bottling. Rhône-like, with rounded spicy fruit and good bite. Well worth trying.

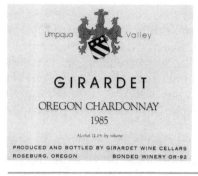

Umpqua Valley

GIRARDET

OREGON CHARDONNAY
1985

Alcohol 12.5% by volume

PRODUCED AND BOTTLED BY GIRARDET WINE CELLARS
ROSEBURG, OREGON   BONDED WINERY OR-92

GLEN CREEK WINERY
Salem   (1982)
4,000 cases

Thomas Dumm's interest in wine led him from owning a successful retail wine shop in southern California to amateur winemaking to buying property in Oregon for his own winery. One of number of new wineries in the Eola Hills west of Salem, Glen Creek has a ten-acre vineyard that includes Cabernet Franc, a grape often used in Bordeaux blends and favored for its soft, fruity qualities. Dumm hopes to make a big-style Cabernet Franc, which he is convinced will not have the problems with vegetal flavors that Cabernet Sauvignon has in Oregon. Comparing the Eola Hills to the better-known Dundee Hills across the valley, Dumm contends Eola has "better soil and a better microclimate."

The success story here is the Whole Cluster Pinot Noir, a wine made by the true carbonic maceration method of Beaujolais: The uncrushed berries are fermented whole, with the fermentation itself, plus the weight of the grapes, eventually bursting them. The maceration technique is meant to produce a red wine with very fresh, grapy flavors, and the Glen Creek version is a marvelous example, with loads of spicy, grapy fruit and lush softness. Dumm hasn't made much of this wine, but it's been so successful that production is being increased. In contrast, the regular Pinot Noir is bigger, harder, and more tannic than is typical in the Willamette—a wine that will probably need some time to show its best.

Other wines are less impressive. Dumm describes himself as fan of Chablis, but his Chardonnay is fruity and quite simple. The Sauvignon Blanc used to be a typically aggressive wine, but the newest vintage has been toned down with considerable sweetness. The Celeste white wine is a blend of two-thirds Müller-Thurgau with one-third Gewürztraminer and combines an intense floral nose with very light fruit. Very much an experimenter, Dumm was also one of the first in the Northwest to put his wine in large boxes for restaurants.

CELESTE ($) ★★ Mostly Müller-Thurgau, with an intense taffylike nose and crisp, clean fruit. Very light body.

CHARDONNAY ($) ★★ Forward, fruity, soft, and simple.

GEWÜRZTRAMINER ($) ★★½ An assertive dry Gewürztraminer, with lychee nut in the nose, good body, and some bitterness.

PINOT NOIR ($$$) ★★★ Tough and angular, lots of tannin, earthy flavors—needs time.

PINOT NOIR, WHITE ($) ½ Lovely salmon color, but the earthy nose seems a little off. Nice crispness.

PINOT NOIR, WHOLE CLUSTER ($) ★★★½ Delightful grapy-peppery aromas (almost like a young Rhône), with utterly fresh fruit and soft texture. There should be more of this in Oregon.

HENRY ESTATE WINERY
Umpqua   (1978)
13,000 cases

Although Scott Henry's family has been farming in the Umpqua Valley for more than a hundred years, it was his years working in California as an engineer in the aerospace industry that convinced him to try growing grapes. When Henry returned to the Umpqua Valley to plant his thirty-acre vineyard, Hillcrest Vineyard had already been in operation nearby for fifteen years, so Henry wasn't starting completely from scratch. Nevertheless, he considers himself something of a rogue in the wine business, having adopted some unusual practices, like planting his vines on bottom land and using exclusively American oak for aging his wines. (He takes pains to point out that he uses American oak not to save money but because he really prefers the flavors, and because he thinks the public prefers the flavors, which are more assertive and spicy than those of French oak.)

The winery is far from fancy, but Henry takes care with winemaking details, and the wines are well made. Although the Pinot Noir has won some impressive awards, it's arguable that the use of American oak has been less successful with this variety than with, say, Chardonnay—it lacks the velvety quality of the best from the state. On the other hand, those who like their wines oaky may find the barrel-fermented Chardonnay to their taste, and it seems to age nicely. Gewürztraminer, though it probably will never be a big seller, may be Henry's most successful wine—it sacrifices some of the aromatic quality of the grape for more body. This dry wine is closer to an Alsatian Gewürztraminer than most American versions.

A botrytised Riesling is the newest addition to the line; while it's won some awards it seems fairly simple.

CHARDONNAY ($$) ★★★ Aggressively oaky, ripe flavors, spicy, slight harshness. Not a subtle wine, it will appeal to those who like rough and ready Chardonnay.

GEWÜRZTRAMINER ($$) ★★★½ A very ripe, appley nose, with full spicy flavors, lots of fruit, and good weight. An impressive example.

MÜLLER-THURGAU ($$) ★★ Unusually strong flavors for this varietal, with an earthy aroma. Slightly sweet.

PINOT NOIR ($$) ★★½ An intense, oaky, sweetish nose with a bit of greenness, not heavy, but some harshness.

PINOT NOIR BLANC ($$) ★½ More of a rosé, really: dark color, quite sweet and full-flavored.

RED TABLE (ALSO CALLED EARLY HARVEST PINOT NOIR) ($) ★ One hundred percent Pinot Noir. Light, soft, some caramel flavors.

RIESLING, BOTRYTIS ($$) ★★ Straightforward apple flavors with some leafy undertones, medium sweet.

HENRY ESTATE

1984

ESTATE BOTTLED

UMPQUA VALLEY

OREGON PINOT NOIR

HIDDEN SPRINGS WINERY
Amity   (1980)
3,000 cases

Two families, the Byards and Alexandersons, own and run the winery, using grapes from the twenty-acre vineyard first planted by the Byards in 1973. The winery, on the crest of a hill in the Eola chain, grew out of Don Byard's interest in home winemaking, and the scale remains very small. The wines, though clean, have rough edges and betray the absence of a professional winemaker. And they are not inexpensive.

Although Hidden Springs' first Pinot (the 1980) attracted some attention and awards, the most recent vintage sampled (1985), while good, was not exciting. The fruit is accurate but the wine seems rather unyielding. The white wines are also decently made but, again, don't have much charm or interest. The one wine of modest interest is the Cabernet Sauvignon, which, while it shares the slightly underripe character of others from the Willamette, has more body and a rounder feel than the Pinot and is reminiscent of a light Bordeaux. (Nevertheless, it probably won't appeal much to lovers of California Cab.)

CABERNET SAUVIGNON ($$$) ★★½   An olivey, green pepper nose with decent fruit and a bit of tannin. Pleasant in a light style.

CHARDONNAY ($$) ★½   Very oaky with just a bit of ripe apple flavor. Tart and harsh.

PINOT NOIR ($$$) ★★½   A light cherry nose with lean, rather green fruit—quite straightforward.

RIESLING ($) ★½   Pleasant green apple fruit, dry, crisp—but not much there.

HILLCREST VINEYARD
Roseburg   (1963)
12,000 cases

Although Richard Sommer began the current Oregon wine boom in the early sixties with his small winery in southern Oregon's Umpqua Valley, his wines are no longer in the forefront. Perhaps it's because Hillcrest's principal varietals, Riesling and Cabernet, are not the wines that Oregon has become noted for, or perhaps it's because the winemaking has lacked consistency. (The winery seemed to go through a bad patch in the late seventies and early eighties, turning out a number of flawed wines.) The winery is still trying to revive its reputation and sales.

Still, Hillcrest has some things going for it. Most important, its vineyards, now totaling thirty-five acres, have some of the most mature vines in the state, and mature vines make good wine. Moreover, Philip Gale, who has been with the winery for some time and is now winemaker, seems to be bringing a more professional and consistent approach to the wines.

Although Hillcrest acquired a reputation for Cabernet Sauvignon early on and has long since established that the variety can do well in southern Oregon, many vintages in the last ten years have not been impressive—tannin and sulfur have been the chief culprits. But both have been reduced in the last few years (though Gale still wants to "err on the side of tannin"), so future releases should be more drinkable. Meanwhile, the Riesling, though it's variable, continues to be one of the more solid and interesting ones in the state. And in the very warm '87 vintage, Gale was excited about some very ripe Sauvignon Blanc, which held promise for a Sauterneslike dessert wine.

CABERNET SAUVIGNON ($$) ★★   Most older vintages (newer ones are unreleased) have a sweet, oaky nose, and rather tannic, woody flavors. They age, but not very gracefully.

CHARDONNAY ($$) ★★   A rather nice, oaky nose—but tart, green flavors.

GEWÜRZTRAMINER ($) ★★½   Dry, soft, not a powerful style, but good varietal flavor.

MELLOW RED ($) ★½   An interesting wine, and better than it sounds: a Riesling base, with Cabernet for color. Slightly sweet, with Riesling flavor and a bit of tannin.

PINOT NOIR ($$) ★★   Not terribly varietal, but some pleasant oaky flavors.

PINOT NOIR, EARLY RELEASE ($) ★★   This emphasizes ripe Pinot fruit and is surprisingly tannic.

RIESLING ($) ★★★   Some vintages have been truly excellent, with rich, ripe apricot flavors and very solid acidity and body. Others have been ordinary or candy-flavored. Available wines tend to be older than most Oregon Rieslings.

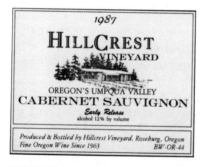

American Wines of the Northwest

HINMAN VINEYARDS
Eugene   (1979)
25,000 cases

Hinman started out as many Oregon wineries have—a small-scale operation begun more or less as a hobby by its creator, Doyle Hinman. But today the winery is set up to be one of the largest in the state, new partners have been added, and the winery's future has been linked with that of Boardman Farms, a large investor-owned vineyard project on the Oregon side of the Columbia Valley. Although there are a few acres of vineyard at the winery near Eugene, most grapes are trucked over from Boardman, which has a warmer, drier climate than the Willamette Valley and has more in common with eastern Washington than western Oregon.

Hinman received his training at Geisenheim, one of Germany's best-known wine institutes, and the German influence is reflected in the wines. Hinman's goal is to let the flavors of the grape come through in the wine, and the emphasis is on a light, crisp, straightforward style—nothing fancy, just well-made wines. Hinman has also been one of the state's pioneers in wine-in-a-box production for sale to restaurants—though unlike most California wineries, Hinman emphasizes premium varietals for this program. As a relatively low-cost producer and seller, the winery hopes to open up new markets for Oregon wine.

This is not the place to look for powerful, complex varietals, but the light, fruity white wines can be a good deal here, including the White Pinot, Tior (an interesting blend of Riesling, Chardonnay, and Gewürztraminer), and a dry Gewürztraminer that is notable for its fresh fruitiness. Red wines have so far been less interesting. Prices are quite modest.

CABERNET SAUVIGNON (WASHINGTON) ($$) ★★
Pleasant oaky nose, somewhat herbal, with good bite.

GEWÜRZTRAMINER ($) ★★★ Dry, fruity, balanced, with a soft, floral nose. Not a "serious" Gewürz, but most drinkable.

PINOT NOIR, WHITE ($) ★★½ Very pretty, with a light, earthy nose, some melon flavors—just off-dry.

RIESLING ($) ★★★ Flowery, peachy nose, with very fresh fruit and good acidity.

TIOR ($) ★★ A blend of Riesling, Gewürz, and Chardonnay, with the latter two providing considerable flavor interest. Medium sweet. A pretty wine.

HONEYWOOD WINERY
Salem   (1934)
12,000 cases

Honeywood's roots go back well before the current batch of small premium wineries, which have developed in the

American Wines of the Northwest

past twenty years. It was opened in 1934, just after the end of Prohibition, and has been in business ever since under a succession of owners, making fruit and berry wines. Though grape varietals were added in 1982, the emphasis is still on fruit, which comes in a huge assortment of varieties and styles, including such rarities as red currant and Hawaiian Tropical (a blend of passion fruit, guava, and papaya). The winery has a huge capacity and could be making a lot more wine than it is, but Honeywood seems to have been left behind in the drive toward top-quality wine in the state. The fruit wines are OK but lack the freshness and bright fruitiness of Oak Knoll, or Paul Thomas in Washington. And the grape wines are mostly light and simple, without the distinctive varietal characteristics of the better Oregon wineries. Still, there's no pretension at this winery, and the prices are low. The best bet is to stick with the berry wines and avoid the more exotic concoctions.

Honeywood recently sold its Salem property; owner Paul Gallick plans to build a new facility and move the winery in 1989. Possibilities include establishing the winery's own vineyard.

CHARDONNAY ($$) ★ Simple, vaguely appley flavors, not much weight, some off flavors.

PINOT NOIR BLANC ($) ★½ Not much Pinot character, slightly sweet, some earthiness.

RED TABLE (PINOT NOIR) ($$) ★★ Quite purple, with a berry nose. Tart, tannic, fruity, quite boisterous.

APRICOT ($) ★ Light, sweet, not much apricot flavor—but decent.

CHERRY ($) Rather like cough syrup.

RASPBERRY ($) ★★ Basic berry flavors, quite sweet and heavy.

STRAWBERRY ($) ★★½ Heavy but accurate strawberry flavors, quite sweet.

HOOD RIVER WINERY
Hood River   (1981)
4,000 cases

A surplus of pears on their farm in the Columbia Gorge provided the impetus for Cliff and Eileen Blanchette to start making fruit wine. They first began planting their twelve acres of vineyard in 1974, about the same time Washington's Mont Elise Vineyards was being planted across the river. The gorge has a climate somewhere between those of the mild western side of the mountains and the hot interior, and varieties like Cabernet Sauvignon and even Zinfandel that do not do well in the Willamette Valley thrive here. In fact, the Zinfandel comes from a tiny local vineyard planted in the 1930s—the current owners didn't know what it was until they asked the Blanchettes, who had it analyzed.

But Chardonnay, made in a full-bodied, oaky style, is the top wine here. It doesn't have the finesse of some of the Willamette Valley Chardonnays but is appealing nonetheless. The red wines, especially the Zin, will surprise those who think that Oregon can produce only good Pinot Noir among the reds, although Hood River's high-alcohol style works best in the warmer vintages, like '85 or '87. The area around the The Dalles, twenty miles toward the warmer eastern part of the state, may turn out to be a fine Cabernet-growing area. Nor should the Sauvignon Blanc, made in assertive herbaceous style with a touch of oak, be overlooked.

While other wineries are increasing blush wine production, the Blanchettes are planning to phase theirs out—too much competition. But they plan to stick with the fruit and berry wines they make, which they still think of as their bread-and-butter wines.

CABERNET SAUVIGNON ($$) ★★½ Oaky nose, pleasant brambly flavors—not deep but nice fruit and quite soft.

CHARDONNAY ($$$) ★★★ Very oaky-buttery nose, tart, quite viscous on the palate—no great depth but nice round body.

GEWÜRZTRAMINER ($) ★★½ Very fruity, rich, appley, very slight sweetness—soft, a bit of spice, fresh.

SAUVIGNON BLANC ($$) ★★★ Nice grassy-herbaceous nose, fresh, fairly full—straightforward and assertive.

ZINFANDEL ($$$) ★★½ Very dark color. Oaky-dusty nose with very ripe, hot flavors and some spice. Not as much fruit as one might like, but powerful, alcoholic stuff.

PEAR ($) ★★½ Intense pear-almond nose, quite sweet and full—but very fresh flavors.

HOUSTON VINEYARDS
Eugene (1983)
1,200 cases

The vineyard is simply that: a vineyard. There's no winery nor any immediate plans for one—the grapes have been custom-crushed, first at another Oregon facility and more recently at the Coventry Vale custom facility in Washington. The vineyard, just five acres, is near Eugene, at the southern end of the Willamette, and it's planted entirely to Chardonnay. But Steve Houston, who's proud to be a fifth-generation grape grower (his father has a vineyard in California's Central Valley), is not out to make a traditional Chardonnay. The goal is as natural a product as possible, so natural yeasts are used, and no oak. The wine turns out soft and fruity and slightly sweet—almost like Chenin Blanc.

CHARDONNAY ($) ★★½ An interesting honeylike nose, with soft, sweet, slightly earthy flavors. Not much like standard Chardonnay, but well made in its own way.

JONICOLE VINEYARDS
Roseburg   (1975)
1,000 cases

This on-again, off-again winery is on again, more or less. Originally begun as a partnership of three couples who had gotten excited about wine in the Napa Valley and had come north looking for suitable land, the winery's production ceased when the partnership broke up. But Jon Marker, one of the partners, rescued the aging wines and started making a little wine again in 1984, using grapes from a now-mature five acres of grapes first planted in the late sixties.

Unfortunately, it's still a hard go. The older red wines sat in oak for four years while the winery was dormant and have lost their fruit completely. The newer wines are full-flavored but awkward and sometimes harsh.

CABERNET ROSÉ ($) ★   A decent Cabernet nose, with rather tart, green flavors.
CHARDONNAY ($$) ★½   Lean and tart, with grapefruity flavors and hints of hay.
GEWÜRZTRAMINER ($$) ★★   A very ripe, lychee nut nose, with slightly sweet, soft flavors. Rather bitter in the finish.
PINOT NOIR (AMERICAN) ($) ★   Excessively oaky, spicy nose, tart, unyielding. OK for oak diehards.

KNUDSEN ERATH WINERY
Dundee   (1972)
41,000 cases

This winery, under the name Erath Vineyards, was (along with Eyrie Vineyards) one of the very first in the

Willamette Valley. But unlike Eyrie it has continued to grow, to the point where it is now not only the largest winery in Oregon but one of the largest producers of Pinot Noir in the United States (16,000 cases in 1987), making more than twice as much as nearest Oregon rival Sokol Blosser. Nevertheless, the quality of this varietal remains strikingly high.

Winemaker Richard Erath is a former electronics engineer (why are so many Oregon winemakers former engineers?) who prepared for his wine venture with enology courses at the University of California at Davis. Contacts with Hillcrest's Richard Sommer, as well as experiments in home winemaking with Oregon grapes, led Erath to Oregon, and he planted his first vines in 1969. Frankly surprised at the early success of his Pinot Noir, he has said, "It turned out so well when I didn't know what I was doing, how good could it be when I learned?"

A partnership with Seattle investor Cal Knudsen has allowed Knudsen Erath to become the state's largest winery, and the joint vineyards are extensive—125 acres of prime acreage in the Dundee Hills, with more recently planted. Even so, Erath has been scouring the Oregon countryside, buying up grapes to increase his Pinot Noir production. Erath believes that many more acres of vineyard could produce successful wines in the area. A few years ago Erath's Pinot Noirs were a tough sell, even though the quality has been high (several from the seventies were lovely wines), but now the best sell out quickly. The Vintage Select is sometimes fairly light and delicate but always has excellent spicy qualities and lots of flavor, and its track record indicates excellent aging ability. The winery should also be applauded for making a "regular" Pinot Noir that is modestly priced but wonderfully fruity. (Knudsen Erath used to make a "lower-end" nonvintage Pinot Noir that was always ripe and varietal and an excellent value, but demand for Pinot has apparently put an end to this wine.)

The white wines have seemed less interesting over the years. There have been some fine Vintage Select Rieslings, with full body and good complexity, but the regular Riesling and the Chardonnay lack the richness and intensity of the best from Oregon. The Vintage Select Chardonnay, however, will please those who favor a round, buttery Chard. The sparkling Brut is fuller-bodied and more flavorsome than others in Oregon. All the wines are very reasonably priced and represent fine value in the marketplace.

BRUT (OREGON) ($$$) ★★★½ Lots of bubbles, full yeasty nose, ripe full flavors—not quite elegant.

CABERNET SAUVIGNON ($) ★★½ Herbaceous qualities, but not too assertive—medium body, reasonably round.

CHARDONNAY ($$) ★★★ Has varied from butterscotchy to more haylike and delicate, fairly light body, straightforward. Good value.

CHARDONNAY, VINTAGE SELECT ($$) ★★★½ Very buttery nose, soft, round, with no great depth.

COASTAL MIST ($) ★½ A white wine with an interesting herbal nose, decent fruit, soft.

GEWÜRZTRAMINER ($) ★★½ Dry, light, rather earthy, good bite.

MERLOT ($) ★★★ A full-bodied, warm-flavored, somewhat herbal wine—rough and tannic. Ages well.

PINOT NOIR (WILLAMETTE) ($$) ★★★½ Lots of fruit in this wine, which has a meaty, smoky nose, medium body, and good bite.

PINOT NOIR, NONVINTAGE ($) ★★★ Consistently a good blend, with ripe, pungent, plummy flavors. Fine value. No longer made.

PINOT NOIR, VINTAGE SELECT ($$$) ★★★★★ This has varied from powerful and smoky to more delicate, but is always balanced and spicy, with plenty of flavor interest, even in lighter vintages. Ages beautifully.

RIESLING ($) ★★　Insubstantial, with often rather tired
flavors.

RIESLING, VINTAGE SELECT ($$) ★★★½　Lovely wild-
flower aromas, not heavy but some interesting miner-
ally complexities.

LA CASA DE VIN
Boardman　(1983)

Boardman sits on the Oregon side of the Columbia Val-
ley; there's already one large vineyard here (Boardman
Farms) and the area has considerable potential for further
development. What role this minuscule winery (the pro-
ject of a local lawyer) will play, if any, remains to be
seen—wine has been made in previous vintages but
there's no evidence of it in the marketplace. Wines not
tasted.

LANGE WINERY
Dundee   (1987)
1,000 cases

The news here is Pinot Gris. The Pinot Gris pioneers in
Oregon have never let this wine touch any oak, but Don
Lange, a Californian who worked as assistant winemaker
at several Santa Barbara wineries before migrating north,
thinks Pinot Gris is worthy of oak, so half of his first vintage was fermented in French oak. (The Langes say well-
established winemakers "pointed and laughed" when
they heard what this winery was doing.) The resulting
wine is impressive: rich and round, with a fine balance of
oak and fruit. If this wine is successful in the marketplace
it may mark the beginning of a new style for this grape.
  The Langes came to Oregon out of their love for Pinot
Noir, and that's the variety in their tiny two-acre vineyard
in the Dundee Hills (though Pinot Gris is planned, too).
After looking around for land and trying wines from different parts of the valley, they say "It's no accident we're
in the Red Hills," feeling it's the best for Pinot Noir. Production is small and will remain so—Lange wants to be
able to do it all himself.
  Wendy Lange admits that '87 was a scramble, as they
bought the property just in time for the crush; the Pinot
Noir and Chardonnay in barrel seem a bit awkward, but
the success of the Pinot Gris suggests this as a winery to
follow.

PINOT GRIS ($$) ★★★★   Big, rich apple-oak nose, lovely
  fruit, rounded wine—quite soft.

LAUREL RIDGE WINERY
Forest Grove   (1986)
9,000 cases

Laurel Ridge is Reuter's Hill Winery reincarnated (by a completely new company). And Reuter's Hill, in turn, began life as Charles Coury Vineyards, which was planted in the mid-sixties as one of the earliest premium grape ventures in the Willamette. (The site is that of perhaps the oldest vineyard in Oregon, planted near Forest Grove in the late 1800s by German immigrant Frank Reuter, who thought the Willamette could be "America's Rhineland.") Both these earlier efforts failed as businesses, although they made some rather nice wines. The new venture combines the original thirty-acre vineyard, now owned by the Dowsett family, with a more recently planted fifty-acre vineyard near Dundee, in the heart of Pinot Noir country, owned by the Teppola family. The combined eighty acres should allow sizable production.

The winemaker is Rich Cushman, formerly of Chateau Benoit, where he gained a reputation for fine sparkling wine and distinctive Sauvignon Blanc. The plan calls for Laurel Ridge to start with white table wines but eventually to focus on Champagne-method sparkling wine as its flagship. The initial sparkling wine is Riesling-based, but there is a vintage Pinot Noir–based sparkler currently aging.

Cushman brings a professionalism to this new enterprise that bodes well. The initial releases, while not always exciting, are clean, technically sound wines, the most interesting of which is the austere Sauvignon Blanc–Semillon blend.

GEWÜRZTRAMINER ($) ★★   Flavors are clean and varietal but quite strong and a little bitter.

RIESLING ($) ★½ Light, bready flavors, tart, slight sweetness.

RIESLING, SELECT HARVEST ($$) ★★ Straightforward apple fruit and medium sweetness—but it lacks richness.

SAUVIGNON BLANC/SEMILLON ($$) ★★½ A lean, tart, earthy wine with fairly aggressive flavors. Should be good with seafood.

CUVÉE BLANC ($$) ★★ Champagne method Riesling. Decent fruit, but it seems a little heavy-handed. Medium sweetness.

LUMIERE VINEYARDS *See* ROGUE RIVER VINEYARDS

MIRASSOU CELLARS *See* PELLIER

MONTINORE VINEYARDS
Forest Grove (1987)
5,000 cases

If it achieves its plans, Montinore will easily be Oregon's largest winery, with the potential of changing the state's image as a collection of small ultrapremium wineries. Already the scale of the vineyards dwarfs others in the Willamette: 430 acres of vines planted, with 138 dedicated to Pinot Noir ("by far the largest Pinot Noir vineyards in Oregon," according to manager Jeff Lamy) and 14 acres to Pinot Gris, making that the largest single planting of the variety in the United States. The elaborate vineyard, designed with a variety of different trellising systems and densities of planting, is frankly an experiment. It includes a number of varieties not normally cultivated in this area (like Sauvignon Blanc and Chenin Blanc) and different plots with different exposures—Lamy isn't sure what will work. "We'll learn as we go along."

The operation has drawn critical comment from other local producers, who think failed experiments may damage Oregon's already solid reputation. Lamy shrugs off such comments, convinced that the soil (similar to that at other fine vineyards), the site, and the growing procedures will prove out. To suggestions that the site is a marginal one for wine grapes, Lamy counters that great wine has always come from very marginal areas. Only time will tell.

Lamy's background is more in business and real estate than viticulture and enology, and the first wines, from the fine 1987 vintage, showed mixed results for his winemaking. The Pinot Gris in particular (slightly sweet) may not please those used to the dry, aromatic Pinot Gris of other properties. Several of the wines, while decently made, would benefit from more varietal fruit, but this may develop as the vines, first planted in 1983, begin to mature.

The first vintage was crushed at a nearby facility, but 1989 should see the completion of the first phase of what eventually will be a 300,000-gallon winery, including substantial sparkling wine production (from Pinot Noir that doesn't ripen enough for red wine). Chardonnay, Pinot Noir, Sauvignon Blanc, and Chenin Blanc are yet to be released, as well as an extremely sweet late-harvest Riesling.

MÜLLER-THURGAU ($) ★★ Very light flowery aromas—pleasant, but not showing strong character.
PINOT GRIS ($$) ★½ Slightly sweet, slightly weedy, a bit harsh—a disappointment for those who know what this variety can do.
RIESLING ($) ★★ Quite a sweet style, with a pungent, green apple nose.

ROSÉ ($) ★★   Perhaps the most interesting wine, 60 percent from the Cascade hybrid, with strawberry aromas and some wild flavors, very soft.

MT. HOOD WINERY
Government Camp   (1974)
2,000 cases

Longtime fruit and berry winemaker Lester Martin has sold most of the equipment and the wine to Gary Hood and Doug Whitlock, who plan to continue in the same fashion, relocating the operation to Government Camp. They began crushing in 1988, with blackberries, blueberries, raspberries, and huckleberries. Wines not tasted.

MULHAUSEN VINEYARDS
Newberg   (1979)

Although the address is Newberg, Mulhausen sits in rather splendid isolation from other local wineries, on the north side of the Chehalem Mountains, where the thirty-acre vineyard sits on a fairly high but protected hillside. The winemaking has seemed somewhat isolated as well, and the quality has not matched that of most of Mulhausen's neighbors. Owner Zane Mulhausen is an engineer by background who turned his winemaking hobby into a full-time vocation.

The wines have limited availability and tend to be older, which is unfortunate, as they often seem tired and a little dirty. The exception is the Pinot Noir, which, while over-oaked, is decently made.

As this book went to press, the vineyard and winery, which had been in financial straits, had been sold to an out-of-state investor.

CHARDONNAY ($$) Not a clean wine—oxidized and chemical-tasting.

PINOT NOIR ($$$) ★★ Too much oak, giving the wine an excessively cedary, sweet flavor, which obscures the cherry fruit. Otherwise, a clean wine.

RIESLING ($) ½ An odd nose—tart, lean, not for Riesling lovers.

VIN BLANC ($) ★ Rather piney nose—herbal, not terribly fresh, but with decent fruit and acid.

NEHALEM BAY WINERY
Nehalem   (1973)
4,000 cases

It's definitely not wine country, but the winery *is* on one of the prettiest stretches of the Oregon coast, where it serves the flourishing tourist trade. Originally a fruit and berry winery in a converted cheese factory, it has added a selection of vinifera wines in recent years, mostly made from Willamette Valley grapes. Owner and longtime winemaker Pat McCoy's background is in promotion. (As of 1987, Jeff Daniels is the new winemaker.)

The wines are of little interest: None of the grape wines exhibits much fruit character, or anything else—they are sweet but not fresh.

PINOT NOIR ($$) ★ Some decent berry flavors, soft—OK.

ROSÉ ($$) ½ A blend of Chardonnay and Pinot Noir(?)—mellow, but no character.

WHITE TABLE ($$) ½ Alfalfa scents, off-dry, not fresh.

RHUBARB ($) ★ The nose is decent, but the flavors are sugary.

NISQUALLY RIDGE *See* CHATEAU BENOIT

OAK GROVE ORCHARDS WINERY *See* STEVENS CELLARS

OAK KNOLL WINERY
Hillsboro   (1970)
33,000 cases

"I have spent the past fifty years of my life searching for the world's finest Pinot Noir and yours is among the greatest I have ever tasted." So said André Tchelistcheff, one of California's best-known winery consultants and a close observer of Northwest wine, about Oak Knoll's 1980 Vintage Select Pinot Noir. Wine newsletter publisher Robert Parker also called it "one of the greatest non-French pinot noirs I have ever tasted." High praise for a winery that started out as a small fruit and berry operation, run by a Tektronix engineer and his large family.

Ron Vuylsteke, who has no formal training as an enologist, started as an "avid amateur" making blackberry wine. The winery, housed in an old dairy barn not far from Portland, was founded in 1970, making Oak Knoll one of the older wineries in the state—as well as one of the two or three largest. In the early eighties Oak Knoll was making 80 percent fruit and berry wines; today the mix has changed to 85 percent grape wine, as production has gradually increased. Despite the down-home image, the Vuylstekes have invested heavily in equipment to make wines in the freshest possible style. Oak Knoll wines have always emphasized fruitiness: Some of the early Pinot Noirs had no oak aging in order to preserve the flavors of the grape, and the Pinot Noir still has a ripe fruitiness.

There is no estate vineyard, but Vuylsteke feels he can best maintain quality by choosing carefully from local vineyards, with which the winery has long-term relationships. The white wines are all well made in a fairly light style, with a fruity, oaky Chardonnay. But the Pinot Noir is something else again. Vuylsteke prefers a robust style, and while the regular bottling emphasizes forward fruit, the Vintage Select in good years is one of the darkest, deepest, richest Pinots in the state—a powerful wine of great ripeness that needs time to develop. It represents a considerable contrast to the lighter, rounder, more elegant Pinots that have made Oregon famous, but will appeal to those looking for very flavorful and full-bodied wine.

The fruit and berry wines are not to be overlooked; they are, in fact, some of the best in the Northwest. Slightly sweet but preserving the tartness of the fruit, they all have absolutely fresh flavors.

CHARDONNAY ($$) ★★★ Oak flavors come through, though there's lots of fresh Chardonnay fruit as well. Forward, flavorful, not quite elegant.

GEWÜRZTRAMINER ($) ★★ Light, dry, pleasant, well made, though not terribly varietal.

PINOT NOIR ($$) ★★★ Earthy and cherrylike aromas, fruity, with oak backbone. Good, but not in the same class with the Select.

PINOT NOIR, VINTAGE SELECT ($$$) ★★★★ Very purple, very blackberrylike fruit, very powerful in youth. Rich, concentrated stuff packed with flavor and tannin. More vivacious than elegant.

RIESLING ($) ★★½ Light, rather bready nose with a pleasant tartness. Simple.

TWILIGHT BLUSH ($) ★★½ Really more of a rosé, with bright salmon color and lots of strawberry fruit. Good picnic wine.

BLACKBERRY ($) ★★★ Deep, rich blackberry flavor—it preserves the lovely balance of sweet and tart of the local marionberry (a wild blackberry cross).

LOGANBERRY ($) ★★½   A little sweeter and softer than the blackberry—not quite so distinctive, but well made.

RASPBERRY ($) ★★★½   Raspberry lovers take note: This is intense essence of raspberry. Full-flavored and very fresh.

RHUBARB ($) ★★½   Fresh, tart, slightly sweet—tastes just like rhubarb.

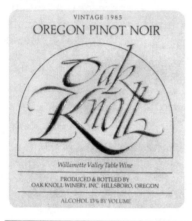

VINTAGE 1985
OREGON PINOT NOIR

Willamette Valley Table Wine

PRODUCED & BOTTLED BY
OAK KNOLL WINERY, INC. HILLSBORO, OREGON

ALCOHOL 13% BY VOLUME

PANTHER CREEK CELLARS
McMinnville   (1986)
1,000 cases

Although its production is tiny, this may well be the only U.S. winery exclusively devoted to Pinot Noir. And owner-winemaker Ken Wright wants that one wine to be distinctive, which, if the first vintage is an indication, it will be. Wright confesses to a love affair with Pinot Noir, which drew him north from California, where he had worked at several wineries, including Ventana. In California he couldn't find in Pinot Noir the "core of fruit" that he feels is so essential.

The Panther Creek Pinot has a core of fruit, and a good deal besides. In addition to fruit Wright is looking for structure and a richer style, letting the wine macerate on the skins after fermentation to extract more color, body, and tannin. He hopes his wines, not as charming as many Oregon Pinots, will be powerful and long-lived. Unquestionably the wine is different, sacrificing subtlety and finesse for weight, spice, and tannic body—it should be fascinating to see how it ages.

Panther Creek owns no vineyards and has been buying grapes from both the Dundee Hills and Eola Hills growing areas. Wright sees real differences: firmer, fruitier wines from Eola and softer, richer, fleshier ones from Dundee. He thinks the two styles blend well but is reserving judgment on whether to continue with a blend or make two separate wines.

PINOT NOIR ($$$) ★★★★ Very intense fruit, with black pepper flavors, tannic and tart—looks promising, definitely a wine for aging. Very different style from most.

PELLIER (MIRASSOU CELLARS OF OREGON)
Salem (1985)
15,000 cases

Pellier was the name of the founder of the Mirassou winemaking clan of California. Now one member of the extended family, Mitch Mirassou, has migrated north to try his hand at Oregon wine, using the Pellier name to avoid confusion with the California winery. A former California grower, he has planted a vineyard that at forty-five acres is relatively large, with plans for more plantings. The location is the Eola Hills just north of Salem, an area that seems to have a slightly warmer growing season than vineyards farther north. Like many Willamette wineries,

Pellier is committed to Riesling as a popular varietal; unlike most, it is also trying to make a go of Cabernet Sauvignon.

Conventional wisdom has it that the Willamette is too cool for Cabernet, but the Mirassous feel it is a matter of finding the right location and using the right growing techniques. Initial bottlings show the definite herbal-vegetal flavors of cool-climate Cabernet, but the wine is well made (it may need really hot years to bring out the best flavors). The first Pinot Noir, from the warm '85 vintage, seems a little awkward, but it has the structure that with time may permit it to develop nicely. The quality of the other wines, made in a straightforward style, is somewhat variable, the Gewürztraminer being the most pleasing.

CABERNET SAUVIGNON ($$) ★★ Definitely on the green, herbal side. Dusty nose, tart, tannic, but well made given the fruit.

CHARDONNAY ($$) ★★½ Very appley nose, good fruit with straightforward flavors and some oak. Little complexity.

GEWÜRZTRAMINER ($) ★★★½ Dry style, with a subtle, spiced apple nose, full flavors and good body. One of the better examples around.

PINOT NOIR ($$$) ★★★ Tart and tannic; there's good fruit but a weedy edge to it—give it some time to settle down.

PINOT NOIR BLANC ($) ★ More character than the Blush, but with some odd herbal flavors. Quite sweet.

RIESLING ($) ★★ First effort seemed odd, but the newer release is better—nose of clover, slightly sweet, tart, simple.

SPRING VALLEY BLUSH ($) ★ Quite pale, tart, same herbal qualities as the Blanc—not exactly what one expects in a blush.

PONDEROSA VINEYARDS
Lebanon (1987)
350 cases

One of just three wineries in the Northwest to make certified sulfite-free wines (and the only one in Oregon), Ponderosa's selling point is "totally natural" products. A very small and very family-oriented operation, the sixteen-acre vineyard has been planted slowly and is not yet in full production. Owner-winemaker Bill Looney believes his site south and east of Salem is a little warmer than the northern Willamette; certainly the indigenous Ponderosa pines, which give the vineyard its name, suggest a drier and slightly warmer area than Douglas fir country.

Making whites without sulfites is a bit tricky: The acids must be high to preserve the wine, so Looney finishes them off a bit sweet to balance the natural tartness. Both wines are pleasant, though both lack strong varietal character and have some odd flavors in the finish. Look for Pinot Noir to follow. The winery adds two caveats about these wines: They do throw a bit of sediment, and they should be kept at cool temperatures. One might add that they probably should be drunk young.

CHARDONNAY ($$) ★★   Light fruit with good crispness and a touch of sugar—funny finish.
SAUVIGNON BLANC ($) ★½   Not much varietal character, slightly sweet with balancing acid—also finishes not quite clean.

PONZI VINEYARDS
Beaverton   (1974)
7,000 cases

The vineyard sits in low-lying farmland just a few miles from the high-tech Portland suburb of Beaverton. But if the setting is pedestrian, the wines are not: Ponzi is one of the half-dozen best wineries in Oregon, judged by its entire lineup. Unfortunately, production is small, and owner Richard Ponzi is committed to making his wines widely available, so the best ones can be hard to find.

Ponzi's background is in engineering (he used to design rides for Disneyland), but a desire to work on the land—an effect of the countercultural sixties—brought the Ponzi family to Oregon, where making wine seemed like a romantic prospect. They planted their twelve-acre vineyard in 1970 with relatively few varieties, including the then-experimental Pinot Gris, a white cousin of Pinot Noir. (They also buy some grapes from other local growers and plan to purchase additional acreage for vines.) Their uncompromising approach is to produce completely dry, balanced food wines—there are no tourist-oriented sipping wines here.

Like David Lett at Eyrie and Richard Erath at Knudsen Erath, Ponzi has been making consistently fine Pinot Noir for a number of years, good weather or bad, though it went largely unnoticed for quite a while; the wines, deeply structured and quite meaty, have proven to hold up very nicely over time. Ponzi notes that the Oregon "pioneers" like himself, Erath, and Lett initially modeled their efforts on Alsace, where several of them had spent time. Only after the unexpected success of Pinot Noir did the focus shift away from the Alsatian varieties Riesling and Gewürztraminer. Chardonnay is completely barrel-fermented and shows lovely fruit. (There is to be a Reserve Chardonnay as well.) Ponzi is one Oregon winemaker who feels success with Chardonnay will come not from finding the perfect clone but from working more effectively with the grapes available now. Pinot Gris may be the most interesting wine—it achieves richness and complexity without any oak aging. Ponzi has no doubt that Pinot Gris will prove to be a major variety in the state, though so far it trails behind a number of others in acres planted. The Riesling is also noteworthy: one of the best dry dinner-style versions of this grape in the Northwest and an excellent accompaniment to crab and clams. Other wineries make dry Riesling, but somehow Ponzi manages to extract more fruit and body from his.

Prices of these wines have always been moderate and have not risen as precipitously as those at other fashionable Oregon wineries.

CHARDONNAY ($$) ★★★★ Just beautiful: Ripe, apple-butterscotch flavors are nicely melded. There is a fine touch of spice and good length on the palate.

PINOT GRIS ($$) ★★★★ A serious white, with lots of bright, spicy, tropical fruit flavors, considerable strength, and a Chardonnay-like feel—but without oak.

PINOT NOIR ($$) ★★★½ Not as complex as the Reserve, but lots of solid fruit and round flavors, with substantial oak. Good value, ages well.

PINOT NOIR, RESERVE ($$$) ★★★★★ One of the best. A muscular wine, with dark color, oaky smoky aromas, some herbal accents, and loads of fruit. Ages extremely well.

RIESLING, DRY ($) ★★★★ Rich nose of grapefruit and bread. Perfectly dry, with full body and crisp acidity. A model of dry Oregon Riesling.

REUTER'S HILL WINERY *See* Laurel Ridge Winery

REX HILL VINEYARDS
Newberg   (1983)
12,000 cases

A first-class facility from tasting room to barrel room, immaculately kept and arrayed with the best equipment, Rex Hill is doing several things differently than other wineries. Buying Pinot Noir grapes from a number of different area vineyards, the winery releases its wines under separate vineyard designations—as many as seven from one vintage. And owner Paul Hart likes the effect of oak on his Pinot Noirs, so they spend more time in barrel than those elsewhere in Oregon, with the result that they are released about a year after most other Willamette Pinots.

Hart would even like to add a few vineyards to his lineup, looking for them in the Dundee Hills or Chehalem

Mountains, which he feels have the exposure, wind protection, and drainage to make great wine. Though pleased with his success, Hart says, "We're not yet making my kind of wine"—wine not just of power but of elegance. He actually favors the lighter vintages over the really ripe ones and is not afraid to downgrade vineyard wines that he doesn't feel meet his standards. (Pinots that don't make the cut are blended into "Willamette," "Oregon," or nonvintage wines.)

First winemaker David Wirtz, a local vineyard owner, helped establish Rex Hill's reputation, and new winemaker Lynn Penner-Ash, who has worked at Warren Winiarski's Stag's Leap in Napa, promises to carry on in the style already established by the winery.

In 1983, there were three vineyard-designated wines, Archibald, Maresh, and Dundee Hills; in 1984 only one, Medici; but in 1985 there were six. Although the vineyard-designated Pinots are all different, there are some common strains, including a pronounced though not harsh oaky character (from a mixture of French oaks) and velvety softness. Preferences will vary, but certainly the Maresh and Archibald vineyards, both in the heart of the Dundee Hills, are producing first-rate wine, with the Maresh a little heavier and rounder and the Archibald revealing more delicate and earthy flavors. The other notable wine is the Medici, a big tannic wine with smoky tea aromas. Not everyone will agree with the concept of all these different bottlings (and consumers may find them a little hard to keep track of), but hard-core Pinot fanciers will love the chance to compare the differences.

Consumers may also be interested in the fact that older vintages of both Pinot Noir and Chardonnay are available (at higher prices), because the winery releases them over a multiyear period with the hope of making them available to wine lovers closer to the point at which they will be mature—a policy to be commended. (And given the longer oak aging, most of these will require good bottle age to show their best.)

The latest additions to the lineup are an oak-aged Pinot Gris, which will delight lovers of this wine with its dramatic flavors and full body, and a dessert wine blended from Riesling and Sauvignon Blanc.

CHARDONNAY (WILLAMETTE) ($$$) ★★★½ Oaky, butterscotch nose with soft flavors—nicely rounded. Very drinkable.

ENCORE (?) ★★★½ Blend of two-thirds Riesling and one-third Sauvignon Blanc. Rich honey in the nose, but lighter Riesling fruit on the palate. Semisweet but not heavy; not rich like Sauternes, but interesting.

PINOT GRIS ($$) ★★★★ Aged in oak. Very ripe, pungent apple nose, tangy, full-bodied, with lots of fruit—a big wine. Pinot Gris lovers will adore it.

PINOT NOIR (ARCHIBALD) ($$$) ★★★★½ Leathery, earthy tones, sweet oak—not as weighty as, say, Maresh, but good tannin.

PINOT NOIR (DUNDEE HILLS) ($$$) ★★★ Soft, caramelly, rounded oaky flavors, but lacks the flavor interest of the others.

PINOT NOIR (MARESH) ($$$) ★★★★½ Ripe, true black cherry nose, very solid, round, tannic.

PINOT NOIR (MEDICI) ($$$) ★★★★ Smoky, oaky nose, deep peppery fruit, tannic.

PINOT NOIR (OREGON) ($$) ★★½ Light, fruity, some spice.

PINOT NOIR (WILLAMETTE) ($$$) ★★★½ More plummy and less elegant than the single-vineyard wines, but with rounded, spicy flavors and some tannin.

PINOT NOIR (WIRTZ) ($$$) ★★★★ Nicely balanced, with oaky-cherry nose and a bit of tannin.

RIESLING ($) ★★½ A very light nose, with grapefruity flavors and a nice tingle.

REX HILL
1985
OREGON
PINOT NOIR
ARCHIBALD VINEYARDS
PRODUCED AND BOTTLED BY
REX HILL VINEYARDS BW-OR-91
NEWBERG, OREGON
ALCOHOL 13½% BY VOLUME

ROGUE RIVER VINEYARDS
Grants Pass   (1983)
4,000 cases

A grab bag of wines, with everything from varietals to jug wines to grape and fruit coolers, under several different labels. The winery is run by four partners and their families, who have settled in the Grants Pass area of southern Oregon in what could pass for a sixties-style commune. They did their apprenticeships in California's Central Valley, and the California influence shows: Many of the wines and coolers are made from juice trucked up from down south. The winery also purchases grapes from a number of southern Oregon vineyards for its premium varietal wines. (The partners admit their real interest is not in growing grapes. They have only seven acres of young vines planted here, though more acreage is planned, perhaps in the Ashland area.) Although Rogue River's capacity could make it one of the larger wineries in the state, it has gone very much its own way in its winemaking.

The emphasis here is on marketing—exploring consumer tastes to find niches for inexpensive wines with unique accents. Thus the white wine flavored with apricot and strawberry, as well as the varietal coolers; the packaging, all done at the winery, is slick and upscale. So far, the coolers (a Chenin Blanc and Cabernet Blush) have been the most successful products, and winemaker Bill Jiron would like to push the production up considerably.

Although the coolers, under the Rogue River label, are quite decent (light and not too sweet), the varietal wines are unimpressive. None of them shows much in the way of varietal fruit, and all lack backbone. The table wines under the Silver Springs label (from California juice) are OK, but even at relatively low prices cannot be considered bargains. And the fruit-flavored table wines, labeled Lumiere Vineyards, which include peach, apricot, almond, and strawberry, seem quite odd indeed.

CABERNET SAUVIGNON ($$) ½ Decent herbal nose, light—but a chemical finish spoils it.

CHARDONNAY ($$) The nose is reminiscent of glue; flavors are not fresh.

GEWÜRZTRAMINER ($) ★ Slight varietal flavor, soft, but lacks freshness.

LUMIERE VINEYARDS APRI BLANC ($) ½ Apricot-flavored white wine. Heavy, sweet apricot nose, with almondlike flavors.

SILVER SPRINGS BLUSH ($) ½ Sweet, cherrylike, dull.

SILVER SPRINGS RED TABLE ($) ★ Sweet berry nose, light, soft, off-dry.

SILVER SPRINGS WHITE TABLE ($) ½ Slightly hot and viscous, flabby flavors.

ST. JOSEF'S WEINKELLER
Canby   (1983)
6,000 cases

Canby, though not far from Portland, is off the beaten wine path, on the eastern side of the Willamette Valley. Although the name and winery architecture suggest German influence, winemaker Joe Fleischmann, a successful retired baker, is Hungarian in background, and his strongest interest is in making powerful, full-flavored reds, including Cabernet Sauvignon and Zinfandel.

Grapes come from a fourteen-acre vineyard and, in the case of the Zinfandel, from California—the local microclimate is a shade warmer than across the valley, which allows better ripening for the Cabernet. Even so, the Cabernets, while well made, are on the lean and herbaceous side, like so many others from the Willamette. The Zinfandel, by contrast, is a big wine, rather rough, with lots of spicy oakiness from Yugoslavian barrels. Pinot Noir, too, is treated like a heavy-duty red and comes off seeming clumsy.

The whites are less successful than the reds. Although Fleischmann is proud of his natural approach to winemaking, these wines have some odd, almost chemical-tasting flavors in the finish and would seem to be best drunk very young. The '87 Gewürztraminer (not tasted) has been renamed L'Esprit and has proven popular.

CABERNET SAUVIGNON ($$) ★★½ Oaky, somewhat herbaceous flavors, fairly soft, on the lean side.
CHARDONNAY ($$) ★★ A nice warm oaky nose, but there's something slightly funny in the finish.
GEWÜRZTRAMINER ($) ½ Rather vegetal, dry, fullbodied. Again, some odd flavors.

PINOT NOIR ($$$) ★★ Dark and full-bodied, oaky and heavy.

RIESLING ($) ★ Good body, but not that fresh. Some off flavors.

ZINFANDEL (AMERICAN) ($) ★★ This comes in a couple of different styles, including one that's slightly sweet. Blackberry nose, lots of oak, quite hot.

SCHWARZENBERG VINEYARDS
Dallas (1986)
4,000 cases

Most Oregon wineries have aimed their wines at the local market first, but the goal of Helmut and Helga Schwarz, both with strong business backgrounds, is to produce light, fruity wines in as natural a way as possible— and make a strong effort to sell them in the eastern market, where Chardonnay and Pinot Noir are much in demand.

The Schwarzes, transplanted Germans, had hoped to buy land in the Napa Valley but were put off by high prices and attracted instead to Oregon's climate, which they reasoned would be like those of the Rhine, Mosel, and Burgundy regions, with which they had been familiar in Europe. The fifty acres already planted with Chardonnay and Pinot Noir (another seventy acres could be added) are almost on bottomland, west of Salem. Feeling that the influence of California is still too strong in the United States, the Schwarzes have hired German-trained enologist Norbert Fiebig to make the wines, as well as to manage the vineyards. Plans call for steady growth to a rather substantial size for the state.

The model for the Chardonnay has been Chablis. The first vintage had no oak in it; consumer response suggested that adding a touch of oak would help, so a small percentage of the wine now spends a short time in French oak. (In contrast, the Pinot Noir, still to be released, is being aged in the traditional fashion.) Although nicely made, this wine stands apart from other Chardonnays in Oregon with its emphasis on soft fruitiness and light body, and many Chardonnay lovers will not find the character in it they are looking for.

CHARDONNAY ($$) ★★ The '87 (oak aged) has some light vanilla and caramel qualities with lean fruit and soft flavors.

SERENDIPITY CELLARS
Monmouth (1981)
1,800 cases

This tiny winery, southwest of Salem, has a rather unconventional line of wines. Owner and winemaker Glen Longshore, who got his start helping Myron Redford at Amity Vineyards, doesn't buy the conventional wisdom about which grapes are right for Oregon, so he has experimented liberally, with some happy results. Serendipity owns no vineyards and buys grapes from growers in the Willamette Valley and southern Oregon.

Most interesting is the Maréchal Foch, a French hybrid scorned by the large wineries, though it is grown extensively in the East. Foch is an early ripener; in the south of France it makes a coarse, heavy wine, but in Oregon's cool climate it becomes more delicate and fruity. It has something of the character of Lemberger, the German grape grown with surprising success in Washington—a sort of mild Zinfandel, though without the same backbone. Longshore is also a promoter of Chenin Blanc. The winemaking here is surprisingly good, given the modest facilities.

CHENIN BLANC ($) ★★★   Longshore is convinced Chenin is a great grape for Oregon; most people would disagree. This wine is melony, off-dry, crisp, with good body.

MARÉCHAL FOCH ($$) ★★★½   A successful wine in consumer judgings—very dark purple and forward with intense plummy fruit and a big nose. A soft wine, lacking a bit in foundation, but very drinkable.

MÜLLER-THURGAU ($) ★★★   A straightforward wine with very fresh apple fruit, good intensity, just off-dry.

PINOT NOIR ($$) ★★★   This wine has been discontinued (surprisingly, it hasn't sold well), which is too bad, since it was well made, with balanced cherry, leathery flavors and a soft, open style.

SEVEN HILLS CELLARS
Milton-Freewater   (1987)
750 cases

The Seven Hills Vineyard, part of the Walla Walla Valley appellation, is close to the Washington border in eastern Oregon. Grapes from these twenty-four acres, a partnership of Jim McClellan and Herb Hendricks, a couple of physician-farmers, have gone into a number of Walla Walla wines, including the excellent reds made by Leonetti Cellar and Woodward Canyon. Excited by the showings their grapes have made, McClellan has had some wine produced at the Waterbrook facility to release under the Seven Hills label.

Son Casey McClellan, a Davis-trained enologist who has worked in the Porto country in Portugal, will be the winemaker, and eventually a new winery will be built, probably on the Oregon side of the border. The vineyard has a little bit of everything, as no one knew what would do well when the vines were planted in 1980, but the winery's focus will probably be on a Cabernet-Merlot blend, Chardonnay, and Sauvignon Blanc. The first releases showed careful winemaking.

OVERTURE WHITE TABLE ($) ★½   Heavy, ripe, almost Muscaty aromas, sweet, some harshness.
RIESLING ($) ★★★   Delicately ripe peachy flavors and well-balanced sweetness mark this nicely made wine.
SAUVIGNON BLANC ($) ★★½   Steely, restrained Sauvignon nose, light body, good balance.

SHAFER VINEYARD CELLARS
Forest Grove   (1978)
8,500 cases

Harvey Shafer is one of the few winemakers in Oregon whose Chardonnay is better than his Pinot Noir—in fact, this Chardonnay should win fans even among diehard lovers of the California version. Shafer began as a grower, planting twenty acres of vineyard in 1973 on a hillside in the Tualatin Valley near Forest Grove. Other wineries had success with his grapes and he decided he wanted to control the whole process. The first vintages were made elsewhere, but since 1981 the wines have been estate bottled. Harvest tends to be a couple weeks later here than at many other Willamette vineyards, which Shafer feels gives the grapes more flavor in warm years, though it causes problems in cool years.

Shafer is well satisfied with the Chardonnay, which is deliciously fruity even in off years and not nearly as lean as some. But while all the wines show careful winemaking and considerable fruit, Shafer doesn't seem quite to have found his touch with Pinot Noir and is still fiddling with the wine, working toward more elegance. Shafer Pinot Noir has tended to be fairly light and fruity, though newer vintages should have more color and depth. The Sauvignon Blanc is moving in the other direction: Older vintages were unabashedly herbaceous, while newer ones are lightly grassy and softer (this is the way consumers seem to prefer them). The Gewürztraminer is one of the notable ones in the state—dry and substantial.

CHARDONNAY ($$) ★★★★ Stylistically quite close to a California Chardonnay, this wine should appeal to almost all Chardonnay lovers. A lovely rich nose of pineapple and oak leads into delicious fruit and crisp acidity. A forward wine that can also age.

GEWÜRZTRAMINER ($) ★★★½ A subdued, nonfloral, lychee nut nose, totally dry, with good weight and nice spice. Some richness.

PINOT NOIR ($$$) ★★★ A fairly ripe, smoky, plummy wine—a little lighter, softer, and less elegant than many.

PINOT NOIR BLANC ($) ★★ Fresh, fruity flavors, pungent, tart.

SAUVIGNON BLANC ($$) ★★★ An aggressive style, with a very herbaceous nose and crisp fruit. More recent vintages are toned down, though.

SHALLON WINERY
Astoria   (1978)
400 cases

It's hard not to think of Paul van der Veldt as a tad eccentric for conceiving of wines like Cran du Lait, made from cranberries and whey, or Lemon Meringue Pie, from lemons and whey. He believes firmly that any winery should make use of local "fruit," and in Astoria the local fruits are blackberries and cranberries, apples and peaches—and cheese. Whey is a cheese by-product and it gives a definite "milky" texture to the wines.

Hard to rate because the flavors are so unique, these wines nonetheless get high marks for technical skill, and one has to admire the adventurousness of van der Weldt's restless experimentation. The straight fruit wines are fresh, dry, and very well made. Available principally at the winery.

BLACKBERRY ($$) ★★★   Made from local wild blackberries, it has a wild and woodsy flavor, light, tart, and dry.
CRAN DU LAIT ($$) ★½   Light plum color, with a unique nose of berries and milk (yogurt with alcohol?).
LEMON MERINGUE PIE ($$$) ★½   A dessert wine, with a soft, lemony flavor and milky aftertaste. Quite sweet.
PEACH ($$) ★★★½   Very fresh peach-pie aroma, fairly dry, tart, very nice.
SPICED APPLE ($$) ★½   Definitely spicy apple, honeyed.

SILVER FALLS WINERY
Sublimity   (1983)
2,000 cases

Less than five years old, Silver Falls has already had more than its share of ups and downs. The nineteen acres of vineyard were first planted in 1974, on the eastern side of the Willamette Valley not far from Salem—an area with few vineyards. In 1983 partner Jim Palmquist began the winery, but after two vintages financial problems forced a shutdown. Now, with the help of new partners, the winery is back in business, intending to concentrate on Pinot Noir and Chardonnay, with an initial crush in 1987.

Wines are available from the earlier vintages, though they show the rough edges of nonprofessional winemaking and the effects of several years of neglect. However, the new Pinot Noir from the 1987 vintage is simple but is decently made. Future plans include the employment of a professional winemaker.

PINOT NOIR ($$) ★★½   Good color, grapy nose and flavors; simple and Beaujolais-like, but the wine is well-made. Great pizza wine.

SISKIYOU VINEYARDS
Cave Junction   (1978)
4,000 cases

One of the blithe spirits of the Oregon wine industry, Suzi David's warmth and good cheer belie the difficult tasks she has faced. She and her husband, Chuck, planted the first vines in this mountainous area in the southwestern corner of the state in 1974. Widowed in 1983, she has carried on operations (with the assistance of a winemaker, Donna Devine) and now exclusively uses grapes from the small twelve-acre vineyard.

The climate in the Illinois Valley is different from that in the Rogue, just a few miles to the east—cooler, with more rain. The Davids made a considerable commitment to Cabernet Sauvignon, but the wines haven't been as successful as Cabernets from the Applegate area (although the winery makes a most pleasant Rosé of Cabernet). Nor has Pinot Noir, the mainstay at so many Oregon wineries, done particularly well. In contrast, whites, especially those best suited for cool climates like Müller-Thurgau and Gewürztraminer, have done very well. Overall results at Siskiyou are inconsistent, a problem perhaps exacerbated by the presence of some older wines in the marketplace.

CABERNET SAUVIGNON ($$) ★   The flavors from an older vintage seem woody and tired, with a leafy nose—not a good example.

GEWÜRZTRAMINER ($) ★★½ Again, the current release is several years old but holding well, with good varietal flavors and weight, good crispness.

MÜLLER-THURGAU ($) ★★★ Fresh fruit with some exotic overtones, quite sweet, but good balance. Very flowery.

PINOT NOIR ($$) ★★ It has varied from tasting pruny and tannic to light and herbal—not bad, just not impressive.

RIESLING ($) ★½ Slightly sweet, clean, not much character.

ROSÉ OF CABERNET ($) ★★½ This shows the Cabernet fruit off better than the regular Cab, with fresh, herbaceous flavors and a slight sweetness.

SOKOL BLOSSER WINERY
Dundee   (1977)
30,000 cases

At ten years, this is one of the oldest wineries in the state, and though its 30,000–case production is small by California standards, it makes the winery one of the largest in the state. The production facility is top-notch, and Bob McRitchie, the longtime winemaker who departed in 1988, helped establish its reputation for making consistently high-quality and appealing wines. He has clearly mastered Pinot Noir: When Oregon Pinot bested French Burgundies at a well-publicized tasting in New York in 1985, both of the top wines were McRitchie's. With McRitchie's departure, owner Bill Blosser, a former urban planner who has been active in promoting the state's wines, has taken over the winemaking. Blosser and wife Susan Sokol Blosser, an academic by background, were among the pioneers of modern Oregon wine, having bought their property in 1971. Sokol Blosser Winery has long made a wide variety of wines, both from grapes grown in its own forty-five-acre vineyard, right in the heart of the Dundee Hills, and from grapes purchased from other Willamette and Washington State vineyards. But the focus is narrowing—Merlot is gone, as are several others—and the list will probably drop further. The best bets are the top-of-the-line wines (although the inexpensive Pinot Noir from Washington grapes is quite serviceable).

As at many other Oregon wineries, demand for Pinot Noir has really taken off; fortunately, production here is considerably higher than elsewhere, and the wines are much more widely available. Sokol Blosser has always made a good, medium-weight Pinot that can age, but more recent vintages have produced a Red Hills Pinot Noir that has deep color and fruit and is one of the most impressive, and powerful, in Oregon. The separate Hyland bottling is lighter and more delicate but more forward and shows equal ability to age. Beginning with the 1987 vintage, there will be three Pinot Noir bottlings: Yamhill County (lighter style), Redland (a blend of the formerly separate vineyard wines), and Redland Reserve.

Chardonnay is the other very successful grape here, barrel-fermented like many others, but showing very forward fruit—the Reserve has more character than the regular bottling. Other whites are good but more ordinary, though the dry Gewürztraminer has on occasion been very good, and the flowery Müller is popular with many.

CHARDONNAY (YAMHILL) ($$) ★★★ Fairly oaky, with tart, appley fruit.
CHARDONNAY, RESERVE ($$$) ★★★★ A beautiful, buttery nose leads into rich fruit—apples and spice. This consistently lovely wine is one of the more forward Oregon Chardonnays, though it seems to hold up well.
GEWÜRZTRAMINER ($) ★★ Has varied from tough and awkward flavors to a rich, applelike nose with dry, tart flavors. In the best years this wine (either Yamhill or Washington) shows good richness and strength.

MÜLLER-THURGAU ($) ★★   Intense, sweet rose bouquet, with slightly sweet, simple fruit flavors. Fine for those who like a big, flowery style.

PINOT NOIR (HYLAND) ($$$) ★★★★   This lovely wine has been somewhat overshadowed by the Red Hills. It has light color, a gentle nose of strawberries and raspberries, but good spice on the palate. Most appealing is the silky texture.

PINOT NOIR (RED HILLS) ($$$) ★★★★   Dark crimson in color in good years, deep raspberry aromas in youth, but this wine, with lots of tannin and solid structure, needs time to develop. Powerful stuff. (But the '86 has been a bit disappointing.)

PINOT NOIR, RESERVE (RED HILLS) ($$$) ★★★★   A big, full-bodied, round wine with soft tannins and tealike aromas.

RIESLING ($) ★★   Fairly simple, straightforward style, with spiced apple flavors, slightly sweet. Occasional Select Harvest wine is more interesting.

STEVENS CELLARS
Rickreall (1987)
250 cases

Stevens Cellars is the brand name for Concord and Golden Muscat wines produced at Oak Grove Orchards Winery, with fruit from owner Carl Stevens's three-acre vineyard near Salem in the Eola Hills. A pie cherry wine (a first in Oregon?) is also planned. Wines not tasted.

STRINGER'S ORCHARD WINERY
New Pine Creek (1984)
100 cases (6,000-case capacity)

It's plum wine and nothing but plum wine (five different types) at this small family orchard, which calls itself "the only wild-plum winery in the world." The setting is high and dry, in the mountains east of Klamath Falls, right on the Oregon-California border (the orchard is actually in California). Wild plums, native to this part of southern Oregon and northern California, cover eighteen acres and used to go into jam, but owner John Stringer is enthusiastic about their characteristically tart and bitter flavors in his "uniquely different" wine. Wines not tasted.

THREE RIVERS WINERY
Hood River (1986)
3,000 cases

Bill Swain is an experienced winemaker (fifteen years in California, first at Charles Krug and then at Cresta Blanca) who came north to start his own winery primarily because he was convinced the Northwest was the place to make Riesling. Most Northwest wineries start with Riesling because it's easy and popular, but Swain, enamored of German wines, sees far greater potential for the grape. His six-acre vineyard, planted mostly to Riesling, is in the Columbia Gorge, which he is convinced is a wonderful place to grow Riesling and Chardonnay.

The wines show an absolutely fresh and crisp fruitiness, though the first vintage was very light in style and perhaps overly subtle. The Chardonnay has an unusual sweetness—the wine wouldn't ferment dry—but has turned out rather nicely. There will also be Pinot Noir, made from locally grown grapes.

CHARDONNAY ($$) ★★½ Rounded, slightly sweet with full and oaky flavors. Unusual, but quite pleasant.

GEWÜRZTRAMINER ($) ★ There isn't much varietal character in this light, clean wine.

RIESLING ($$) ★★ Very light, subtle flavors of peaches come through—slight sweetness balanced with crisp acidity.

ROSÉ OF PINOT NOIR ($$) ★★ Lovely color, with some nice Pinot flavors—light, crisp, fruity.

TUALATIN VINEYARDS
Forest Grove   (1974)
21,000 cases

In all the hoopla over Oregon wine the past few years, Tualatin has gotten less attention than some other newer wineries, probably because it hasn't had a standout Pinot Noir, and Pinot Noir is the hot wine. But the winery has consistently turned out one of the best Chardonnays in the state, its other white wines are all well made, and the Pinot seems finally to be catching up with others in the Willamette Valley. Owner-winemaker Bill Fuller is one of the most respected winemakers in the state, with a solid background in the California wine industry (including nine years at Louis M. Martini) before he came to Oregon, and the winery is one of the more technologically advanced.

Tualatin's large vineyard (eighty-five acres) is one of the older ones in the state, having been planted in the early to mid-seventies. It lies toward the western end of the Tualatin Valley, thirty miles west of Portland and somewhat distant from the mass of vineyards in the Dundee Hills to the south. A warm microclimate here means that grapes ripen a week or so earlier than in other vineyards, a definite advantage in cooler years; it may also account for the richness and depth of the Chardonnay (and the occasional plumminess of the Pinot Noir).

Chardonnay has always been the star here—a ripe, soft, oaky wine made in a forward style that should appeal to almost anyone who likes the grape. It should also convince most folks that Oregon is an excellent place for Chardonnay as well as Pinot Noir—the winery has grafted over some lesser varieties in order to increase production. Although Tualatin's Pinot Noir has occasionally been fine (the 1980, from a cool year, was a big award winner), it has lacked consistency. Now, however, Fuller seems to be solving the mysteries of the grape—not letting the fruit hang as long, for example. The '85 vintage was a breakthrough for this wine, with lots of ripe fruit but not out of balance.

Fuller is also experimenting to find the right techniques for rich, deep, dry Gewürztraminer in the Alsatian style; his own, like much Oregon Gewürz, is dry and spicy, but quite light. But other white wines here are made in a fruity, slightly sweet style that is popular with local consumers.

CHARDONNAY ($$) ★★★ Now in two different versions—a tank-fermented wine with light, appley fruit and a barrel-fermented wine with rather aggressive oaky flavors.

CHARDONNAY, RESERVE ($$) ★★★★½ In warmest years, extremely rich, powerful, with flavors of spiced apples and melons. Oaky, ripe, fat, very long. One of the biggest Oregon Chardonnays.

GEWÜRZTRAMINER ($) ★★½ Fresh apple-lychee nose, light, delicate, with nice spice. Dry.

MÜLLER-THURGAU ($) ★★★½ Rich, flowery nose, cloverlike flavors, fresh, delicate. Very appealing.

PINOT NOIR BLANC ($) ★★½ Crisp, fruity, slightly sweet. Fairly subtle style.

PINOT NOIR, RESERVE ($$$) ★★★★ More forward than many, with round, ripe cherry flavors, good oak, and soft tannins.

RIESLING ($) ★★ Light nose, just off-dry, simple. Slight herbal quality.

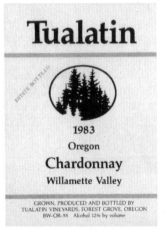

Tualatin

ESTATE BOTTLED

1983
Oregon
Chardonnay
Willamette Valley

GROWN, PRODUCED AND BOTTLED BY
TUALATIN VINEYARDS, FOREST GROVE, OREGON
BW-OR-55 Alcohol 12% by volume

TYEE WINE CELLARS
Corvallis   (1985)
1,500 cases

Oregon State University enologist Barney Watson does research for the local wine industry, experimenting with different grapes and grape clones. Dave and Margy Buchanan own a large farm near the university and, as longtime farmers, have looked for ways to diversify their operation. When they decided to plant grapes, they consulted Watson, whose advice led eventually to a partnership in this winery. The tiny six-acre vineyard is sited on bottomland (unusual for the region) in the central Willamette Valley, and the vines must be carefully pruned and thinned to control vigorous growth. But the wines show very careful and clean winemaking, with fine fruit.

The ubiquitous Chardonnay and Pinot Noir are the leading wines here, though Watson has a special affection for Gewürztraminer as well (the winery has a Reserve Gewürztraminer). The Chardonnay has an appealing balance of fruit and oak, and there is an interesting Pinot Noir Blanc, a truly dry one, with earthy flavors. Plans call for the development of a sparkling wine and continued experimentation with different varietal clones.

CHARDONNAY ($$$) ★★★   A forward wine, with lots of spicy, oaky flavor and crisp fruit. Should develop nicely.
GEWÜRZTRAMINER ($$) ★★½   Fairly light, dry style, with good spice—very pleasant.
GEWÜRZTRAMINER, RESERVE ($$) ★★★ Unusual wine. Flavors of citrus and lychee-nut, with underlying bitterness. High alcohol gives it body. Lightly sweet. Needs age to smooth out.

PINOT GRIS ($$) ★★★ Light nose, with some soft, appley flavors and just a little bite.

PINOT NOIR ($$$) ★★★ The first release showed forward, cherrylike flavors in a lighter style, with a slight earthiness.

PINOT NOIR BLANC ($$) ★★½ An interesting nose— more earthy than fruity. Made in a medium-weight, quite dry style.

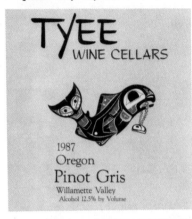

TYEE WINE CELLARS

1987
Oregon
Pinot Gris
Willamette Valley
Alcohol 12.5% by Volume

UMPQUA VALLEY WINERY *See* GARDEN VALLEY WINERY

VALLEY VIEW VINEYARD
Jacksonville (1976)
8,000 cases

If there are good long-term prospects for Cabernet Sauvignon and Merlot in Oregon, it is probably due in considerable part to this small winery, which pioneered a very different viticultural area in the state with its twenty-six-acre vineyard first planted in 1972. The Applegate Valley, not far from Medford and Ashland in far southern Oregon, is ringed by mountains that protect it from rain—it gets about half the rain of the Willamette Valley. High, dry, with warm summer temperatures, it has proven ideal for the ripening of the classic grapes of Bordeaux, even though the growing season is relatively short and killing frosts can be a problem both spring and fall.

The Wisnovsky family came to Oregon from the East Coast via San Francisco, looking for a place to grow grapes, and discovered the beauties of the Ashland area. The first red wines were striking for their power and depth, although even with age they seem rough and overly tannic. But new winemaker John Guerrero has brought a lighter, more forward style to the reds, which most people will find more appealing, and American oak is giving way to French oak in the aging process. Chardonnay also shows promise in the area, and again, the newer barrel-fermented Chardonnays from this winery have considerable character and lively flavors, with lots of oak. Production of this varietal is expanding with grapes purchased from other local vineyards.

CABERNET SAUVIGNON ($$) ★★★½ Newer vintages are medium-bodied, with forward fruit, some herbaceousness, and good balance.

CABERNET SAUVIGNON, RESERVE ($$$) ★★½ Older vintages are still purple, tannic, tart, hard. Powerful but tough.

CHARDONNAY ($$) ★★★ Very big, oaky nose with lots of fruit and forward flavors. Quite lively.

MERLOT ($$) ★★★½ Lovely berry nose, slightly herbal, with a soft oakiness. Again, older vintages are much fuller and more tannic.

PINOT NOIR ($$) ★★½ Oaky, tannic, and a bit raw, but with some good fruit.

ROGUE RED ($) ★★   Mostly Cabernet Sauvignon. Oaky
nose, good fruit, some bite.

VERITAS VINEYARD
Newberg   (1983)
5,000 cases

It's not hard to see why both Chardonnay and Pinot Noir
from this winery have found an enthusiastic following—
the style in both is rich, with lots of fruit. These are more
forward wines than many in Oregon, with the Pinot in
particular sacrificing finesse for full body and plump flavors. The one caveat is that the Chardonnay has not shown
the ability to age very well.

The first Veritas wines were made in 1983 at Sokol
Blosser by winemaker Bob McRitchie (part of a lot shared
with Yamhill Valley Vineyards), but a new facility is now
turning out the wines, with grapes from a number of local
vineyards, including Bethel Heights and Hyland. Veritas's
twenty-acre vineyard is planted with Pinot Noir, Chardonnay, and Riesling, and a bit of Müller-Thurgau. Owner Dr.

John Howieson is an award-winning amateur winemaker (he notes that the scientific aspects of medicine are good background), and the winemaking seems very carefully done, with wines that are well made and emphasize fine fruit and full body.

To deal with the difficult Riesling market, Veritas will experiment with both dry and Late Harvest Rieslings in the future.

CHARDONNAY ($$) ★★★ A rich, full, oaky-yeasty nose, with lots of fruit. Seems best in warm vintages, as the oak is assertive. Drink young.

PINOT NOIR ($$$) ★★★★ A nice nose of cherries, solid straightforward flavors, fairly full style, tannic.

RIESLING ($) ★★½ Ripe, spiced apple or peach-apricot flavors, sweet, soft, a bit flat.

VIENTO *See* AUTUMN WIND VINEYARD

WASSON BROTHERS WINERY
Sandy (1983)
3,000 cases

Although Wasson is best known for its berry wines, it turned some heads in 1987 when the 1985 Pinot Noir won Best of Show at the Oregon State Fair (the blackberry won the same prize in the fruit division, completing a sweep). The Wassons contend that fruit and berry wineries are still treated as second-class citizens, though they argue that making really good fruit wines is more difficult than making good grape wines.

The winery, not far east of Portland on the way to Mount Hood, is the creation of twin brothers, Jim and John, who have been part-time farmers and more recently amateur winemakers. Success at home led to a commercial venture, about evenly split between berries and vinifera, with Jim as winemaker while John manages the farm. There's a fourteen-acre vineyard near Oregon City, but the winery purchases grapes from a variety of vineyards in Clackamas County and the Willamette Valley. The berry wines are unquestionably well made, full-bodied but fresh, lightly sweet but with good acidity. The winery produces them year-round (from frozen fruit, which the Wassons feel works better than fresh) in small batches, so that the wines are always fresh tasting. Berry wines are, they say, "at perfection when they are bottled"—don't keep them.

The grape wines are in a lighter style, emphasizing delicate fruit, the Chardonnay and Pinot Noir having a strong oak component.

CHARDONNAY ($$$) ★★★½ Toasty oak nose, soft round fruit—no great depth but nicely made, and no rough edges.

GEWÜRZTRAMINER ($) ★★★ Enticing nose of exotic fruit, with soft, rather delicate flavors, moderately sweet.

PINOT NOIR ($$$) ★★★ A lighter style than the norm in Oregon, with delicate fruit but a fair amount of oak in the nose.

BLACKBERRY ($) ★★★ Dark, heavy blackberry-pie aromas, good acid.

RASPBERRY ($) ★★★★ Very dark, very fresh, strong pure raspberry scent, full body, lightly sweet but excellent acid.

WEISINGER VINEYARD
Ashland (1988)
1,800 cases

The success of nearby Valley View Vineyard inspired transplanted Texan John Weisinger to plant grapes in 1980 and to build his own winery in 1988. Initial varieties include Gewürztraminer and Cabernet Sauvignon, but Weisinger is experimenting with some Italian varieties in the belief that the warm Ashland area is suitable for Italian-style wines. Siskiyou Vineyards winemaker Donna Devine is also the winemaker here. Wines not tasted.

WITNESS TREE VINEYARD
Salem (1987)
1,500 cases

This brand-new winery planned to release its first wine in late 1988. Owned by Douglas Gentzkow, the thirty-five acres of Pinot Noir and Chardonnay in the northern Eola Hills near Salem were first planted in 1980. The winemaker is Rick Nunes, who has worked at Knudsen Erath, among other places. Wines not tasted.

YAMHILL VALLEY VINEYARDS
McMinnville (1983)
7,500 cases

Yamhill Valley hit the ground running when it released its first vintage of Pinot Noir, the 1983, which was made at Sokol Blosser by veteran winemaker Bob McRitchie. It was selected as one of the Oregon wines in a challenge tasting against French Burgundy in New York in 1985. All the wines were tasted blind, and Yamhill Valley emerged a winner, not only over the Burgundies but over a number of more famous Oregon Pinots as well.

Denis Burger set out in the eighties to find a small piece of property where he could plant an acre of grapes for his homemade wines. He ended up buying 100 acres, which has since expanded to 200, with 50 acres planted, including Pinot Gris (more of which is being planted), making the vineyard one of the area's larger ones. So far, grapes for the Pinot Noir have come from Hyland and Flynn vineyards. Burger, a microbiologist by profession, is the winemaker; members of the Hendricks family are partners.

The carefully designed and spacious winery clearly is intended to be a first-class facility, and all the wines are clean and well made. Pinot Noir is the lead wine, and it shows the effects of Burger's belief in warm fermentation: In ripe years it is big, deep, and tannic, an uncompromising wine that will need age to show its best and that will probably never have the delicacy of many other Willamette Pinots. Of the other wines, the Chardonnay is aggressively oaky and fine in that style; like the Pinot it lacks delicacy in youth and looks to be an ager. The most unique wine is the Elder Blossom. This latter, which the winery claims is a German tradition, is a concoction of Riesling with a small amount of elder blossom extract added, which gives a unique (some would say peculiar) herbal quality to the wine. Not to everyone's taste, but the winery says the wine has proved popular: "Elder Blossom lovers will kill for it."

CHARDONNAY ($$$) ★★★   A firmly oaky style, with very spicy flavors. Oak and acid make it fairly biting—it needs time to soften out.

ELDER BLOSSOM ($$) ★★   A very distinctive, herbal nose and woodsy, floral flavors. There's a slightly bitter aftertaste. You love it or hate it.

GEWÜRZTRAMINER ($$) ★★   Ripe wine, with an apple-vanilla nose, some bitterness. Just off-dry.

PINOT NOIR ($$$) ★★★★   One of the harder and more tannic Pinots around in good years, it has a big cherry-raspberry nose and deep fruit. It's rough-edged and reticent in youth and needs time to develop.

RIESLING ($$) ★★½   A very flowery nose, with intense, warm, appley flavors. Fresh, straightforward, slightly sweet.

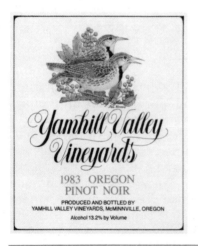

WINERIES NO LONGER MAKING WINE
Big Fir Winery
Century Home Wines
Côte des Colombes
The Honey House
Reuter's Hill Vineyards

9

WASHINGTON WINES
AND WINERIES

ARBOR CREST
Spokane   (1982)
33,000 cases

auvignon Blanc is king here—a startling 40 percent of production—and it has been a big award winner nationwide. That wasn't part of the winery's original plan (wine-maker Scott Harris would rather be known for his barrel-fermented Chardonnays). But Harris has found the key to this wine: French oak aging and a slight residual sweetness, both of which help to tame the grape's sometimes assertive vegetal tendencies. The same style has been applied to the other Arbor Crest wines with good success, and the lush fruit, softness on the palate, and drinkability make them fine restaurant wines (very classy labels don't hurt).

The Mielke family, which owns the winery, has been in the fruit-growing and -processing business for over sev-enty-five years and has the wherewithal for a very classy operation. Arbor Crest bought the innards of a bankrupt California winery and transported them to Spokane. Grapes have come from various vineyards in the Columbia Basin, including Sagemoor, Bacchus, and Stewart, while the Mielkes' own eighty-seven-acre vineyard near Mattawa on the Wahluke slope is maturing (Spokane is too cold for grapes).

UC Davis–trained winemaker Harris, who worked in the California wine industry before coming to Washington, does a very careful job indeed, helped by the winery's first-class approach (e.g., only French oak for aging). The wines are consistently high in quality, especially the whites (look for some absolutely beautiful Late Harvest wines), though reserve bottlings often don't seem substantially better than the regular ones. The first releases of red wines showed the same attention to good fruit in a forward, appealing style, although the Cabernet looks like it should stay the course very nicely. The Merlot, which Harris thinks offers the same potential for success as Sauvignon Blanc, is made in quite a soft and fruity style, ready to drink.

CABERNET SAUVIGNON ($$$) ★★★★ Dark, classic Cabernet nose, deep body with some tannin, but not harsh—it shows the structure needed to age very well.

CHARDONNAY (SAGEMOOR) ($$) ★★★ Lots of oak flavor in this wine, with straightforward fruit, medium body, fairly soft style. The Reserve is a bit oakier and doesn't have the same charm.

JARDIN DES FLEURS ($) ★★ Essentially a blush Riesling, made by adding a bit of red juice to the wine. It's perfectly pleasant.

MERLOT (BACCHUS) ($$) ★★★½ A raspberry nose, lots of fruit, light but flavorful—a lovely, almost Beaujolais-like example of the early drinking style of Merlot that is coming into fashion. As with the Chardonnay, the Reserve is stronger but not that much more impressive.

MUSCAT CANELLI ($$) ★★★ Quite piquant, soft, only slightly sweet, with a nice bite to it.

RIESLING ($) ★★½   A light style, with a Muscaty nose, slight sweetness, and not a lot of depth.

RIESLING, LATE HARVEST ($$$) ★★★★★   Not notably botrytised, but rich and creamy, with lots of ripe, peachy flavors. It's sweet but beautifully balanced. Consistently one of the best in the state.

SAUVIGNON BLANC ($$) ★★★½   A kiss of sweetness and a hint of oak give this wine a lovely, round feel. Not too varietally assertive, just slightly herbaceous. Not really a wine for seafood—it needs something more substantial.

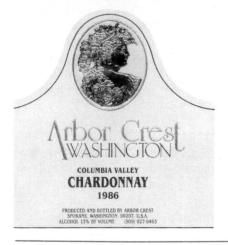

ASSOCIATED VINTNERS   *See* COLUMBIA WINERY

BAINBRIDGE ISLAND WINERY
Winslow   (1981)
1,500 cases

The efforts of Gerard and Joan Bentryn to grow grapes and make wine on their small plot of land on an island in Puget Sound has met with considerable skepticism from natives familiar with the Sound's cool and rainy weather. But the Bentryns are both believers in and energetic experimenters with their grapes, which include a number of vinifera crosses developed in Europe precisely to cope with cool ripening conditions. Originally they also purchased eastern Washington grapes but are proud now to be using only grapes from their own seven acres and from other western Washington vineyards.

The wines are styled in the German fashion, with low alcohol (the grapes have to be able to ripen early, at low sugars) and some residual sweetness. The flagship wine is Müller-Thurgau, which has also been successful in Oregon and combines a very floral character with some exotic flavors—the slightly sweet version seems more successful here. The really surprising wine is Siegerrebe (the only commercial bottling in the United States?), a cross of Gewürztraminer with Madeleine Angevine, itself an old French cross. The Bentryns have managed to make a full-flavored, sweet dessert wine from this early ripener, which has a wilder character than Riesling. Pinot Gris has also recently been planted, and there are even plans for a little Pinot Noir.

The strawberry wine from local fruit, full-bodied and sweet, has developed quite a local cult and sells out very quickly.

FERRY BOAT WHITE ($) ★½ Another Müller, flowery and sweet, with less character than the varietals.

MÜLLER-THURGAU ($) ★★★ Very flowery, fresh and soft, with low alcohol but decent body from some sweetness.

MÜLLER-THURGAU, DRY ($) ★★ Same flavors as the sweeter bottling, but it seems thin without the sweetness.

SIEGERREBE, BOTRYTIS *AFFECTED* ($$$) ★★★★ More flowery than Riesling, sweet with lots of rich, tropical fruit flavors (papaya), lush.

STRAWBERRY ($$) ★★★ Amber color, with a rich, heavy perfume of strawberries—very spicy.

BARNARD GRIFFIN WINERY
Kennewick (1983)
1,000 cases

The Griffin in Barnard Griffin is the same Rob Griffin who helped build Preston's reputation and more recently has overseen Hogue's hugely successful growth (see Hogue Cellars). This winery is his own small venture (in partnership with wife Deborah Barnard), with the goal of making the highest-quality handcrafted wines in limited quantities. Many tiny wineries display the defects of home winemaking, but Griffin is a thoroughly experienced professional who rarely makes a mistake.

Griffin thinks the key to good Cabernet in the state is "don't spare the oak" (he favors American oak for reds), and indeed, all the wines with the exception of the Riesling have a noticeable oakiness without, however, any woody harshness. The Fumé Blanc is fermented in oak and left on the lees for a time to give it greater richness; the result is a wine with toned-down varietal flavors but more complexity. Characteristics of all these wines are accurate fruit, careful balance, full body—and no rough edges. The barrel-fermented Chardonnay shares with the Hogue Reserve a real buttery quality and nice fatness, while the Cabernet is a bit leaner and harder than the Hogue at this point, but shows every sign of evolving gracefully. Distribution of these wines is very limited, but they are well worth searching out.

CABERNET SAUVIGNON ($$$) ★★★★   A lean, tart, spicy wine with lots of oak showing. Not a real heavyweight, but fairly hard yet. Needs time.

CHARDONNAY ($$$) ★★★★   Very appealing buttery nose, with melony fruit. Fairly soft, medium body, fat and round. A winner.

FUMÉ BLANC ($$) ★★★   Newer vintages show a softer style, with less grassiness and more rounded oaky qualities. Lean and crisp—definitely a food wine.

RIESLING ($$) ★★★½   Lots of body, with a rich, lively wildflower nose. Off-dry, but good acidity.

BINGEN WINE CELLARS *See* MONT ELISE VINEYARDS

BISCUIT RIDGE WINERY
Dixie (1987)
350 cases

A Gewürztraminer-only winery doesn't sound like a formula for commercial success these days (hard as the
grape is to grow, it's harder to sell), but retired naval officer Jack Durham is not concerned about commercial
success. He settled in this tiny community in the hills
northwest of Walla Walla because he loved the area, and
he's growing his five acres of Gewürztraminer and making it into a dry wine because that's what he likes to drink.
His years spent in Europe enamored him of the small wine
producers in France and Germany, and he sees his wine
as a very personal statement.

Admitting that "people thought I was nuts" to produce
Gewürz, he is applying some unorthodox methods to the

grape—like putting the wine into old American oak barrels for a short time to "round off the rough edges." The wine is distinctive, if still a little rough—definitely designed to stand up to food.

GEWÜRZTRAMINER ($$) ★★½   Ripe, appley nose with good body and some bite to it—a little bitter.

BLACKWOOD CANYON VINTNERS
Benton City   (1982)
15,000 cases

It's amazing this winery still exists. Essentially a one-man project of owner-winemaker Mike Moore, the winery burned to the ground in a fire in 1985, virtually wiping out a supply of aging wines in storage. Rather than give up, Moore has continued to make wines in a temporary structure, planted more acres of vineyard, and has ambitious plans for a brand-new winery. The fifty-acre vineyard site at the eastern end of the Yakima Valley is not far from Kiona Vineyards on Red Mountain, which has already established a reputation for high-quality grapes (especially Cabernet). Meanwhile, surviving wines from the prefire vintages have shown a distinctive and pleasing style.

Moore trained with Ventana's Doug Meador in California and attributes to him an openness to experimentation and creativity in his winemaking. A firm believer in barrel fermentation and aging on the lees, Moore has used this technique on unlikely varietals like Riesling and Chenin Blanc, with good results. The first wine to draw attention here was a huge, barrel-fermented Semillon, which shows Moore's preference for rich, full-flavored, distinctive wines. (This wine, still available, has stirred controversy but has a solid set of fans. The newer Semillon is a bit toned down.) The big toasty Chardonnay shows much the same approach—if you don't like oak, this is not the place for you.

But it is with Late Harvest wines that Blackwood may prove most successful. Moore scours local vineyards for botrytised grapes no one else wants and has a number of sweet Rieslings as well as a Sauternes-style Sauvignon Blanc. He is ecstatic about a 1986 Riesling that is immensely sweet and thick (he claims his cellarman walked across the open tank of fermenting must).

Blackwood is expanding quite rapidly: Reds (including Pinot Noir) should appear in the next year. There is also a new second label called Windy River Cellars, with less expensive wines designed for the restaurant trade.

CHARDONNAY ($$) ★★★½ Toasty flavors of oak come through in this wine—there's rich fruit, a bit of caramel, and solid body. A lovely wine.

CHENIN BLANC, DRY ($$) ★★★ An unusual wine, after time in oak. A light nose of clover and light, crisp, dry flavors leave a pleasant, rounded sensation.

RIESLING, DRY WHITE ($$) ★★½ Another unique wine: barrel-fermented Riesling with a rich, yeasty nose and light apple flavors. Riesling for Chardonnay lovers?

RIESLING, LATE HARVEST ($$) ★★★★ A rich, light apricot nose with a definite accent of cloves makes this a most interesting wine. There's more body here than in most Late Harvest wines, but all is in balance.

RIESLING, ULTRA LATE HARVEST ($$$) ★★★★ This very sweet (Beerenauslese-style) dessert wine has intense tropical fruit flavors and slight nuttiness—with a very long finish. Very lovely.

SAUVIGNON BLANC, BOTRYTIS (?) ★★★½ This oak-aged wine comes the closest to a French Sauternes that one is likely to find in the United States. It has an intense, honeyed nose, fine weight and complexity, and a long finish. Unreleased.

SEMILLON ($$) ★★★★   Not your ordinary Semillon. The
'83 has a huge, uncompromising nose of green peppers,
full fruitiness, tangy tartness, and a long finish. Power-
ful. (The '86 seems lighter, though.)

BONAIR WINERY
Zillah   (1985)
2,000 cases

This compact little winery in the middle of the Yakima
Valley is very much a family undertaking. School admin-
istrator Gail Puryear has turned his winemaking hobby
into a serious enterprise with the help of wife Shirley and
children. The wines show careful attention to winemak-
ing details and the neat and tidy approach emphasized by
consultant Mike Januik (now with Snoqualmie). The
flagship wine is Chardonnay (the five-acre vineyard is de-
voted to this variety), made in traditional big, oaky style,
but with plenty of fruit. Puryear is a believer in the lees
contact and malolactic fermentation that give the wine
that soft and buttery feel. For those who want to compare
two different styles, the Outlook Chardonnay, tank-fer-
mented, is more straightforward and fruity than the bar-
rel-fermented Puryear Chardonnay. Both wines are great
values.
   The Riesling is also very well made, and a Cabernet will
be released in the future. Although there is no track record
to look at here, the first results were most promising. This
will be one of the small wineries to watch carefully.

CHARDONNAY (OUTLOOK) ($$) ★★★   Softer, more applelike flavors than the Puryear, straightforward fruit
with a dab of oak.
CHARDONNAY (PURYEAR) ($$) ★★★★   A buttery, soft,
balanced wine, with open, warm flavors. Lots of fruit

and oak here, in plump style, should please most Chardonnay lovers.

RIESLING ($) ★★★   The style is the same as for Chardonnay—fat and ripe. Lovely apricot nose, soft, with good body.

SUNSET (BLUSH) ($) ★½   Nose of wildflowers and sweet herbs, tart, good fruit.

BOOKWALTER WINERY
Pasco   (1983)
6,000 cases

Jerry Bookwalter is an experienced hand in the grape business, having managed for many years the huge Sagemoor Farms vineyard, which has supplied grapes to many wineries, as well as orchards in both Washington and California. As one might expect, he is one of many who believes that "the wine is made in the vineyard."

Bookwalter's work as a vineyard consultant keeps him well informed about the state's grape crop, and he prefers not to own his own vines but to pick and choose grapes from a number of vineyards in the Columbia Valley, a strategy well suited to the current oversupply of wine grapes in Washington. Wines are made both at his own small facility and at other custom-crush wineries. (A new, larger facility opened in 1988.)

Bookwalter's aim is to make "consumer-oriented" wines. The fruity white wines are in a ripe, soft style: The Chenin Blanc has shown some inconsistency from year to year but the Riesling has been a steady performer—ripe and fat. The Chardonnay, surprisingly, seems just a bit lean and light, but the Cabernet has lots of good fruit and good body in a straightforward style. Like many in eastern Washington, Bookwalter is also making sparkling Riesling, but this one doesn't have the zip of some others.

CABERNET SAUVIGNON ($$$) ★★★ Lots of fruit and oak in the nose, still fairly tart and tannic—it may need some time.

CHAMPAGNE ($$) ★½ A big burst of bubbles with fruity Riesling flavor, but it finishes flat, slightly earthy.

CHARDONNAY ($$) ★★½ Light nose and rather tart flavors, with good balance.

CHENIN BLANC ($) ★ This has been very good in the past, but the current release, while sweet, tastes tired.

MUSCAT BLANC ($) ★★ Appealing, appley nose, but it falls a bit flat.

RIESLING ($) ★★★½ A wine for those who like their Riesling voluptuous. Rich, ripe, peachy flavors—quite soft.

RIESLING, LATE HARVEST ($$) ★★½ Pearlike flavors, rather tart and angular.

CAROWAY VINEYARDS
Kennewick   (1983)

Although Caroway Vineyards has retained its bond (federal license to make wine), it is not currently producing any wine.

CASCADE CREST ESTATES
Sunnyside   (1987)
70,000 cases

A partnership group, including President Toby Halbert and operations manager Bob Fay, has entered into a long-term relationship with a group of growers who own 250 acres in the Sunnyside area. Halbert spent ten years with Chateau Ste. Michelle, where he worked on both the production and marketing ends of things (helping to build the Chateau's powerful national marketing network). He believes marketing is a key to success for the Northwest and wants to emphasize a selection of "fighting varietals": fruity white wines ("the best the Northwest has to offer") at good prices. Having bought a lot of almost brand-new equipment and oak barrels from bankrupt Haviland Winery on the cheap, and using an old dairy plant in Sunnyside, Halbert hopes to keep production costs low.

To do national marketing, production must be fairly high—this ambitious new winery crushed 170,000 gallons at Langguth (under Mike Januik's supervision) its first year, with plans for expansion to an eventual 500,000. Although as yet there is no permanent winemaker, Mike Wallace, formerly of Hinzerling, is acting as consultant in 1988.

The style of the initial releases was appealing, if not

remarkable, with all the wines tasted emphasizing fresh varietal fruit and an easy-drinking style. Although the emphasis is on young whites, premium whites and reds are also in the plan.

GEWÜRZTRAMINER ($) ★★ Fruity, appley, medium sweet—simple but pleasant.
RIESLING ($) ★★½ Ripe nose of apple and peach, fresh, pleasant.
SEMILLON BLANC ($) ★★ Fruity style, with just a touch of grassiness and slight sweetness.

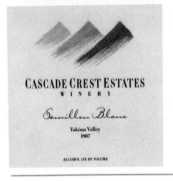

CASCADE MOUNTAIN CELLARS
Ellensburg   (1986)
4,000 cases

Although Washington wineries have long sought to convince wine drinkers that the state's Chenin Blanc is on a par with the lovely wines of Vouvray in France, Cascade Mountain is the first winery to label a Chenin Blanc as "Vouvray." Whether this will turn out to be a marketing winner is unclear; as good as Washington's Chenins are, they still haven't found the elusive richness that French Vouvray has.

Jürgen Grieb came to Washington from Germany in 1983. A graduate of a German winemaking institute, he had been working for the huge Langguth firm in Germany and was sent to the Northwest to make wine for its American operation (since sold to Snoqualmie Winery). His own small winery (housed in an old railroad depot) will focus on whites in what he calls the "German style—light and fruity." Grapes are purchased from Columbia Valley vineyards, and the first vintage was produced at Worden's Winery.

Initial releases were pleasant and well made, with the "Vouvray" showing the plump fruitiness and wildflower aromas that make Chenin a popular grape in Washington.

CHARDONNAY ($$) ★★   Rather unctuous style, with tart fruit; one-dimensional.
VOUVRAY (CHENIN BLANC) ($) ★★½ Fresh, fruity, wildflower nose, crisp.

CAVATAPPI WINERY
Kirkland   (1984)
500 cases

Production is minuscule, as the goal of restaurateur Peter Dow is only to produce enough wine to sell in his popular Italian café. A true house wine being very much an Italian tradition, Dow is pursuing another Italian tradition by growing Nebbiolo (a northern Italian grape used in making the great Barolos and Barbarescos) on an acre and a half at the Red Willow Vineyard at the west end of the Yakima Valley. The vines have grown vigorously, and his first harvest of these grapes was in 1987. Meanwhile, the winery is turning out quite a tasty Sauvignon Blanc, which has some Semillon blended in—available only at the winery. A tiny amount of Cabernet is also in the works.

SAUVIGNON BLANC ($$) ★★★ Crisp, restrained, rather
steely flavors that should suit seafood just fine.

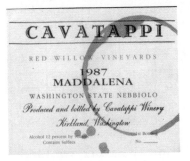

CHAMPS DE BRIONNE
George   (1983)
9,000 cases

The winery has a spectacular perch on cliffs overlook-
ing the Columbia River, squarely in the middle of the
state. But it's far from the fertile grape-growing regions of
the state—this is largely alfalfa country. Nevertheless,
Vince and Carol Bryan suspect that it's precisely these
inhospitable conditions that will make their vines pro-
duce outstanding grapes, just as the rocky and gravelly
soils of Europe produce the best wines. So far the wines
have shown a soft balanced quality rather than varietal
intensity.

The vineyard is large, 130 acres, and planted to a num-
ber of varieties, including Pinot Noir—the Bryans feel
their site is similar to those of Burgundy vineyards for
heat and soil. (The first release of Pinot Noir did not im-
press.) The best wine here is probably the Cabernet-Merlot
blend, a fruity, accessible wine that most people would
find very palatable. Other wines, while well made, are

unremarkable. The Brut sparkling wine was made as a still Riesling at the winery, shipped to Weibel in California to have bubbles added, and returned to the winery for bottling—a trek that will probably become more common. The result is a pleasant Riesling sparkler.

Swiss-trained winemaker Cameron Fries makes no apologies when he describes his own taste in wine as "popular taste." He wants to make light, soft wines and feels many Washington wines are too high in acid. "Making 'pleasant' wine is not a bad goal." Indeed.

BRUT ($$) ★★½ Light, clean, appley flavors, with light bubbles.

CABERNET-MERLOT ($$) ★★★ Pleasant oaky nose, ripe berry flavors, and a bit of spice. Very soft and drinkable.

CHARDONNAY ($$) ★★½ Light, slightly vegetal flavors—well made but not terribly weighty, with a touch of oak.

GEWÜRZTRAMINER ($) ★½ Light nose, semisweet, nothing special.

PINOT NOIR ($$) ★★ Flavorful, with some interesting ripe, woody qualities. Strong, not elegant.

RIESLING ($) ★★½ Spicy fruit, slightly sweet, fresh, tart, and simple.

SEMILLON ($) ★★½ Balanced, delicately fruity, citrusy flavors. Good seafood wine.

CHATEAU STE. MICHELLE
Woodinville and Grandview   (1968)
450,000 cases (capacity)

In many parts of the United States, Washington wine *is* Ste. Michelle; this company's superb marketing has introduced many wine lovers to the idea of wine from the "rainy" Northwest. Fortunately, the quality is high for a winery of this size—it dwarfs all other Northwest wineries except sister winery Columbia Crest, though it is still far smaller than California's largest.

Ste. Michelle's roots go back to 1934, when two companies, Nawico and Pommerelle, began to make sweet wines from Concord grapes and other fruit. These two merged to become American Wine Growers, and in the fifties the winery planted its first vinifera grapes, beginning with Semillon and Grenache. André Tchelistcheff, a fabled California wine consultant who made Beaulieu Vineyard's reputation, was brought in to oversee the winemaking. By 1967 the enterprise was ready for a new label, Ste. Michelle, for an emerging line of grape varietals; it was these wines, along with those of Associated Vintners (now Columbia Winery), that first attracted national attention to premium Washington wine. In 1974 the winery was sold to U.S. Tobacco (the king of smokeless tobacco), which began pumping in considerable money to expand production and make the facility top-of-the-line, building in the process an impressive-looking chateau-style winery. Today Chateau Ste. Michelle is under the umbrella of Stimson Lane, the tobacco giant's wine and spirits business, which includes Columbia Crest and two small California wineries as well as Whidbeys brand liqueurs and port (all operated separately). Ste. Michelle has 900 acres of its own in the Yakima and Columbia valleys, but it also purchases a lot of grapes, going a long way toward setting state grape prices in the process. Supervising winemaker is Peter Bachman, who has an extensive background in both the Northwest and California.

Ste. Michelle has always been committed to premium varietal wines, and despite its huge growth, it has maintained high quality standards—the wines are not always the most striking examples in their class, but you rarely get a bad bottle. The best of the varietals are excellent value, as well. The flagship wine is Johannisberg Riesling, which Ste. Michelle has managed to produce on a large scale as a very fresh, crisp, fruity wine year in and year out. Of the other whites, Sauvignon Blanc and Semillon stand out—both do a fine job of balancing fruit with the herbaceous character of these grapes, and both wines have the crispness to be fine seafood wines. Surprisingly, the Chardonnay has been a little disappointing, without the character and fruit that one would like to see, although the new Cold Creek Vineyard wine from the 1986 vintage shows a more refined style.

The Ste. Michelle Cabernet Sauvignon has never gotten the attention it deserves, probably because it often doesn't show particularly well in youth, needing some years to rub off the tannins. Some of the older vintages are drinking very nicely, and the more recent releases are showing better balance when young. (But the Reserve Cabernet retains very hard qualities.) And 1983 seems to have been a breakthrough vintage for the Merlot—the Chateau Reserve is quite excellent.

Among the many firsts at the winery is Washington's first *méthode champenoise* sparkling wine, the Blanc de Noir, which is released well aged and is very well made. (A new label, Domaine Ste. Michelle, has been developed for a line of sparkling wines.) The winery produced a legendary Ice Wine in the seventies, long since gone, but both the Late Harvest Riesling from Hahn Hill Vineyard and the Select Cluster Riesling are among the biggest and richest dessert Rieslings in the state.

The winery also produces a line of inexpensive jug wines under the Farron Ridge label.

BLANC DE NOIR BRUT ($$$) ★★★½ Six years on yeast gives this vintage-dated sparkler good body, with tart fruit, delicate flavors, and some richness.
CABERNET BLANC ($) ★ Slightly sweet, with some Cabernet flavor, rather heavy.

CABERNET SAUVIGNON ($$) ★★★★ A consistently good, solid Cabernet. Intense, rather hard berry-oaky flavors and tannins give way with age to a round plumminess. Excellent value.

CABERNET SAUVIGNON, RESERVE ($$$) ★★★★ Even bigger than the regular Cab, with more vanilla oak in the nose—tart, hard wine. Many will prefer the regular bottling.

CHARDONNAY ($$) ★★ Light, tart, somewhat woody flavors—not as much fruit as one might like.

CHARDONNAY (COLD CREEK) ($$$) ★★★½ Haylike aromas, with restrained fruit and nice oak overtones; not really complex, but very nicely balanced, and more elegant than previous Chardonnays here.

CHARDONNAY, RESERVE ($$$) ★★★ Light nose of butterscotch, with restrained flavors—not big, but balanced.

CHENIN BLANC ($) ★★ Nice balance of sweetness and acid with some wildflower aromas.

MERLOT ($$) ★★★½ Very tasty indeed, with a balance of berry and oak flavors. Older vintages were occasionally harsh and hot, but the most recent ('83) is velvety.

MERLOT, CHATEAU RESERVE (RIVER RIDGE) ($$$) ★★★★ The '83 is certainly the best Merlot from the winery—big, rich, and thick, with lots of vanilla oak in the nose, chocolaty flavors, and excellent weight. A winner.

PINOT NOIR ($$) ★★★ Leathery-earthy nose, rich, tannic, spicy, but a bit rough.

RIESLING ($) ★★★½ At its best, lovely apple-pear nose, delicate fruit, very fresh, nice crispness—what a Riesling should be.

RIESLING, LATE HARVEST (HAHN HILL) ($$) ★★★★½ A very dense, rich wine, with a lovely balance of sweetness and acid. Powerful rather than delicate.

RIESLING, SELECT CLUSTER ($$$) ★★★★½ Definite apricot flavors, with thick, rich, straightforward fruit. Muscular sweet Riesling.

SAUVIGNON BLANC ($$) ★★★½   New releases are less aggressive, with subtle herbaceous flavors and crisp acidity.

SEMILLON ($) ★★★½   A bit lighter and fruiter than the Sauvignon, with flavors an interesting balance of citrusy fruit and herbs. Ripe, soft. (There's also a slightly sweet Semillon Blanc.)

DOMAINE STE. MICHELLE BRUT ($$) ★★½   Tart, rhubarby flavors, light fruit—not nearly as distinguished as the Blanc de Noir.

FARRON RIDGE RED TABLE ($) ★★   Great pizza wine, not too heavy, with decent fruit, a hint of sweetness, but good acid.

FARRON RIDGE WHITE TABLE, DRY ($) ★½   Pearlike aroma, soft, decent fruit, medium body—not as interesting as the red.

WHIDBEYS PORT ($$) ★★   A port-style wine from Cabernet Sauvignon; it has heavy, spicy, slightly vegetal flavors—not elegant but lots of flavor.

CHINOOK WINES
Prosser   (1984)
1,500 cases

Chinook is a pocket-sized operation whose wines can be hard to find. But they are worth seeking out, as they are all extremely well made and appealing in style. Indeed, they are almost paradigms of what people mean by "restaurant wines"—fruity, accessible, balanced, without rough edges, and with flavors that marry well with food.

The quality is no surprise, as the winery is run by two widely respected professionals in Washington's wine industry. Kay Simon has been a consultant to various wineries for a decade (getting a number of respected small producers off the ground), while husband Clay Mackey has worked as a vineyard manager. There's no vineyard here, which gives them the opportunity to pick and choose their fruit.

Crisp acidity and fresh fruit are the watchwords. The Chardonnay and Sauvignon Blanc really do what they claim to do—go well with the Northwest seafood cuisine. All the whites see time in French oak, which seems mostly to round out the flavors rather than to add an assertive oakiness. These whites have been the specialty, but the first releases of Merlot showed good fruit and depth, and there's a sparkling Riesling that is quite tasty, too.

CHARDONNAY ($$) ★★★   Light, toasty aromas with a nice balance between apple and oak flavors—not a heavyweight but most enjoyable.

CHARDONNAY, RESERVE ($$$) ★★★★   Spicy, oaky nose, with big, warm, fat flavors. This is a full-bodied wine, but shows considerable finesse.

MERLOT ($$) ★★★½   Starts off with a subtle raspberry nose. Oaky, plummy, slightly herbaceous character. Fairly rich.

SAUVIGNON BLANC ($$) ★★★   A light and subtle example of this wine, with an emphasis on balance rather than assertive fruit. Slight herbaceousness, tart.

TOPAZ ($$) ★★½   A blend of Semillon and Sauvignon Blanc (in proportions varying from year to year), with citrusy, herbaceous flavors. Light, tart—a pleasant food wine.

COLUMBIA CREST VINEYARDS
Paterson   (1984)
500,000 cases (capacity)

Columbia Crest was the name Ste. Michelle chose in 1984 for its second-label blended wines—which were so successful that now the name has been extended to a full line of varietals made at what used to be Ste. Michelle's immense River Ridge Winery on the banks of the Columbia at Paterson. For the Northwest it's an astonishingly large operation: 2,000 acres of vineyard dot the desert in huge green irrigated circles, and the largely underground winery stretches for many football fields of space. The whole thing cost $26 million to develop, courtesy of cash-rich parent company U.S. Tobacco (smokeless tobacco). Although Columbia Crest still produces less than Ste. Michelle, it clearly has the capacity to be the largest winery in the Northwest.

For all that money Columbia Crest got a very technically advanced facility, and the aim of the winery is clearly to make very fresh, fruity varietals in a soft and appealing style. Overall, they are perhaps a bit less intense in flavor than the Ste. Michelle wines (which tend to run a dollar or so higher in price), more rounded, with a touch more sweetness, though a couple of the wines (especially Chenin Blanc) are more appealing than their Ste. Michelle counterparts. Winemaker Doug Gore was formerly assistant winemaker at Ste. Michelle, where he oversaw red wines, and he has considerable California experience. His talent with reds shows through here particularly—both the Cabernet and the Merlot are excellent wines in their price classes and stand up well to much more prestigious bottlings.

The parent company has spent a bundle of money to promote these wines, and the packaging is very slick—but the wine is just fine. Several of the new varietals are clear successes, especially the Chenin Blanc and Semillon, both loaded with fresh fruit flavors and a nice measure of tartness. The Chardonnay is also a nice example in the soft, fresh fruit style. The blended table wines are also surprisingly good. The white is an especially interesting blend, combining the delicacy of Riesling with the floral qualities of Muscat and the spice of Gewürztraminer—lots of flavor in a medium-sweet wine.

Even more impressive were the first releases of reds, from the difficult '84 vintage. Both Cabernet and Merlot, in slightly different styles, are very appealing wines with very rounded character.

CABERNET SAUVIGNON ($$) ★★★½   Attractive nose of berries, oak, and herbs. Not a big wine, but it shows beautiful balance and grace.

CHARDONNAY ($$) ★★★   Spiced-apple flavors, fruity, with lots of acidity—forward and simple. Good value.

CHENIN BLANC ($) ★★★   Rich honeyed flavors with a lovely sugar-acid balance.

GEWÜRZTRAMINER ($) ★★   Fresh apple flavors, soft—not much intensity.

MERLOT ($$) ★★★   Big nose of chocolate and berries, fruity, tannic, slightly hot.

RIESLING ($) ★★   Decent Riesling fruit, but a bit soft and lacking backbone.

SAUVIGNON BLANC ($) ★½   A vegetal nose without much redeeming character. Quite dry.

SEMILLON ($) ★★★   Clean, fresh hay aromas, good fruit, just off-dry—a very pleasant wine.

VINEYARD RESERVE WHITE ($) ★★   A zippy, medium-sweet wine with interesting floral characteristics and good body.

COLUMBIA RIVER CELLARS *See* PRESTON WINE
CELLARS

COLUMBIA WINERY
Bellevue (1967)
40,000 cases

After undergoing a considerable transformation in the
last five years, Columbia seems to be finding its stride. Not
that there have been any problems with quality here—the
wines have always been first-rate. But it's been difficult to
figure out what the winery wanted to focus on (it probably
has the longest list of wines in the state, under two separate labels). Now a strong emphasis on top-quality Cabernet Sauvignon has emerged, alongside a commitment to a
solid line of medium-priced varietals that have long represented good value.

This is the winery, then named Associated Vintners, that
helped put Washington wines on the map (see "A Brief
History" in Part One.) A group of home winemakers,
mostly from the University of Washington, outgrew their
basements and did their first commercial crush in 1967
(before the great majority of current California wineries,
one might note). Under previous winemaker Lloyd Woodburne, they had an uncompromising approach that emphasized absolutely dry, European-style dinner wines
(mostly whites). The AV Gewürztraminer was the flagship
wine—not quite Alsatian, but dry, medium-bodied, spicy,
crisp, and very ageworthy. (A recently tasted '77 Gewürztraminer was still showing very nicely.) The other whites
were also fine—light, delicate, long lasting. But the reds,
Cabernet and Pinot Noir, never quite seemed to get off the
ground.

AV outgrew the energies of its amateur owners, and in 1979 David Lake was taken on as winemaker. Lake is a Master of Wine, a prestigious title in the English wine trade, and apprenticed in the Northwest under David Lett at Eyrie. Under Lake, the quality of the reds showed quick improvement—indeed, Lake's first vintage, 1979, produced a huge, hard, tannic Cabernet released under a special Millennium label, suitable for aging until the year 2000. Lake continues to feel that Washington will make its name more for Cabernet than anything else. As production has grown (ownership was expanded in 1984 to include majority investor Dan Baty, and the name changed), some concessions have been made in the form of a more popular, fruity style of Riesling and Gewürztraminer. (There is still a dry Gewürztraminer, for the die-hard fans, under the Woodburne label.)

But the single-vineyard bottlings of Cabernet have gone from strength to strength, though they can be quite hard when young (Lake makes no apologies for solid acids and tannins in his young wines). Three different Cabernets, from Red Willow, Otis, and Sagemoor vineyards, show strikingly different fruit, but all three are characterized by depth, good structure, and the need for aging. The Red Willow, from an out-of-the-way vineyard surrounded by Indian reservation land at the western end of the Yakima Valley, is probably the best, and most Bordeaux-like (it has shown well in tastings with the Bordeaux First Growths). Lake is experimenting with Merlot and Cabernet Franc from this vineyard to see what different blends might produce. Meanwhile, the regular Cabernet and regular Chardonnay (1,000 cases of the '84 Chardonnay went to England on the recommendation of wine writer Hugh Johnson) are good values. (Lake is still tinkering with the Wyckoff Chardonnay, moving toward complete barrel fermentation.) Also noteworthy is the Semillon, which has evolved from an intensely herbaceous, citrusy wine to one that shows a bit less varietal fruit but is rounder and more balanced. Made in a dry but fruity and slightly grassy style, it is an excellent wine for light seafoods and continues to be an outstanding value.

The winery has dedicated its Woodburne label, in honor of its first winemaker, to wines that will probably find a more limited audience. The dry Gewürztraminer (not made every vintage) is usually very good and quite subtle. And Lake is still experimenting with Washington State Pinot Noir, from both sides of the mountains, to try to find the right formula. The current Pinot, while lacking the perfume of most Oregon versions, is quite approachable.

Columbia also makes a number of table wines, which appear under a variety of special labels, as well as some generic restaurant wines, which turn out to be surprisingly good (the only decent value in some restaurants).

In late 1988 Columbia completed a purchase of the former Haviland winery facility in Woodinville. Columbia will benefit both from increased space and from much better visitor facilities.

CABERNET SAUVIGNON ($$) ★★★½ Tannic and deep in good years, with chocolate and spice on the nose. Not complicated, but lots of fruit. Good value.

CABERNET SAUVIGNON (OTIS) ($$$) ★★★★ Rich, tart, taut wine in youth, with classic Cabernet flavors and a slight herbal, almost minty, accent that some find off-putting (but remember Martha's Vineyard).

CABERNET SAUVIGNON (RED WILLOW) ($$$) ★★★★★ An austere, closed, oaky nose when young, with classic underlying structure and excellent balance. Should develop for a long time.

CABERNET SAUVIGNON (SAGEMOOR) ($$$) ★★★★½ More straightforward than either Otis or Red Willow, with bunches of spicy blackberry fruit and lovely oaky-vanilla flavors. More accessible, though quite dense; it should age well.

CHARDONNAY ($$) ★★★   Light, crisp fruit with a touch of oak—rather haylike aromas, like a nice Mâcon. Very pleasant.

CHARDONNAY (WYCKOFF) ($$$) ★★★½   A very concentrated wine, with thick butterscotch aromas, considerable spiciness and weight. Fairly chunky and tart in youth, definitely a wine to age.

CHENIN BLANC ($) ★★½   Light, crisp, flavors of wildflowers and grapefruit.

GEWÜRZTRAMINER ($) ★★   The new style is soft, slightly sweet, with a nice lychee nose and no bitterness. It's pleasant enough but won't excite fans of the old wines.

MERLOT ($$) ★★★   A warm, oaky nose with some berry flavors, good tannin in a balanced, drinkable style—though it's a little harder than many others. Takes some time to develop.

RIESLING ($) ★★½   Very nice, pear-apple nose, spicy, slightly sweet, a little soft.

RIESLING, CELLARMASTER'S RESERVE ($) ★★½   This has tended to be an early-release wine in a low-alcohol style, with some sweetness and lots of peachy fruit. Fairly simple.

SEMILLON ($) ★★★½   Excellent seafood wine—lean, balanced, good backbone but not assertive. Citrusy flavors with some grassiness.

WOODBURNE GEWÜRZTRAMINER ($$) ★★★½   Lovely restrained nose, with apple fruit. Dry, lasts well. Made only in certain vintages.

WOODBURNE PINOT NOIR ($$) ★★★   A nice earthy nose, with slight greenness, slightly harsh, but good roundness of flavor and feel.

COOLEN WINE CELLARS
South Colby   (1986)
350 cases

Dick Coolen, a masonry contractor, would like to see about six or seven acres of vines at his Puget Sound site, but so far there's just a half acre, so grapes are purchased from eastern Washington, Oregon, and California. Right now these red grapes are going into a full-bodied red table wine. The Madeleine Angevine and Siegerrebe planted in the vineyard are destined for a Champagne-method sparkling wine. Wines are available only at the winery; not tasted.

COVENTRY VALE
Grandview   (1983)
400,000 cases (capacity)

Wine buyers with sharp eyes may notice that a number of Washington wines with unfamiliar names were produced and bottled in Grandview. They were made at a winery that is one of the largest in the Northwest yet until recently had no wines on the market under its own name. Coventry Vale is essentially a first-class winery for rent: wineries just getting started that have no facilities yet, wine brokers who buy grapes and turn them into wine—those are the folks who make use of Coventry Vale.

Now, in addition to its custom-crush service, Coventry Vale is in the sparkling wine business, with a line of four different "Champagnes" based on the Riesling grape. Owners David Wyckoff and Don Toci, who also have 650 acres of vineyard between them, felt that there was a market niche for Northwest *méthode champenoise* wine that was not being filled—clearly the number of different styles offered is meant to fill the niche snugly. The wine is being made a little at a time from a reserve of Riesling set aside for this purpose, with the rosé getting its color from a small addition of red juice. The best of these wines, all of which are quite frothy, is the Blanc de Blancs Brut, which is just slightly sweet and shows off the Riesling fruit quite attractively. The wines are all well priced.

There is also a line of inexpensive and unremarkable white varietals under the Washington Discovery label, as well as a line of restaurant wines.

CHAMPAGNE BLANC DE BLANCS BRUT ($$) ★★½ Lots of bubbles with fresh fruit flavors, but, despite the name, not quite dry. Light, crisp—the Riesling comes through.
CHAMPAGNE BLANC DE BLANCS EXTRA DRY ($$) ★★½ Good bubbles, decent fruit, not as zippy as the Brut.
CHAMPAGNE DEMI-SEC ($$) ★★ A sweeter "dessert-style" sparkler, but the fruit seems a little tired.
CHAMPAGNE EXTRA DRY ROSÉ ($$) ★★ Lots of fruit and flavor with good bubbles. Riesling with a touch of red wine. Bit of a soda pop finish.

ÉSTATE BOTTLED
1985

MÉTHODE CHAMPENOISE
Columbia Valley Champagne
BLANC DE BLANCS
BRUT
ALCOHOL 12% BY VOLUME
PRODUCED AND BOTTLED BY
COVENTRY VALE WINERY, GRANDVIEW, WA BW 99
NET CONTENTS
750 ML.
CONTAINS
SULFITES

COVEY RUN VINTNERS
Zillah and Kirkland   (1982)
38,000 cases

What's in a name? Covey Run began life as Quail Run but ran into trouble with a preexisting California winery named Quail Ridge—the name change came after a court action. Clearly it hasn't hurt, as the winery is one of the fastest growing in the state. Owned by a partnership of a number of Yakima Valley farmers, the winery owes much of its success to manager Stan Clarke, who not only is a well-trained viticulturist but also has worked tirelessly to promote the wines. The current winemaker is David Crippen.

In just five years Covey Run has established its reputation as one of the best medium-sized producers in the state. A very broad array of wines is offered, and all are well made, well priced, and styled to please a wide audience. The Chardonnay in particular has gained a reputation as a forward, delicately fruity wine that will satisfy most palates—it comes in several bottlings with different levels of oakiness. The reds, Cabernet Sauvignon and Merlot, are big and fruity. But in addition to the standard offerings, there are several unusual wines, including Aligoté, Lemberger, and Morio-Muskat.

The Aligoté is unique—a lesser white variety from Burgundy grown on just one 2-acre patch of vineyard in the state. The winery has experimented with the grape, trying out oak aging and barrel fermentation. The wine turns out lighter than Chardonnay, but it ages surprisingly well, and the winery touts it as a fine seafood wine. Lemberger, from a German grape, Covey Run makes into a soft, very fruity red (no oak) with lots of flavor. Morio-Muskat, a little-grown Sylvaner–Pinot Blanc cross, offers considerable pungency in a sweet wine.

Although the winery hasn't gotten much recognition for sweet wines, it has some lovely ones. The regular Riesling is pretty ordinary, but the sweeter Rieslings from the Mahre and Whiskey Canyon vineyards are packed with lovely, straightforward fruit and are very modestly priced. At the other end of the price spectrum is an Ice Wine from the 1986 vintage, which is quite splendid and certainly one of the most powerful sweet Rieslings produced in the state.

Not only does Covey Run have a second facility for sparkling wine production in a Seattle suburb, but in 1987 it introduced a new label Zillah Oakes. These releases are advertised as "varietal wines at everyday prices"—the winery openly aspires to cut into California's dominance in the low-end premium wine field, and there are plenty of grapes to do it. All the Zillah Oakes wines have a light, fresh, fruity style and all are well priced.

ALIGOTÉ ($) ★★★ Like a light Chardonnay, but more flowery. Very fresh, with nice tartness. An all-around good light-food wine. Newer vintages are a bit heftier.

BRUT ($$$) ★★½ Good, prickly bubbles, but the Riesling fruit seems a little tired. Quite soft.

CABERNET SAUVIGNON ($$$) ★★★½ Very dark, with a big, chocolaty-oaky nose and rough, tannic flavors.

CAILLE DE FUMÉ, LA ($) ★★★½ A proprietary name (*caille* means "quail") for a Sauvignon Blanc–Semillon blend. Softened by oak, this has a lovely balance of fruit and herbal flavors and is refreshingly light.

CHARDONNAY ($$) ★★★ Delicate fruit, fairly light and crisp. Quite Mâcon-like.

CHARDONNAY (WILLARD FARMS) ($$) ★★★★ An earthy nose, with a rich balance of fruit and oak, and a long, tart finish. Not strong, but lovely.

CHENIN BLANC ($) ★½ Soft, indistinct flavors, a bit of honey.

LEMBERGER ($) ★★★½ Lots of color and blackberry fruit, with a definite black pepper accent. Soft and forward.

MERLOT ($$) ★★★ Big berry nose, but soft on the palate—not deep, but very appealing.

MORIO-MUSKAT ($) ★★★½ A definite tropical fruit nose, but the Muscat quality is not overwhelming and the sweetness is well balanced.

RIESLING ($) ★★½ Soft, peachy flavors, medium body, good acid, but nothing special.

RIESLING (MAHRE) ($$) ★★★★ A very ripe apricot-peach nose, rich, sweet, soft, with some earthy undertones.

RIESLING (WHISKEY CANYON) ($$) ★★★★ Lovely, sweet peaches-and-cream flavor, with a bit of cinnamon spice.

RIESLING ICE WINE ($$$$) ★★★★★ Spectacular sweet wine. An almost nutty nose, with very full flavors, clove-like spice, and great acid to carry it for quite a while. Expensive.

ZILLAH OAKES CHARDONNAY ($) ★★ Delicate apple fruit with good bite.

ZILLAH OAKES MUSCAT CANELLI ($) ★★ Fresh, green apple flavors, light and pleasant.

ZILLAH OAKES RIESLING, LATE HARVEST ($) ★★½ A very popular wine, with soft peachy fruit and medium sweetness.

COVEY RUN
1986
ALIGOTÉ
YAKIMA VALLEY
PRODUCED AND BOTTLED BY COVEY RUN VINTNERS, ZILLAH, WASHINGTON
ALCOHOL 12.5% BY VOLUME, B.W-WA. 96

DOMAINE STE. MICHELLE *See* CHATEAU STE. MICHELLE

EATON HILL WINERY
Granger

No wine yet available. Plans call for this Yakima Valley winery to make its first crush of Riesling in 1988 in a converted and restored cannery.

FACELLI WINERY
Redmond (1988)

This new winery crushed small amounts of Chardonnay, Sauvignon Blanc, Semillon, Riesling, and Merlot from the 1988 harvest. Grapes are coming from both Sagemoor Farms and Ciel du Cheval Vineyard in eastern Washington.

The reason to take note of this new operation is the owner and winemaker, Louis Facelli. Facelli first gained a reputation in Idaho for making excellent, ripe, and flavorful Riesling and Chardonnay at the winery that bore his name—but the other investors sold it from underneath him. More recently he became winemaker at Haviland—just before that enterprise went bankrupt. He is sole owner of the new winery, and the wines should bear watching.

FIDALGO ISLAND WINERY
Anacortes (1986)
1,700 cases

If finding a market niche with a unique product is the way to success, Fidalgo Island is on the way—it's one of only two wineries in the state (Lost Mountain is the other) making wine without the use of sulfites. Sulfites are used almost universally in the wine world to preserve flavors and prevent spoilage, but some people, including owner and winemaker Charles Dawsey, are allergic to them, and the federal government, beginning in 1988, requires all wineries to label their wines containing sulfites. Dawsey has had his tested by the feds—no sulfites, so no warning label.

Dawsey, who's retired, says he was drawn into the wine business by friends who kept wanting to buy his home-made wine. He continues to tinker with his winemaking process, which he keeps to himself, except to allow that oak flavoring is part of his secret. He's not entirely happy yet with his wines, which lack freshness. Availability is limited, but these wines may be worth searching out for those who are sulfite-sensitive.

CABERNET SAUVIGNON ($) Dark and heavy, harsh, hot—not very drinkable.
RIESLING ($) ½ The first vintage was flowery and had good body, but was rather flabby, with some peculiar flavors, especially in the finish.

E. B. FOOTE WINERY
Seattle   (1978)
1,000 cases

The Foote wines seem less and less available—Gene Foote, a Boeing engineer who started as a home wine-maker, doesn't seem much interested in the marketing side of the business. Nor is he trying to make wines in a popular style. All the wines here, mostly white, are completely dry and not terribly fruity. (The lack of fruit is accentuated by the fact that most current releases are at least five years old.) Nevertheless, there is a small but enthusiastic following for Foote's full-bodied, pungent Gewürztraminer, the dry Riesling is sturdy and clean, and all the wines are reasonably well made and modestly priced. (Lack of filtering does lead to some problems with bottle variation.) The 1985 vintage saw a break with Foote's hard line on sweetness, as he made a small amount of Late Harvest Riesling in a semisweet style.

The tiny winery is in a semi-industrial section of Seattle, while the grapes come from several Yakima Valley vineyards with which Foote has long-term relationships.

CHARDONNAY ($$) ★½   Aged in Limousin oak, it has quite woody, hard flavors and not much finesse. Medium body.

GEWÜRZTRAMINER ($) ★½   Variable. It is usually floral and strong-flavored, with quite a bite, but it can have some peculiar flavors. Always dry.

PINOT NOIR ($$) ★   Some varietal fruit, but dominated by very earthy qualities. Woody.

RIESLING ($) ★½   Quite dry, with rather hard fruit and solid body—there's not much varietal fruit, but it makes a decent dry white.

RIESLING, LATE HARVEST ($$) ★★ A nice apricot nose, but the fruit is rather clumsy and the finish is bitter.

FRENCH CREEK CELLARS
Woodinville (1983)
4,000 cases

Like a number of wineries that have grown out of home winemaking operations, French Creek Cellars has had trouble maintaining consistency with its product. The aim of the winery has been to make traditional European-style dry dinner wines, so even Riesling and Muscat have been finished in a bone-dry style (though recently these have gotten sweeter). Hans Doerr, a German-born University of Washington professor, is the partner who oversees the winemaking, and his approach is uncompromising. Both whites and reds tend to be full-bodied, tart, alcoholic, oaky, rough in their youth, but designed for aging.

Fining and filtering seem to be at a minimum, so the wines are variable and often a little cloudy. French Creek, located in a Seattle suburb that has a growing colony of wineries, buys all of its grapes—including Pinot Noir from Oregon vineyards and Cabernet Sauvignon from the excellent Otis Vineyard in the Yakima Valley. The 1987 vintage saw the first, minute amounts of Washington-grown Petite Sirah, a pioneering effort.

CABERNET SAUVIGNON ($$) ★★★½ A fat, tannic wine, rather closed in, but with hints of strong blackberry fruit.

CABERNET SAUVIGNON, RESERVE ($$$) ★★★ Very dark purple, vegetative–green pepper nose, lots of oak, hot, powerful but not complex.

CHARDONNAY ($$) ★★½ Definitely an oak wine, with bready nose and full, tart flavors. Fairly thick.

LEMBERGER, RESERVE ($$) ★★★½ Lovely raspberry–black pepper nose, soft, lots of fruit, crisp.

MERLOT ($$) ★★½ Vanilla-blackberry nose, plummy flavors, deep hot fruit. Lots of body.

MUSCAT CANELLI ($$) ★½ A lively Muscat nose, perfumed, soft, low acid, slightly sweet.

RIESLING ($) ★★ Slightly sweet, decent fruit, good tartness.

RIESLING ICE WINE ($$) ★★★ Although not sweet enough for traditional Ice Wine, this has the thick, tart, nutty flavors of this style.

SEMILLON ($) ★ Intense, vegetal nose marks this wine, which lacks balance. There is also a sweet Late Harvest version.

GORDON BROTHERS CELLARS
Pasco   (1983)
2,500 cases

The slopes of the Snake River, a few miles out of Pasco, is the location of this eighty-five-acre vineyard, one of the most respected in the state. The Gordon brothers, Jeff and Bill, are potato farmers who decided to diversify into grapes in 1980, only to run into the current grape glut in the state. With a small winery they can make wine from grapes that don't fetch a good price on the market; fortunately, they planted the right varieties, including Merlot, Chardonnay, and Cabernet Sauvignon, and left out Riesling, which is overplanted. Jeff Gordon keeps on top of the grape-growing business as director of the state growers' association, which has worked hard to find homes for all the grapes (in 1987, a bumper crop found its way to California, the Midwest, and Japan, as well as state wineries).

Jeff Gordon is also the winemaker and, despite lack of experience, shows a steady hand. All the wines are well made, have good balance and fruit, and are in a forward, drinkable style. The Merlot, especially, has been a big prizewinner—it shows tart, cherrylike fruit and is considerably lighter than many Merlots, a good style for this sometimes difficult grape.

The unusual wine is the moderately sweet Sauvignon Blanc, which Gordon says people like because it has more flavor than Riesling. He's the only one making wine like this, but sometimes it doesn't hurt to be different. Those who like their Sauvignon Blanc light and crisp should look elsewhere.

CHARDONNAY ($$) ★★★ A very forward, appealing wine, with an oaky-buttery nose, and rich, soft, apple fruit. Well rounded.

CHENIN BLANC ($) ★★½ Pungent apple nose, good fruit, nice bite.

MERLOT ($$) ★★★½ Fresh, tart, bright cherry fruit, with nice oak flavors—a good example of the forward style.

RIESLING ($) ★★½ Rich, spiced apple fruit—some tendency toward overripeness.

SAUVIGNON BLANC ($$) ★★ There's lots of herbaceous Sauvignon flavor, but the moderate sweetness is disconcerting. Good acid, but not really a dinner wine style.

HAVILAND VINTNERS
Woodinville   (1981)

The ambitions of founder George de Jarnatt were not small: This young winery described itself as "Washington's premier limited production, world-class winery." But de Jarnatt's expertise ran more to promotion than winemaking, and the wines never matched the claims. Rapid expansion, including an elaborate new production facility, led to the winery's financial collapse in late 1987. Remaining wines and the winery's equipment were sold off in 1988, and Columbia Winery purchased the facility.

HINZERLING VINEYARDS
Prosser (1976)
3,000 cases

Hinzerling was the first small winery established in the Yakima Valley (earlier wineries trucked their grapes across the mountains to Seattle area facilities). The Wallace family moved across the mountains to settle in Prosser and realize winemaker Mike Wallace's dream. Wallace was one of the first winemakers native to the state to have been thoroughly trained as an enologist, at the University of California at Davis, and he was instrumental in getting the young wine industry off the ground. Ironically, Hinzerling's production, never large, has fallen in the past several years, as the wines have faced greatly increased competition in the marketplace. In 1988 the Wallaces sold the winery to Californian Don Allen, but the leading influence at the winery will probably be Allen's brother-in-law, Bill Broich. Broich, the original winemaker at Idaho's Ste. Chapelle, has established a reputation especially for Chardonnay, and the new emphasis will be on whites.

Wallace's wines were shaped not by the market but by his own uncompromising standards. The largest portion of the twenty-three acres of vineyards is committed to the classic grapes of Bordeaux—Cabernet Sauvignon, Merlot, Cabernet Franc, and Malbec. The Cabernet Sauvignon (which in some vintages has some Merlot in it) is a great wine for the patient—tough and unyielding in youth, it develops fine complexity with age. (The '77 is still going very strong.) This wine is underpriced and overlooked. In addition to the regular Cab, there's a Cabernet-Merlot-Malbec blend that is more forward, with lots of fruit and a softer touch.

Of the whites, the Gewürztraminer is a fine, ripe example, and there are some excellent Late Harvest wines. Wallace was one of the first in the valley to make sweet dessert wines from botrytised grapes and has some memorable wines to his credit, including one fabulous wine called Die Sonne from Gewürztraminer grapes allowed to dry out in the sun. Pungent and aggressive young, this wine has aged very graciously.

A second label, Prosser Falls, is in use for some white wines.

ASHFALL WHITE ($) ★★ Lively, lots of flavor, slightly sweet.

CABERNET-MERLOT-MALBEC ($$) ★★★½ The nose is slightly weedy at first, but opens into rich, spicy, oaky flavors with more pronounced fruitiness and less tannin than the regular Cab.

CABERNET SAUVIGNON ($$) ★★★★ In youth, dark, tough, lean, tannic. But with age the wine develops complex spice while retaining powerful fruit. Always long-lived.

CHARDONNAY ($) ★½ Pungent, woody, and slightly weedy—it doesn't have the fresh fruit of most others.

GEWÜRZTRAMINER ($) ★★★ Varies from slightly sweet to totally dry, but always spicy, tart, full-flavored.

RIESLING, LATE HARVEST ($$) ★★★½ Older vintages are lovely, with an old Riesling nose and lots of rich, honeylike flavors—not too heavy.

SONNE, DIE (GEWÜRZTRAMINER) ($$$) ★★★★½ The '77 is an amazing old sweet Gewürztraminer with huge flavor, excellent spice, and great weight. The '85 is dense, nutty, viscous, and spicy.

HOGUE CELLARS
Prosser (1982)
60,000 cases

In five years Hogue has become one of the best-selling and highest-quality producers in the state—an extraordinary success story. The members of the Hogue family are no strangers to success, having built up a prosperous and diversified farming business on their 1,200 acres of land in the Yakima Valley (200 of which are now planted with grapes). They jumped into the wine business with a stylish Chenin Blanc and Riesling (made by Mike Conway of Latah Creek), which proved immediately popular and which have been models for other developing wineries. But increasingly, the winery is emphasizing more prestigious varietals, like Chardonnay, Fumé Blanc, and Cabernet Sauvignon, as well as a Champagne-method sparkling wine.

Hogue winemaker Rob Griffin (who also has his own small winery—see Barnard Griffin) has been making wine in Washington longer than most, having started with Preston Cellars in 1976. Griffin has a solid background from training at UC Davis and while at Preston established a reputation especially for fine Chardonnay and Fumé Blanc. His trademark has always been very fresh fruit and clean, technically excellent winemaking, and the Hogue commitment to a first-class product supports this approach. And Griffin has demonstrated the ability to handle a large number of varietals and maintain quality in a large facility.

The Chenin Blanc and Riesling continue to be fine examples of these varietals in the state, though increased production seems to have taken a little varietal intensity out of the wines. The Fumé Blanc shows a character rather similar to the trend-setting Sauvignon Blanc at Arbor Crest—with the herbaceous quality of the grape toned down by judicious use of American oak, which plumps the wine up a bit, too (the Hogue wine has a bit more backbone than most). There's a real contrast between the regular and Reserve Chardonnays—the former (a great bargain) should appeal to those who like ripe Chardonnay fruit while the latter, completely barrel-fermented in French oak, is great for those in love with a big, buttery oak style.

Hogue's very first Cabernet Sauvignon, a 1983 Reserve, took Best of Show at the large Atlanta Wine Festival. It is a monster wine with loads of fruit and lots of spicy oak (Griffin prefers American oak for the reds because of the more intense, "showier" oak character it imparts to the wine). Red wines have been in limited production here, but that is changing, and there are now regular as well as Reserve bottlings of both Merlot and Cabernet Sauvignon.

Hogue was also one of the first in the state to produce a Champagne-method sparkling wine made primarily from Riesling grapes. With the '86 vintage Griffin had developed a very attractive style for this wine, toning down the fruitiness of the Riesling with the addition of a little Chardonnay. It's hardly French Champagne but has a very appealing character of its own.

All the wines are reasonably priced.

BRUT ($$$) ★★★★   Most recent style shows a lovely, subdued nose of apples and melon, with lots of bubbles and good body.

CABERNET SAUVIGNON ($$$) ★★★   Fairly light color with forward berry-oaky nose. Fruity, tart, light tannins, straightforward.

CABERNET SAUVIGNON, RESERVE ($$$$) ★★★★½   Intense blackberry-vanilla nose, very full body—but surprising softness. Solid tannin and acid without harshness. Lovely.

CHARDONNAY ($$) ★★★½   A hefty wine with lots of rich, appley fruit and a bit of oak. More emphasis on fruit than in the Reserve.

CHARDONNAY, RESERVE ($$) ★★★★   An intensely buttery nose, with a soft feel to it—the fruit really gives way to oak. Lovely texture, though perhaps not as complex as one might like.

CHENIN BLANC ($) ★★★½   One of the best examples of this grape. Light, balanced, with wildflower aromas and fine crispness. Just a bit of prickle on the tongue.

FUMÉ BLANC ($$) ★★★★   A rather fat Fumé, with a subdued, grassy nose, forward fruit, good tartness, and a rounded feel from light oak aging.

MERLOT ($$$) ★★★½   Intense nose with good fruit, some spice, and fine balance. Softer than the Cabernet.

RIESLING ($) ★★★   Pears and wildflowers in the nose, lively, fresh flavors—fairly lean.

RIESLING, LATE HARVEST (MARKIN) ($$) ★★★★ Forceful, rich, sweet wine—tons of fruit and spice. Not really delicate or complex, but very tasty.

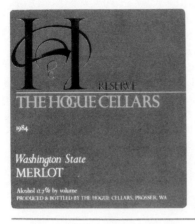

HOODSPORT WINERY
Hoodsport (1980)
12,000 cases

Sixty percent of production at this little winery, well off the beaten track on the Olympic Peninsula, is fruit and berry wines, with the remaining 40 percent grape wines (most of the grapes come from eastern Washington, including the excellent Kiona Vineyard). Dick Patterson, who owns the winery and makes the wine, began as a hobbyist (he still teaches part-time at a nearby community college). The wines are sound in quality, if not exciting, with the style of the grape wines emphasizing straightforward fruit flavors. The one stand-out wine is the raspberry—fresh and luscious without being heavy. It's hard to fault the gooseberry wine—it tastes like gooseberries, nice if you like that fruit. The winery recommends it with spicy Asian cuisine.

The most unique Hoodsport wine is the Island Belle, a red wine from a native American grape. Some identify

Island Belle with the Campbell Early grape, while others contend it is a cross. In any case, the grapes come from some of the oldest vineyards in the Northwest, on Stretch Island in South Puget Sound. First planted in the late nineteenth century, the vineyards survived Prohibition and prospered until rising land values and competition from eastern Washington and California ruined the market for the grape. But the Pattersons began purchasing it for their winery in 1981 and have made a small amount every year since. Island Belle has the "foxy," grapy character of labrusca grapes, though considerably toned down.

Rapid increases in production and sales have led to ambitious plans for expansion, including two possible new facilities in the South Sound area.

CHARDONNAY ($$) ★★★ The emphasis is on fresh apple-melon fruit, with quite viscous body and a good oakiness.

GEWÜRZTRAMINER ($$) ★★ Floral, sweetish, soft, fruity.

ISLAND BELLE ($$) ★★½ A bright red wine with a "foxy," grapy nose and lots of tart flavor. Fairly dry—interesting if not elegant.

MERLOT ($$) ★★★ Good berry nose with considerable fruit and body—without oak flavor.

RIESLING ($) ★★ Light wildflower nose, just off-dry. Clean flavors.

GOOSEBERRY ($) ★★ Wild forest aroma of gooseberry, with a balance of tart and slightly sweet. Distinctive.

LOGANBERRY ($) ★★★ Bright red, with a very fresh nose—fairly sweet but not heavy.

RASPBERRY ($) ★★★★ Lovely, fresh, crisp flavors—slightly sweet. A truly delicious example.

CHARLES HOOPER FAMILY WINERY
Husum   (1985)
1,000 cases

After more than twenty years in Europe, having discovered the pleasures of German wine, the Hooper family returned to the United States to settle in the Columbia Gorge and make wine. Their six-acre vineyard, planted largely to Riesling, is on a very steep slope high in the hills, looking south across spectacular scenery toward Oregon's Mount Hood. Charles and son Chris are basically amateur winemakers, without formal training, though they did gain some experience in German vineyards. Production is tiny, and the winery is very much a family enterprise.

The wines are fruity, if not as fresh as those made in larger commercial wineries. (A new facility is in the works.) Most interesting are the Chardonnay, from a mixture of Oregon and Washington fruit, and the Riesling, which shows more of a piney than applelike character.

CHARDONNAY ($$) ★★   Interesting herbal nose, some nice viscous fruit, slight oak character—not really classic flavors, but decent.

GEWÜRZTRAMINER ($) ★   Dry, fairly biting, a bit tired out—good body.

RIESLING ($) ★½   A somewhat piney nose and fairly full body—dry and tart, slightly harsh, not that fresh.

HORIZON'S EDGE WINERY
Zillah   (1983)
3,000 cases

This small winery has attracted little attention so far, but its first releases of Chardonnay (the wine it plans to specialize in) showed great promise. Owner-winemaker Tom Campbell has worked at a number of other Yakima Valley wineries, including Ste. Michelle and Stewart, and helped start Montana's first winery (Mission Mountain). He is a devotee of barrel fermentation, aiming more for richness and complex flavors than fresh fruit in his wines.

Despite its small size, the winery has several different bottlings of Chardonnay (you have to check the fine print on the label to know which is which). Chardonnay from the Celilo Vineyard in the Columbia Gorge is quite different from the others—not only is it a different clone, but the climate is cooler. Most Chardonnay lovers will probably favor the wines from Yakima Valley or Columbia Valley grapes. Chardonnay also provides the base for a Champagne-method sparkling wine, which has the toasty richness of the other Chardonnays.

The initial release of Cabernet Sauvignon showed some promise, though the remaining wines are unremarkable. Still to come is Pinot Noir. Campbell is convinced Pinot grown in cooler sections of the Yakima Valley (his own twenty-acre vineyard is north-facing) can have the elegance of Oregon Pinot Noir.

CABERNET SAUVIGNON ($$$) ★★½ Deep purple-red, ripe, oaky nose, lots of flavor. It has the strong, spicy quality of American oak, with lean, rather herbal fruit. Still tart, it needs some age.

CHAMPAGNE ($$$) ★★★ One hundred percent Chardonnay, this wine has the toasty nose of the other Chardonnays, is quite tart, and has lots of fine bubbles. A good sparkler.

CHARDONNAY (CELILO) ($$) ★★½ An interesting, slightly stewed nose, fruity and tart. There's not much oak showing and the wine seems fairly simple.

CHARDONNAY (FAIR ACRE) ($$$) ★★★½ A very appealing wine in a soft, ripe, toasty oak style, made from

Yakima Valley grapes. Flavors are assertive but not harsh. Needs some time to smooth out. The best of these bottlings.

CHARDONNAY (GREEN LABEL) ($$) ★★½ The entry-level Chard here, with pleasant, crisp varietal fruit and fresh flavors. Well made.

CHARDONNAY (MCKINNON) ($$$) ★★★ Lighter, oakier, softer, more open than the Fair Acre, with appley fruit and nice balance.

GRENACHE ($) ½ Made in a light blush style, it tends toward vegetal, bell pepper flavors, with slight sweetness. It will probably seem very odd to most blush lovers.

RIESLING ($) ★★ Light, fruity, crisp, not notable.

HUNTER HILL VINEYARDS
Othello   (1984)
4,000 cases

The location is somewhat isolated from the rest of the Columbia Valley wineries, northeast of the Wahluke Slope, a good twenty miles from the river. Twenty-eight acres of vineyard were planted in the early eighties by commercial pilot Art Byron, and a new winery was completed in time for the 1987 crush (previous vintages were made at another local winery). It's too early yet to know whether this subregion will be favorable for wine grapes—based on limited samples, the wines have seemed ordinary. (Gary Graves of Pacific Crest recently became consulting winemaker.)

CHENIN BLANC ($) ★ Light color and nose, slightly sweet, not much character.

RIESLING ($) ★★ Scents of wildflowers and clover, with fairly full body and sweetness.

HYATT VINEYARDS WINERY
Zillah   (1987)
8,500 cases

The newest winery in Zillah (fast becoming the center of mid–Yakima Valley winemaking), Hyatt is frankly an effort by owner Leland Hyatt to deal with an oversupply of grapes from his seventy-three-acre vineyard. Hyatt shakes his head over the recent prices for wine grapes (he gets more for his Concords than for some varieties of wine grapes). The plan is to process some bulk wine to sell to other wineries while keeping the best to bottle under his own label, as well as the label of his winemaker, Wade Wolfe, a noted viticulturist.

Wolfe, who used to work for Ste. Michelle and now acts as vineyard consultant for a number of properties, is most interested in dessert wines and will release these under a separate label. His most unusual project is Black Muscat, a little-planted red Muscat grape grown only in one nearby vineyard, which he has made into a fortified, heady sweet wine.

Hyatt will concentrate on higher-end wines, including Chardonnay, Sauvignon Blanc, and Merlot (Wolfe feels the earlier-ripening Merlot does better in the cooler sections of the Yakima Valley). Barrel samples of the wines showed considerable promise; first releases were in the fall of 1988.

JOHNSON CREEK WINERY
Tenino   (1984)
2,000 cases

One of a very small number of intrepid vineyardists in western Washington, Vince De Bellis has planted mostly

Müller-Thurgau, a cool-climate grape, in his three-acre vineyard southeast of Puget Sound. While the vines mature he is buying grapes from the good-sized Brookside Vineyard in southwest Washington, as well as warmer-climate grapes from small growers in the Yakima Valley. Although he hopes to specialize in Müller-Thurgau, a wine that has proved surprisingly popular, the winery makes a fairly full line of white and red varietals.

The winery, in the European tradition, is alongside the popular restaurant that wife Ann runs, and much of the wine is sold through the restaurant. The De Bellises, long-time home winemakers, got the itch for a commercial winery when they entered a national amateur wine competition as a lark and won three first prizes. The wines are all decently made and fairly priced, without being fancy. The Müller-Thurgau, full-flavored and earthy, is a very nice example of this little-known wine, while the new Cabernet Sauvignon has lots of straightforward flavor.

CABERNET SAUVIGNON ($$) ★★★ Lots of lively oak-berry flavors, fresh and straightforward. Good drinking.

CHENIN BLANC ($) ★★ Pungent nose of tropical fruit, with fresh fruit and some liveliness.

MERLOT ($$) ★★ Ripe, oaky blackberry nose, spicy, tannic, rough and ready.

MÜLLER-THURGAU ($) ★★★½ Earthy-flowery nose—almost Muscaty; off-dry, strong-flavored, with more body than is typical.

PINOT NOIR ($) ★★ A very light-styled Pinot, with a ripe cherry nose, good acid, and a slight harshness. Not for aging.

RIESLING ($) ★½ Apple nose, slightly overripe flavors, decent acid.

RIESLING, PINK ($) ★½ Salmon color, quite sweet, decent fruit.

KIONA VINEYARDS
Richland   (1980)
8,500 cases

Kiona has been a consistent award winner in national competitions, attracting attention as one of the consistently best small producers in the state. A thirty-acre vineyard was planted in 1975 in a previously wild section of hills (known locally as Red Mountain) at the warm eastern end of the Yakima Valley, and it has proved a fine site for grapes: Kiona grapes, particularly Cabernet Sauvignon, have made impressive wines under labels like Woodward Canyon and Quilceda Creek. More recently a number of other new vineyards, like Blackwood Canyon, have been established in the area.

Kiona is the product of a partnership between Jim Holmes, a longtime home winemaker who describes winemaking as a "compelling hobby," and John Williams, an experienced farmer. Clearly the fruit is excellent, and the wines have all been well made. Riesling and Chenin Blanc are made in a light, soft style, but the barrel-fermented Chardonnay is very serious wine, not heavy, but with lots of well-rounded flavors.

Lemberger is Kiona's most interesting contribution to the state's wine lineup. A German variety, this red grape makes light, unremarkable wine in its native land. But in the Yakima Valley it has the character of a big red wine without the harshness of Cabernet. "It's ideal for those who would like to have a red but might be put off by it," says Holmes. Kiona's version is very pleasing, with dark colors, a rich raspberry nose, and soft smooth flavors. Production is small, but other area vineyards are beginning to plant the grape.

Holmes is also enthusiastic about Cabernet, believing

(with others) that the region will become a premier area for this varietal. His Cabernet, aged in French and old American oak, is dark, rich, and spicy—appealing when young but very ageable. It's one of the better ones in the state and, like all the wines, reasonably priced.

Rosé lovers will appreciate the very tasty Merlot Rosé.

CABERNET SAUVIGNON ($$$) ★★★★ Very rich, deep, chocolaty nose, thick and full of fruit, with delightful spice. Tart and strong. The aggressive flavors are not to everyone's taste.

CHARDONNAY ($$) ★★★★ Lovely, rich aromas of melon and toasty oak. Good weight but rounded flavors and nice spice. Barrel-fermented. Excellent value.

CHENIN BLANC ($) ★★ Light nose, tart, grapefruity flavors.

LEMBERGER ($$) ★★★★ Fresh and full of raspberry fruit, with a good hint of oak. The wine is deceptive—the tannins are soft, but there is surprising weight here, and it ages quite well.

MERLOT ROSÉ ($) ★★★ Fresh, fruity, but with considerable backbone.

RIESLING ($) ★★★ This has a light, pleasing spritz on the tongue, with baked-bread aromas. Moderate sweetness and full body.

RIESLING, LATE HARVEST ($$) ★★★ Straightforward apple-pie or grapefruity flavors, slightly harsh feel. Smooths out with age.

Kiona
1983
ESTATE BOTTLED

Yakima Valley
CHARDONNAY

PRODUCED AND BOTTLED BY KIONA VINEYARDS WINERY
BW-WA-73 WEST RICHLAND, WASHINGTON, ALCOHOL 12.5% BY VOLUME

F. W. LANGGUTH WINERY *See* SNOQUALMIE WINERY

LATAH CREEK WINE CELLARS
Spokane (1982)
15,000 cases

In 1982 Mike Conway, a winemaker who had apprenticed at Parducci in California, struck a deal with Mike Hogue, a Yakima Valley farmer who wanted to diversify into the wine business. Conway would make wines for Hogue and in turn Hogue would help finance Conway's own winery. The plan turned out well for both—Conway's touch, especially with Chenin Blanc, helped Hogue establish a quality reputation early, and Conway now is running his own show at Latah Creek. Latah is a small winery by California standards, but Conway doesn't classify himself as a "boutique" winemaker, aiming for a specialized market. Instead, he takes Parducci (of which he is a frank admirer) as a model: to make consistent, drinkable wines in a popular style and at a fair price. He may get written off by the snobs, but the fact is the wines, if not really distinctive, are fresh, fruity, and very well made.

The winery is outside Spokane—not a grape-growing area—so grapes are purchased from vineyards in the Yakima Valley and the Wahluke Slope. All the wines have an attractive fruit quality, and almost all are finished with just a bit of sweetness to make them more appealing. Chenin Blanc is the grape that Conway has really made his mark with, both at Hogue and at Latah Creek—it is livelier and more delicately fruity than most Chenins, with a faint spritz on the tongue from trapped carbon dioxide. A recent release was a Reserve Chenin Blanc, surely the first in this country (Chenin Blanc is not a big seller). Conway made some very attractive Fumé Blanc originally, but has switched to Semillon, which he feels is even better. Like many successful Sauvignons, it is finished with a tad of sweetness and a hint of oak.

Conway made some excellent Merlot early on and then dropped it from his repertoire for several vintages. Now both Merlot and Cabernet are in production, with Merlot the more successful. Also of interest here is the Maywine, a traditional German wine of Riesling flavored with the herb woodruff, which imparts a tangy, woody flavor. It's something of a curiosity but can be a refreshing change of pace.

CABERNET SAUVIGNON ($$$) ★★½ A decidedly oaky and closed-in wine, dark-colored—it needs some time.

CHARDONNAY, FEATHER ($) ★★ Light, fruity, appley, pleasant.

CHENIN BLANC ($) ★★★½ Lively, grapefruity flavors, with some prickle on the tongue and excellent crispness. A model Chenin Blanc.

CHENIN BLANC, RESERVE ($) ★★★½ Richer and sweeter than the regular bottling, with less assertive fruit and good balance.

MAYWINE ($) ★★½ Riesling flavored with woodruff. Dusky color, with definite herbal spiciness. Interesting and good.

MERLOT ($$) ★★★★ A full-bodied wine showing excellent berry fruit and good tartness—ages nicely. One of the best examples in the state.

MUSCAT CANELLI ($) ★★★½ This is not a terribly sweet or full-flavored Muscat, but it has lots of floral character, light body, and nice acid.

RIESLING ($) ★★ Fairly simple applelike flavors, with good bite.

RIESLING, LATE HARVEST ($$) ★★½ Flowery nose, with fresh crisp flavors, moderately sweet.

SEMILLON ($) ★★★ Soft, lively, with fruity-grassy nose. Rounded, subtle flavors.

L'ÉCOLE NO. 41
Lowden (1983)
2,000 cases

The Fergusons, Jean and Baker, make no bones about the style of their two principal wines, calling them "big, gutsy wines . . . not for everyone." The winery, one of several in the Walla Walla area, is a retirement project for the couple; Jean is the winemaker, with skills mostly picked up from summer enology courses at UC Davis. Production in the old schoolhouse that is home to the winery is small, and L'École has no vineyards, buying grapes mostly from Gordon Brothers and Balcom and Moe. The Fergusons look for grapes with a high degree of ripeness and sugar (picking after almost everyone else), to give the wines richness and power—and usually high alcohol.

This winery has eschewed the better-known Riesling, Chardonnay, and Cabernet in favor of Semillon and Merlot, two grapes that the Fergusons feel do particularly well in the area (Baker is still convinced that Semillon has probably the most promise of any white grape in eastern Washington). The Semillon has almost a yellow color from long skin contact and is aggressively varietal and heavy; the Fergusons call it a "red wine drinker's white wine." The Merlot is quite incredible: a purple monster of high alcohol and biting tannin. The question is whether time will tame and smooth it out before the fruit fades away. Don't look for elegance or finesse here, but if you're tired of taste-alike commercial wines and have a palate that can absorb powerful flavors, these wines may be appealing.

There's also quite a pleasant Chenin Blanc for the tourists.

MERLOT ($$$) ★★★½ A controversial wine: dark, cloudy, with heaps of fruit and very hot, alcoholic flavors—will age tone it down? Some love it and some don't. It may be better from lighter vintages.

SEMILLON ($) ★★ A very full, heavy, sharp-flavored style—but it comes off rather flat and charmless, for all its flavor.

WALLA VOILÀ (CHENIN BLANC) ($) ★★½ Fresh, appley, medium sweet, a bit of spritz.

LEONETTI CELLAR
Walla Walla (1978)
1,700 cases

Gary Figgins figures he has devoted twenty years to making the quintessential red wine, and he has come remarkably close. A Walla Walla native, he was strongly influenced by his Italian grandfather, a home winemaker. Figgins began making wine at home, shared his dreams with friend and fellow drill sergeant Rick Small (now of

Woodward Canyon), and finally made his first commercial vintage of Cabernet Sauvignon in 1978.

Cabernet Sauvignon and Merlot are the whole story at this tiny winery, but they are a big story. That first Cabernet, which is aging beautifully, was named Best in the Country by a national wine consumers' magazine, and the wines have become expensive and very much sought after. Figgins has kept his enterprise on a small scale, maintaining a regular full-time job until 1988, and making wines literally in his cellar. (He is slowly building himself a little winery out in back.)

Figgins and Small share much the same approach to their red wines. Both must purchase essentially all their red grapes (Figgins has just one acre of very vigorous Merlot) from growers in the Walla Walla, Columbia, and Yakima valleys. Both use all new French cooperage for aging their wines, and both are looking for a big, deep wine with long aging potential. One significant difference: Figgins likes to blend Merlot into his Cabernet, and vice versa, while Small's Cabernet is nearly 100 percent. Blending seems really at the heart of Figgins's work ("building complexity," he calls it), the different lots of Cabernet and Merlot from different vineyards complementing each other, filling in gaps and smoothing out rough edges. While the wines are massive, they don't seem angular or harsh but have a rounded, complete feel.

The Leonetti Merlot is very good, certainly one of the best in the state, with lots of bright berry flavor, though it's occasionally bothered by a herbal tinge. But the Cabernet is extraordinary, one of those wines that improves for several days after the bottle is opened. It may be the most powerful in the state, and should require considerable aging. Although a believer in blends, Figgins has produced a spectacular Cabernet from the Seven Hills Vineyard, just south of Walla Walla, near Milton-Freewater (the vines are actually in Oregon). And soon to be released is his first Reserve Cabernet, from the '83 vintage, an incredibly powerful wine. Very French in style, it may prove to be his best yet and certainly rates high marks.

Though the number of acres remains small, the Walla Walla area has tremendous potential for red grapes (Figgins notes that the Seven Hills Vineyard gets the same number of heat units as St. Helena in the Napa Valley) and he would like to see more planted.

CABERNET SAUVIGNON ($$$$) ★★★★★ A classic Cabernet nose, though closed in. Huge, ripe chocolaty-berry flavors, with lots of tannin and great spice. Yet all is in balance. A premier Washington Cabernet.

CABERNET SAUVIGNON (SEVEN HILLS) ($$$$) ★★★★½ An absolutely classic Cabernet, with cedary, cigar-box scents and huge, mouth-filling body. Should be a blockbuster.

CABERNET SAUVIGNON, RESERVE ($$$$) ★★★★★ A mountainous wine, dense and extraordinarily rich. Cedary, spicy, very oaky. This will stand up to any Cabernet, anywhere.

MERLOT ($$$) ★★★★ Very deep color, with a herbal-berry nose and rich, spicy fruit. Tremendous potential here, as the tannin and vegetal qualities fade.

LOST MOUNTAIN WINERY
Sequim   (1981)
500 cases

Don't look for Lost Mountain in the wine country. It sits in the fir-covered hills of the Olympic Peninsula, where former research chemist Romeo Conca has his retirement home. Conca takes his Italian heritage seriously and has been making full-blown, rather rough-edged red wines—the kind that go so well with hearty Italian *cucina*—for a number of years, first as an amateur and now commercially. Owning no vineyards, Conca will go far afield for the kind of grapes he wants: Cabernet and Merlot from eastern Washington, Pinot Noir from Oregon, and Zinfandel and Petite Syrah from California's Dry Creek Valley in Sonoma.

Lost Mountain's first releases were decidedly rustic—tart, tannic, and oxidized. But newer vintages have shown much more freshness and drinkability, while maintaining a full-bodied style—zesty and alcoholic—for immediate enjoyment. Conca uses only old oak for aging, so the emphasis is on fruit flavors. The Lost Mountain Red (which Conca cheerfully calls "Dago Red") is an interesting blend of red grapes with some Muscat, the pungent aromas of which add to the fruitiness of the wine.

Conca wants as natural a product as possible and uses no sulfites in his wines, so they are best drunk young.

CABERNET SAUVIGNON ($$) ★★½ Plum-cherry nose, fruity, somewhat harsh.

LOST MOUNTAIN RED ($) ★ Very purple, very aromatic, very alcoholic.

MERLOT ($$) ★★★ Lovely, fresh, spicy blackberry flavors. A very forward and fruity wine. Delightful.

PETITE SYRAH–ZINFANDEL (DRY CREEK) ($$) ★★½
Raspberry nose, fresh fruit with nice bite.
PINOT NOIR (WILLAMETTE) ($$) ★★½ Bright color,
spicy cherry nose, full-bodied and slightly sweet. Very
Italian in style.

LOWDEN SCHOOLHOUSE WINERY *See* L'ÉCOLE No. 41

MERCER RANCH VINEYARDS
Alderdale (1984)
1,700 cases

Certainly one of the premier Cabernet vineyards in the
state, Mercer Ranch is now producing small quantities of
estate wines, and they promise to be excellent. The Mercers are an old family (more than 100 years) in these parts,
and the 132-acre vineyard occupies but a small parcel of
the family's 30,000-acre ranch in the Horse Heaven Hills.
This is a spectacular and empty ridge of hills that sits
between the Yakima Valley and the Columbia. Dry-farm
wheat and sheep were all the land would support until
private irrigation arrived twenty years ago; now the deep
soils support a variety of vegetable crops. Don Mercer, an
architect by background, returned from the Puget Sound
area to help with the family's irrigation project, and in
1972 he planted the first vines—mostly Cabernet, since his
own tastes ran to red. Although the mailing address is
Prosser, the vineyard lies just a couple of miles from the
Columbia, not far downriver from the Columbia Crest
vineyards at Paterson.
The Mercers still sell over 90 percent of their grapes, and
Mercer Ranch Cabernet has gone into some of the best-
known wines in the state, including Woodward Canyon

and Quilceda Creek. These wines from the "Old Block" (Block 1) Vineyard share a dense, concentrated, tannic quality with some minty overtones—all destined for long lives. Why this particular block should be so distinct is unclear, but Don Mercer thinks that the deep outcropping of heavier, claylike soil on which the vineyard grows may be the answer. Mercer also has one of the largest blocks of Lemberger (here called Limburger, an alternative spelling) in the state, much of which again is sold to other wineries.

From 1985 to 1987 the Mercer Ranch wines were made by Steven Redford, the talented but mercurial brother of Amity's Myron Redford, who has now left. Redford's first batches of Cabernet for Mercer Ranch turned out extremely well—both the Old Block wine and the more delicate and fruity wine from Sharp Sisters Vineyard. The Limburger, which the Mercers feel is the perfect match for lamb, is in a serious style, though Mercer is contemplating releasing some without oak aging to test the market (the grape makes inherently soft wine). And although reds are the first order of business here, not to be overlooked is an absolutely excellent Muscat Canelli, packed with flavor.

CABERNET SAUVIGNON (MERCER RANCH BLOCK 1) ($$$) ★★★★ A very big, tough, almost minty wine, with lots of tannin—should be great.

CABERNET SAUVIGNON (SHARP SISTERS) ($$$) ★★★½ More forward than the Old Block, softer, but with tight Cabernet character.

LIMBURGER ($$) ★★★★ Lots of fruit, varying from berry to plummy. A big wine, but with a velvety feel. Quite approachable.

MUSCAT CANELLI ($$) ★★★★ Wonderful intense aromas of sweet melon—not too flowery. Sweet, but lots of acid. Very tasty indeed.

SADIE LOUISE (BLUSH) ($) ★ Pungent, light, off-dry.

MERCER RANCH
VINEYARDS

1984
Limberger
Columbia Valley

Cellared and bottled by Mercer Ranch Vineyards Inc.,
Prosser, Washington   Alcohol 12.7% by volume.

MONT ELISE VINEYARDS
Bingen   (1975)
7,000 cases

Chuck Henderson established the first winery (originally called Bingen Wine Cellars) in the Columbia Gorge in 1975, planting grapes on fifty-five acres of vineyards high above the Columbia River, and his pioneering efforts have led to more vineyards and several newer wineries. The windswept gorge, spectacularly beautiful, has a climate somewhere between the hot, dry conditions of eastern Washington and the cool, moist weather of the western part. Not surprisingly, Gewürztraminer, which loses some character in heat, does well in the gorge, producing a wine with good spice. The winery could be making more Gewürz than it is; unfortunately, the market for dry Gewürztraminer is slim. Mont Elise has also had good success with Chenin Blanc.

Henderson's emphasis has always been on growing the grapes—his background is in growing fruit. But the winery, housed in an old fruit warehouse, is not one of the more up-to-date facilities in the state. Now, while Chuck senior tends the vineyards, his son Charles junior, trained in enology at California's Davis campus, has taken over the winemaking, and he may bring a more professional approach to wine production.

Although Pinot Noir was one of the original plantings, the wine has never come out very well, so production is now being steered into a sparkling Blanc de Noir, as well as lighter picnic wines. The first vintage of sparkling wine spent more than three years on the lees before release, much longer than most Northwest sparkling wines, but similar to the aging that French Champagne gets. The style is lean and tart, but the wine is very nicely made. There is a successful red wine, Gamay Beaujolais, made in a very light, grapy style that has been consistently popular (the winery has trouble keeping up with demand). All the wines are reasonably priced.

BLANC DE NOIR BRUT ($$$) ★★★ It's Brut, all right. This dry and very tart wine really needs some food to accompany it. But there are fine bubbles, some good Pinot aromas, and decent body.

CHENIN BLANC ($) ★★½ Pungent nose of clover, quite sweet and full-bodied.

GAMAY BEAUJOLAIS ($) ★★½ Pink-red color, very grapy nose with light, tart fruit. Fine wine for a summer picnic.

GEWÜRZTRAMINER (MONT ELISE VINEYARD) ($) ★★★½ Dry, tart, spicy. Good apple fruit without floweriness, some richness. Can be a bit harsh. There is also a bottling from Celilo Vineyard, which is not as good.

PINOT NOIR ROSÉ ($) ★★½ Rather nice, strawberry-rhubarby nose, soft, slightly heavy.

RIESLING ($) ★½ Very pungent, apricoty nose, medium sweet, quite full—occasional nuttiness. Could use some finesse.

MOUNTAIN DOME WINERY
Spokane   (1984)
300 cases

Very much a home-style operation, this tiny family winery's goal is to make top-quality vintage Champagne-method wine from two-thirds Pinot Noir and one-third Chardonnay—grapes come from the Moreman Vineyard, near Pasco. The first vintage was crushed in 1984 and is still aging on the lees, with no date set for its bottling and release. The owner and winemaker is Michael Manz. First release is planned for 1992. Wines not tasted.

MOUNT BAKER VINEYARDS
Deming   (1982)
9,500 cases

Every western Washington vineyard is an expression of individual determination; Mount Baker's is the product of Al Stratton, a retired physician. Stratton experimented with numerous grape varieties on behalf of the nearby Washington State University Research Station, and the vines in commercial production represent the fruit of that research. Müller-Thurgau, a German cross; Madeleine Angevine, an old French cross; and Okanogan Riesling, a Canadian grape (yes, that's right) are the principal local plantings. The Okanogan Riesling (not a true Riesling) is nothing to get excited about, but the other two are always interesting and flavorful, if not to everyone's taste. The winery's style for whites stresses flowery fruit and fairly full body.

Though the twenty-five-acre vineyard is hardly large, it is the biggest of any Puget Sound winery growing its own grapes. Its northerly location, almost on the Canadian border, looks suspect, but the Nooksack Valley, nestled up against the Cascades, lies in the "rain shadow" of the Olympic Mountains, so it's actually a little drier and gets slightly more sunshine than most of the rest of western Washington.

Mount Baker may be in the "banana belt," but for late-ripening grapes like Cabernet Sauvignon and Riesling it must go to eastern Washington. The Cabernet (temporarily out of production) has proved surprisingly good for a winery that has devoted itself to soft white wines. The Chardonnay has been rather clumsy.

Perhaps most impressive have been the sweeter wines, especially the Select Cluster Riesling, which is very sweet and quite luscious.

Partner and winery manager Jim Hildt has been active in selling wines in Japan—not surprisingly, Mount Baker's plum wine has proved a huge success among Japanese consumers. Another good sign for the winery is recent federal approval of a Nooksack Valley appellation, which may attract some more serious attention to this unique growing area.

As this book went to press, Al Stratton had decided to relinquish his share of the winery, which was looking for additional investors, so its future course is somewhat uncertain.

CABERNET SAUVIGNON ($$) ★★★   Soft, oaky, slightly vegetal, very forward and pleasant.

CHARDONNAY ($$) ★★   Has varied from very oaky to light and somewhat vegetal. Recent vintages show some improvement.

GEWÜRZTRAMINER ($) ★★   Less assertively varietal than most, soft, off-dry.

MADELINE ANGEVINE, RESERVE ($$) ★★★½   A fascinating nose of tropical fruit, sweet, but quite light and crisp.

MÜLLER-THURGAU ($) ★★★   Flowery, nicely balanced sweetness, bit of spritz—very attractive.

RIESLING, SELECT CLUSTER ($$$) ★★★★   Very sweet, but there's more than sugar—apple-like fruit with some nice complexity. Delicious.

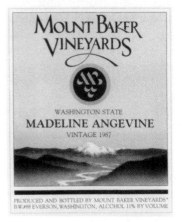

NEUHARTH WINERY
Sequim   (1979)
1,500 cases

Sequim, on the rainy Olympic Peninsula in western Washington, seems an unlikely location for a winery, but this small place is the pet project of a retired California grape grower, Gene Neuharth. Neuharth is not trying to do anything too fancy, just make good, consistent wines that reflect the fruit of the grape and that will accompany food. He is careful in his choice of grapes ("I know what good grapes taste like"), ages all the wines including Riesling in a combination of French and American oak, and takes care that each wine is clean. The results have been impressive—Neuharth has been making excellent wine since the first vintage.

Although Sequim is in what is optimistically termed the peninsula's "banana belt," it's too cold to grow grapes (though Neuharth has a number of experimental hybrids planted). Grapes for the wine come from Sagemoor Farms near Pasco in eastern Washington. The Chardonnay and Cabernet Sauvignon are both noteworthy: The Chardonnay is beautifully oaky and balanced, while the Cabernet, though it doesn't have the weight of some others, has a lovely cedary nose and plenty of flavor—balance is its keynote. All the wines here are relatively lean, have sturdy acid backbones (they show best with food), and age well.

CABERNET SAUVIGNON ($$) ★★★★ Lean, balanced, with lots of sweet oak and some slight herbaceous qualities. Not a knockout wine, but excellently made.

CHARDONNAY ($$) ★★★½ Rich oaky-lemony nose; not a big wine, but very good structure.

DUNGENESS RED ($) ★★½ A wonderfully fruity wine with fresh cherry flavors made in Beaujolais style, from Merlot.

DUNGENESS WHITE ($) ★★ Flowery nose, slightly sweet fruit, with some extra body from oak.

MERLOT ($$) ★★★ Light, herbaceous nose with a bit of blackberry, tart and spicy.

RIESLING ($$) ★½ This oak-aged wine has pungent, cooked-apple aromas, lots of flavor, and medium sweetness. Unusual.

NEUHARTH

19 Washington 80
Cabernet Sauvignon
Aged in Oak
PRODUCED AND BOTTLED BY
NEUHARTH WINERY, INC.
SEQUIM, WA BONDED WINERY NO. WA-74
ALCOHOL 12.6% BY VOLUME

NEWTON AND NEWTON VINTNERS *See*
WHITTLESEY-MARK

NORTHWEST DAILY
(1986)

These wines, which were made for a local *négociant,* are no longer in production, although they may still be found in the marketplace.

CABERNET SAUVIGNON ($) ★★   A bit of vanilla oak and some Cabernet character, light and soft.

CHARDONNAY ($) ★½   Not much varietal character, though there's some wood.

CHENIN BLANC ($) ★★½   A ripe, floral bouquet with solid fruit—a nice wine.

RIESLING ($) ★   Not nearly the character of the Chenin—candylike in the nose.

WHITE TABLE ($) ★★   A lively blend, with a flowery nose and good, tart fruit.

OAKWOOD CELLARS
Benton City   (1986)
3,000 cases

This small, new winery outside of Richland is another
that grew out of the enthusiasm of a home winemaker—in
this case Robert Skelton, a chemical engineer. Skelton has
a tiny three-acre vineyard of Riesling, but most of the
grapes are purchased from various Yakima Valley locations, including reds from vineyards on nearby Red Mountain (already acquiring a reputation for Cabernet). The
cramped winery is short on space and equipment, but the
confident Skelton has improvised and is aiming for top-
quality wines in a traditional big style.

Best bets here are the barrel-fermented Chardonnay
(Skelton is experimenting with American oak as well as
French), in the ripe, fat style, and the regular Riesling,
which has lots of nice, full fruit flavors. The first release
of Merlot was boisterously flavorful, but samples of Cabernet and Lemberger to come showed some promise—these
wines should be big and oaky. Skelton is also planning a
dry-style Riesling.

CHARDONNAY ($$) ★★★½   Some nice, toasty, ripe pine-
apple flavors—oaky and fairly rich. Quite appealing.

MERLOT ($$) ★★   Cherry and oak flovors, some sharp-
ness. Zesty, not refined.

RIESLING ($) ★★★   Haylike aromas accompany strong,
appley fruit. The style is full and fruity, with good acid.

RIESLING, LATE HARVEST ($$) ★   Some piney flavors,
could be fresher.

ROSÉ OF CABERNET ($) ★   Rather herbaceous, crisp,
fresh—OK.

OREGON CHAMPAGNE CELLARS *See*
WHITTLESEY-MARK

PACIFIC CREST WINE CELLARS
Marysville   (1985)
500 cases

Despite the small size, this winery has not stinted on first-rate equipment—there's a strong belief here that high tech can make a difference. On the other hand, winemaker and partner Gary Graves, a TV broadcaster turned enologist, also believes in high-quality grapes and is working with the vineyards in the Yakima Valley from which he buys to improve quality by reducing yield. Graves is a self-described "Chardonnay freak" who hopes to make a big, barrel-fermented Chardonnay in the Burgundian style. He is also producing Late Harvest Riesling and Gewürztraminer in a higher-alcohol style than is usual ("I'm notorious for alcoholic wine"), letting them sit in the tank for at least a year to acquire needed age. Initial releases of these sweeter varietals showed a tendency toward very ripe wines, but the winemaking seems competent.

Current capacity is small, about 5,000 gallons, but Graves hopes to move the winery, now in a small town north of Seattle, perhaps to an eastern Washington location and eventually increase capacity to the 30,000-gallon range.

GEWÜRZTRAMINER, LATE HARVEST ($$) ★★★ Although slightly harsh, this wine has lots of ripe lychee flavors with interesting clove accents. Medium sweet.
RIESLING ($) ★★★ Very ripe wine—flowery, full-flavored, with balanced sweetness.

PONTIN DEL ROZA
Prosser   (1984)
4,000 cases

A long-established Yakima Valley farming family has recently turned to winemaking, using grapes from its own small vineyard and from other vineyards on the Roza, a section of south-facing slope in the middle of the valley. The first wines were made at nearby Coventry Vale, but Pontin has its own facility now. Youthful Scott Pontin, trained at UC Davis, is the winemaker, while other members of the family all seem to be involved, in the Italian tradition (Scott's Italian grandfather arrived in the valley in the twenties).

Like many small wineries just getting started, Pontin has had uneven results. The whites tend to the simple and sweet. Some of the Chenins have been very pleasant, in a soft picnic style. But other wines have not fared as happily and have seemed clumsy or overripe. The wines also seem to have the problem of tasting old rather quickly. Nevertheless, if you like sweet whites with lots of fruit, these may fit the bill.

CABERNET SAUVIGNON ($$) ★★ Sweet oaky nose with rather biting, herbaceous flavors. OK for oak lovers.

CHARDONNAY ($$) ★ This wine shows signs of improvement. The fruit is decent though not terribly varietal. Soft.

CHENIN BLANC ($) ★★ Light, apple-flower nose, pleasant flavors, off-dry style.

RIESLING ($) ★ This is not bashful wine. Ripe apricot flavors, quite sweet and rather cloying, as it lacks acid. Not always fresh.

ROZA SUNSET ($) ½   This blush wine based on Chenin and Riesling has a funny, earthy nose—pepper and stewed vegies.

PORTTEUS VINEYARDS
Zillah   (1986)
2,000 cases

The Portteus family (Paul senior and Paul junior are the owners, with Paul junior the winemaker) avoided the problems of the many Yakima Valley growers when it eschewed Riesling and Chenin Blanc in favor of Chardonnay, Cabernet, and Semillon in its vineyard. The 36 acres of vines, planted in 1982, sit on a ridge above the valley floor—at 1,400 feet this is one of the loftier vineyards in the area, which helps it avoid the worst of winter frosts. Paul Portteus, Jr., had actually hoped to find land in California when he conceived the idea of starting a winery ten years ago, but the Seattle native liked the idea of being closer to home.

Portteus, whose knowledge comes largely from hands-on helping at several local wineries, is aiming for the upper end of the market, with a Chardonnay 100 percent fermented in French oak (he's looking for a ripe style) and Cabernet (he prefers the more aggressive American oak for this wine). Of interest, too, is a small patch of Zinfandel that seems to be growing just fine. First vintage was in 1986, with the wines to be released in late 1988 or early 1989. Production will probably grow to something over 10,000 cases. Wines not tasted.

PRESTON WINE CELLARS
Pasco   (1976)
55,000 cases

Bill Preston was a highly successful farm-equipment dealer who enjoyed his trips to the Napa Valley so much he decided to try making his own wine in the desert near Pasco. Preston Cellars, for years the state's second-largest winery after Ste. Michelle, established a solid reputation while Rob Griffin (now at Hogue Cellars) was making the wines. Griffin made some exciting Chardonnays in the early years (including a '77 that won many awards) and also showed a firm command of Fumé Blanc and Riesling. Since Griffin's departure the winery has lived through a succession of winemakers; Wayne Marcil, formerly of Covey Run, was made winemaker in time for the 1988 crush. If Marcil stays, his track record of well-made wines, especially whites, bodes well for the winery.

The 180 acres of vineyard were first planted in 1972. The hot surrounding country has none of the green lushness of the Yakima Valley, but the vines are kept very green, and cool, by overhead sprinklers. (Unfortunately, this kind of watering makes the vines more vulnerable to winter frost.) Preston's initial success was based as much on novelty and its pioneer status as on quality and marketing skill—as competition has gotten stiffer and newer wineries have received the acclaim, sales have suffered.

The list of varietals is long, and the wines have not always been consistent in the last several years, a problem compounded by slow sales, since some of the whites on the market are clearly too old. (One advantage, though: Reds available already have considerable bottle age.) There has also been a proliferation of lower-end proprietary blends with names like Desert Blossom.

If you stick with the basics here, you can do very well. The Fumé Blanc, aged in oak, will appeal to those who like an assertive Sauvignon Blanc—it has always been one of the better ones in the state. The Chardonnay, which used to be light, lemony, oaky, now has riper fruit flavors. There is also a confusing assortment of Late Harvest Rieslings in different bottlings—some of these can be fine in a straightforward, grapefruity way and are worth trying when the price is right.

Second-label Columbia River Cellars wines are inexpensive, and the Merlot, very ripe, has consistently been a good value.

CABERNET SAUVIGNON ($$) ★★   A soft but rather hot wine that tends toward the herbal, with some berry fruit.

CHAMPAGNE ($$$) ★★   Made from Riesling, it is fruity and frothy, but a bit sweetish and lacking acid. Expensive.

CHARDONNAY ($$) ★★★   The latest one ('86) has very ripe apple aromas, a nice hit of oak, and some bite. Straightforward and flavorful.

DESERT BLOSSOM ($) ★   Very exotic fruit, soft, sweet, "hot-tub wine."

FUMÉ BLANC ($$) ★★★½   Ripe, intense, full of herbaceous fruit—it's quite an aggressive style. Partisans of this style will love it. Well made.

RIESLING ($) ★★   Used to be one of the best, characteristically ripe and full-flavored, with lots of appley fruit, but recent vintages have seemed less interesting.

RIESLING, SELECT HARVEST ($$) ★★★   Straightforward grapefruity flavors, medium sweet.

COLUMBIA RIVER CELLARS MERLOT ($) ★★   Pleasant, woody, rounded flavors with lots of body. A fine, simple wine.

PROSSER FALLS *See* HINZERLING VINEYARDS

QUAIL RUN VINTNERS *See* COVEY RUN VINTNERS

QUARRY LAKE WINERY
Pasco (1985)
20,000 cases

Balcom and Moe Vineyard is one the largest and best-established independent vineyards in eastern Washington, with 110 acres of vines just north of Pasco and more being planned. Now, in what was originally a joint venture with the enormous Langguth Winery, it is producing its own wines. Balcom and Moe began in the potato business (it supplies Wendy's, among other large customers, and has extensive apple and cherry orchards as well), but grapes represented a way to diversify, as they did for Hogue Farms, or the Symms Ranch in Idaho.

American Wines of the Northwest

The vineyard was first planted in 1971, and for years Balcom and Moe supplied grapes to many Washington wineries. Finally, manager Maury Balcom, trained in viticulture and enology in California, decided it was time to make his own wines. Lacking his own winery, he has used the state-of-the-art facility at Langguth to crush, ferment, and bottle the wines, with his own separate location for aging. The initial releases seemed decidedly awkward, but the wines have improved steadily with a little age, and with newer vintages Balcom has demonstrated a surer style. The Chardonnay especially, 30 percent barrel-fermented, has attracted national attention—its fresh, balanced flavors make it a perfect restaurant wine. The first Sauvignon Blancs were pretty unyielding, but the '87 has more fruit and rounder flavors. All the wines are in a lighter, more subtle mold than is standard in eastern Washington.

The initial releases of reds also showed promise—especially a well-structured Cabernet that asks to be aged. Both Cabernet and Merlot avoid the herbal flavors of so many Washington reds: Balcom (who likes to spend lots of time in the vineyard) is convinced that careful management of irrigation and thus foliage canopy is the key to this problem. With reasonable prices and dedication to careful grape growing, Quarry Lake is a winery to watch.

CABERNET SAUVIGNON ($$) ★★★½ Tight, tart, and tannic style in its first offering (1985)—shows good structure and some berry flavors. Age.

CHARDONNAY ($) ★★★ Strong improvement over the last several years: The latest release is light, balanced, with hints of oak and lemon. A fine food wine.

CHENIN BLANC ($) ★★½ Light, off-dry, some pleasant wildflower aromas.

RIESLING ($) ★★½ Light, tart, fresh, appley—quite pleasant.

SAUVIGNON BLANC ($) ★★★   Style still evolving: The most recent release shows more fruit, with slight grassiness and sweetness. Good acid, great with seafood.

QUILCEDA CREEK VINTNERS
Snohomish   (1979)
900 cases

Cabernet Sauvignon is Quilceda Creek's one wine, and what a wine it is. Since the first vintage (1979) won the Grand Prize at the Enological Society of the Pacific Northwest's competition in 1983, this winery has gone from strength to strength. In 1987, in a blind tasting pitting Washington Cabernets against some of Bordeaux's top wines, the '83 Quilceda finished second overall. It's perhaps not surprising to learn that the old pro behind this operation is André Tchelistcheff, who created Beaulieu Vineyard's great Cabernets and got Ste. Michelle started. Tchelistcheff is uncle to Alex Golitzin, a chemical engineer who turned his home winemaking experiments into a commercial winery at Tchelistcheff's urging. The results have been first class and have put Quilceda Creek in an elite group of other small state wineries producing deep-flavored, long-lived Cabernet Sauvignon that can stand with the best in the world.

Quilceda Creek is in Snohomish, just north of Seattle. Currently, the winery is purchasing grapes from both Kiona Vineyards and Mercer Ranch Vineyards, both in the Yakima Valley, both acknowledged as among the best sources of Cabernet Sauvignon in the state. The wine, unfiltered and unfined, is a powerhouse, loaded with deep blackberry fruit. There are no apologies for the tons of tannin or the pronounced oak character, although the wines are held back until four years after the vintage. Even so, they need considerably more time to develop.

CABERNET SAUVIGNON ($$$) ★★★★★ Absolutely black in youth, with a huge, spicy oak nose, deep blackberry fruit, lots of spicy tannin. Very ripe. World class. Will need lots of time to be at its best.

REDFORD CELLARS
(1978)
600 cases

Redford Cellars has gone for ten years without a winery to call its own. Stephen Redford, a true Northwest winemaker, since his interests span the Columbia, started out making a blend of Cabernet Sauvignon and Merlot from Washington and Oregon grapes at his brother Myron's winery, Amity Vineyards, in Oregon. Attracted to eastern Washington by its potential for Cabernet Sauvignon, Redford in 1985 became winemaker for grape grower Don Mercer, when the latter decided to start his own winery. Using the Mercer Ranch facility, Redford continued to make his Cabernet-Merlot blend, plus a varietal Cabernet Sauvignon, from grapes purchased from various vineyards in the Yakima and Columbia valleys (though he uses Oregon fruit when he can find it—the Merlot for the '84 blend, for example, all came from Oregon). In 1988 Redford parted company with Mercer and at press time was still looking for a facility in the Seattle area where he could set up shop. Though a talented winemaker, he has not been able to attract backing for his own winery.

Redford's model is Bordeaux, and the blend of grapes is based on Bordeaux tradition. (The earlier vintages were aged in American oak, but recent ones have been in French.) The wines are not blockbusters but have the virtues of balance and smoothness.

CABERNET-MERLOT ($$) ★★★½ A rich, warm, oaky nose, with considerable body. Lean, tart, balanced.

RUSHCUTTER BAY *See* PAUL THOMAS

SETH RYAN WINERY
West Richland   (1986)
300 cases

A tiny home-based winery run by the Brodzinski and Olsen families, Seth Ryan hopes to focus on specialty Rieslings. The year 1988 should see releases of several experimental lots of wine, including an oak-aged Riesling. There will also be Chardonnay and Gewürztraminer.

RIESLING ($) ★½ Solid body and some flowery qualities, but it doesn't seem entirely fresh.

SADDLE MOUNTAIN WINERY   *See* SNOQUALMIE WINERY

SALISHAN VINEYARDS
La Center   (1976)
4,000 cases

Salishan stands practically in the shadow of Mount St. Helens, in a hilly area along the Columbia, north of Portland, that had never been planted to grapes until Joan and Lincoln Wolverton arrived in the early seventies. They were looking for a climate approximating that of the Willamette Valley, forty miles to the south, and while their harvest is usually a week or so behind the Willamette vineyards, the same varieties, especially Pinot Noir, do well here. Though western Washington had been written off for any but hybrid grapes, the Wolvertons planted 12 acres, and there are now 200 or so acres of vines in the hills around Salishan.

Salishan impressed wine lovers early on with delicious Pinot Noirs from the warm vintages of 1978 and '79—they were Burgundian-style wines with delicate texture but big, smoky noses. These early vintages were actually made at several Oregon wineries, in the days when the Wolvertons were still commuting from Seattle to tend the vineyard. Since 1982 Joan Wolverton has been making the wines, and while they have had difficulties with the weather in several vintages, '85, '86, and '87 were all fine years.

The wines here are in a totally dry, fairly austere style. The Pinot Noir tends to be a bit lighter and gentler in texture than Willamette Pinots (some liken it to Volnay). Besides the Pinot, the most interesting wine is the dry

Chenin Blanc; although Chenin is a cool-climate grape in France's Loire, it is little planted in cool areas in the United States. While it doesn't get terribly ripe in the Wolvertons' vineyard, the wine is richly fruity, with tangy flavors that make it great with seafood—a lovely wine. Chardonnay is a bit iffy here—the climate is pretty marginal—but can be very good in the warm years. All the Salishan wines are modestly priced.

CHARDONNAY ($$) ★★★   Quite a lean style with plenty of oak and fruit that varies from lemony to appley. Very much a food wine.

CHENIN BLANC, DRY ($) ★★★★   Rich, grapefruity, bready nose with lots of flavor in a very dry style. Crisp acidity makes it great with seafood, and it actually needs some age to develop.

PINOT NOIR ($$) ★★★½   In the best years, this has light color but a round, smoky, oaky bouquet and silky textures. Always tart, in some years it is a bit green and unyielding. Produced in different lots.

RIESLING, DRY ($) ★★★   Fresh, lemony, grassy nose; light, delicate, quite dry. Not quite the depth of the Chenin.

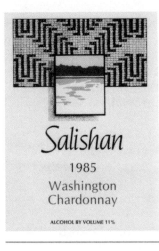

Salishan
1985
Washington
Chardonnay

ALCOHOL BY VOLUME 11%

SALMON BAY WINERY
Woodinville   (1982)
4,500 cases

Salmon Bay, under the name Vernier, got off to a rocky start from which it is gradually recovering. Seattle sommelier Bruce Crabtree, with strong connections to the local restaurant industry, decided with some friends to make wines they could sell to restaurants. But Crabtree didn't prove successful as a part-time winemaker, and he has started over, with a new name and professional help with the wines.

The winery is still in transition. Winemaker Louis Facelli, who made a fine reputation in Idaho, brought out many of the current releases but then moved on to Haviland Vintners. Salmon Bay has just moved to a new location in suburban Woodinville and is currently hunting for a new winemaker—the '86 and '87 vintages were made at eastern Washington wineries. Grapes come from several eastern Washington vineyards.

The current wines, moderately priced, are a slightly mixed bag, with the Chardonnay tasting best. Not a big Chardonnay, and not heavily oaked, it nevertheless has nice melony fruit and medium body. The reds have their origins in less happy times, but they're perfectly decent. Look for newer vintages to be improved.

CABERNET SAUVIGNON ($$) ★★   The flavors are rather tired out and woody, but there's good body.
CHARDONNAY ($$) ★★★   Tart, okay, melony flavors—fresh, straightforward.
MERLOT ($$) ★★   Ripe, soft, but the flavors are a bit weedy.
RIESLING, SELECT ($)   The '85 is foul and should be avoided.
SAUVIGNON BLANC ($$) ★½   There's lots of flavor, but it doesn't quite all hang together. Sharp.

SNOQUALMIE WINERY
Snoqualmie   (1983)
SADDLE MOUNTAIN WINERY
Mattawa
330,000 cases (capacity)

Snoqualmie was the creation of Joel Klein, a strong-willed and enthusiastic bear of a man who helped shape Washington's wines in the seventies as the first winemaker for Chateau Ste. Michelle. He left Ste. Michelle in 1983 to start his own winery in the foothills of the Cascades (not far from Seattle), with ambitious plans for a large winery turning out wines with broad appeal—lighter-bodied, fruity, quite soft. Then in 1986 Snoqualmie bought control of the large (now up to 800,000 gallons), technologically sophisticated F. W. Langguth Winery (now called Saddle Mountain) in Mattawa, near the Columbia River. Built in

1981, Langguth had represented a large commitment by the big German wine company of the same name to produce Riesling from Washington grapes, but the wines ran into stiff competition from the locals and the Germans never quite figured out the marketplace.

The amalgamation of Snoqualmie and Langguth (producing the perhaps unfortunate nickname of Snoguth) makes it the fourth-largest winery facility in the state, after Columbia Crest, Ste. Michelle, and Coventry Vale. (For now, all the wines, including Snoqualmie's, are being made at Mattawa, although ambitious expansion plans call for a new production facility at Snoqualmie's original site outside Seattle.) But much of the winery's capacity has been turned over to custom-crushing grapes for other operations. The F. W. Langguth label, never terribly successful, will be phased out for all except a small selection of Late Harvest Rieslings. Instead, the winery has introduced a list of inexpensive varietals under the Saddle Mountain name, which are intended to be "good-tasting, affordable wines." The Snoqualmie line will remain slightly upscale, without forsaking an approachable style.

Klein is no longer the winemaker, and Mike Januik, a very successful winemaker at Stewart Vineyards (and well known for excellent late-harvest wines), has been hired to run the Mattawa facility. With Langguth came 280 acres of young vines on the Wahluke slope, a relatively warm section of the Columbia Basin, but the winery also has contracts with a number of growers in the Yakima and Columbia valleys.

With all the changes taking place at this winery, it is perhaps misleading to comment on the wines. Certainly one would hope for improvement in the Langguth and Saddle Mountain lines—the Langguth Rieslings have been quite ordinary and the Saddle Mountain varietals inconsistent at best. (Most recent Saddle Mountain releases, under a redesigned label, show marked improvement.) The Snoqualmie wines, though well made, have seemed a shade light and are quite soft; Klein believed in harvesting his fruit later than most, to achieve greater maturity, and bucked the trend to higher-acid wines. This seems to work very nicely for Chenin Blanc, which shows some richness, and Semillon, full of ripe flavors. The reds are quite forward and fruity. A new Fumé Blanc has been very successful.

CABERNET SAUVIGNON ($$) ★★★ Very forward and fruity (berries) with good structure.
CHARDONNAY ($$) ★★½ Light nose (a little oak), soft, not much varietal intensity.
CHENIN BLANC ($) ★★★½ Intriguing nose of clover, slightly sweet, with soft, restrained fruit. More interesting than most.
FUMÉ BLANC ($$) ★★★ A nicely grassy nose with rounded fruit and a hint of sweetness. Well made.
MERLOT, RESERVE ($$) ★★★ Intense, jammy nose with soft, forward fruit and a bit of oak.
MUSCAT CANELLI ($) ★★★ Pungent Muscat nose, with lovely balance of sugar and acid. Very tasty.
RIESLING ($) ★★½ Full, apple-apricot nose, straightforward.
SEMILLON ($) ★★★ Intense nose of honey and hay. Soft, round. Good light-food wine.

LANGGUTH RIESLING, SELECT CLUSTER ($$$) ★★★★ Extremely sweet and nectarlike, with creamy texture. Heavy, but good balance.
LANGGUTH RIESLING, SELECT HARVEST ($$) ★★½ Full, sweet flavors, but without much delicacy or balance.

SADDLE MOUNTAIN CHARDONNAY ($) ★★½ Very warm, appley fruit, light and soft on the palate. A very nice example of fruity Chardonnay.

SADDLE MOUNTAIN GEWÜRZTRAMINER ($) ★★½
  Sweet, fruity style, with good body and some underlying
  spice.
SADDLE MOUNTAIN RIESLING ($) ★★   Big nose, but not
  that fruity.

STATON HILLS VINEYARD
Wapato and Seattle   (1984)
35,000 cases

One of the fastest-growing wineries in the state, Staton
Hills has hit the market with a large number of reasonably priced wines under a variety of labels. The quality,
with a couple exceptions, is fairly ordinary, but owner
David Staton, a savvy and experienced businessman, has
done some innovative things to sell his wine. He introduced the idea of "Pink Riesling"—Riesling with a small
amount of red juice added to give it a little extra color and
flavor—to compete with California blush wine (and to
help deal with the state's Riesling glut). He has been one
of the pioneers in selling Washington wine in the Far East
(speaking Japanese certainly helps), producing special labels for wines in Japan. And he has decided to challenge
New York and California in the inexpensive bulk Champagne business. The state's industry could use a few more
leaders with his enthusiasm and sense of vision. In 1988
vineyard holdings had reached 300 acres, and the winery
was planning to increase production yet again. The winemaker is Rob Stuart.
  The small vineyard lies in a warm south-facing section
of the narrow (and generally cooler) western end of the
Yakima Valley, and Staton has used several different innovative trellising techniques to encourage better ripening.
Given the first-class winemaking facility that Staton has,
one would wish that the wines were a little more impressive. The wide range of offerings may dilute the quality of

individual wines. Best bet is a fresh and fruity Sauvignon Blanc. The semisweet whites are made in a popular style, while the dry whites are clean but sometimes seem to lack varietal fruit. The red wines so far have been fairly tough and unyielding—surprisingly, Pinot Noir (from Oregon) may be the best of these.

A partnership with wine label artist Sebastian Titus has produced two additional labels: Status and Titon, and the Ridgemont label has also been used for wines from California grapes. A small satellite winery operates in downtown Seattle, mainly to provide a tasting room facility.

CABERNET SAUVIGNON ($$) ★★½ Sweet oak nose, with herbal tones dominating, quite soft.

CHARDONNAY ($$) ★½ Light, woody flavors, without much varietal fruit.

CHENIN BLANC ($) ★★ Very tart, a hint of oak in the finish—thin fruit.

GEWÜRZTRAMINER ($) ★★★ One of the nicer wines here—good varietal fruit, tart, zippy. Slightly sweet.

MUSCAT CANELLI ($) ★½ Thick Muscat flavors, sweet and viscous. A bit heavy-handed.

PINOT NOIR (OREGON) ($$) ★★★ Ripe, oaky flavors with a bit of tannin—quite soft.

RIESLING, JOHANNISBERG ($) ★★ Simple fruit, crisp, light.

RIESLING, PINK ($) ★★ Good fruit, sweet, but there's enough acid here to balance the sugar. Merlot and Baco Noir give the color. All in all, a nicer wine than it sounds.

SAUVIGNON BLANC ($) ★★★ Best of the dry wines— nice, ripe, spicy flavors with lots of fruit.

SEMILLON ($) ★★ Fruity, light, tart, simple—slightly herbaceous.

RIDGEMONT CABERNET SAUVIGNON ($) ★★ Good, oaky nose, lean tannic flavors.

STATUS CHAMPAGNE, PINK ($) ½   The price is right, but there's not much fruit and some chemical flavors. The Brut is about the same.

TITON CHARDONNAY ($) ★   This lean wine has oaky, mushroomy aromas and tart flavors. Cleanly made but not terribly varietal.

STEWART VINEYARDS
Sunnyside   (1983)
8,500 cases

Although the winery has been open only since 1983, Dr. George Stewart planted his first vineyard back in the late sixties, on Harrison Hill near Sunnyside in the Yakima Valley, a historic site that had been home to early grapevines during the thirties and then to Associated Vintners' first vineyard in the early sixties. Stewart was also the first to plant vinifera grapes on the Wahluke Slope near the Columbia River north of the Yakima Valley, an area that has since seen many more acres of vineyard planted. The Wahluke is warmer than the Yakima Valley and a good home to varieties like Muscat that are more susceptible to the cold. Before the winery opened, grapes from the seventy acres of vineyards were used for several fine wines at other wineries.

The original winemaker was Mike Januik, a well-trained professional from the University of California at Davis enology program, who demonstrated a deft touch with Late Harvest Riesling and made some fine fat Chardonnays (which haven't aged very well). The winery now has a deserved reputation for appealing, ripe, fruity wines at good prices. New winemaker Scott Benham apprenticed with Rob Griffin at Hogue Cellars and plans largely to carry on in the same style, looking for perhaps a bit more subtlety and complexity in the Chardonnay through barrel fermentation.

There is little to quarrel with in the wines here. Although the Cabernet Sauvignon, while well made, lacks the depth of some others, the whites are uniformly fresh and fruity. The Chardonnay is a model for this wine made in a plump, popular style (drink it up young). The Late Harvest Rieslings are some of the very finest in the state, with consistent richness of flavor and excellent balance— there is little doubt that they can match flavors with the best dessert Rieslings from anywhere in the world (at much lower prices).

CABERNET SAUVIGNON ($$) ★★½ Bright red, fairly oaky, with a dusty nose. Not a heavyweight—cleaned up a little too much?

CHARDONNAY ($$) ★★★½ Ripe, toasty-oaky nose, with lots of apple. Rich, viscous, tangy, ripe. A very open and appealing wine with a long finish. Excellent value.

GEWÜRZTRAMINER ($) ★★½ Light, varietal fruit, with soft, fresh flavors. Very slight sweetness.

MUSCAT CANELLI ($$) ★★★½ Lovely, deep, rich Muscat nose—tart and fresh on the palate. Full-flavored style.

RIESLING, JOHANNISBERG ($) ★★★★ Rich nose, heavier than most, with peachy flavors and soft acidity. A Riesling lover's Riesling, not shy on flavor.

RIESLING, LATE HARVEST ($$$) ★★★★★ Very sweet and quite delicious, with intensely ripe apricot flavors, some spice, and fine acid balance. Hard to resist. Excellent year in and year out.

RIESLING, WHITE ($) ★★ Medium sweet, with ripe, spiced peach nose. Good acid, but the fruit seems to drop off a bit.

TAGARIS
Othello   (1987)
15,000 cases

Michael Taggares's Greek grandfather (who spelled his name Tagaris) planted some of the first grapes in the Columbia Valley in 1911, and the Taggares family today holds the largest Concord grape acreage in the world. Now the grandson has a 120-acre vinifera vineyard, first planted in 1982, on the Wahluke Slope north of the Columbia River—at 1,300 feet one of the higher vineyards in the state. The leading variety initially will be Chardonnay, but the winery also has high hopes for Cabernet Sauvignon as well as for Pinot Noir (planted on a north-facing slope to lengthen the growing season).

Winemaker Peter Bos has a varied background in the wine industry, having served as cellarmaster at Preston under Rob Griffin (now at Hogue Cellars), managed vineyards for Balcom and Moe, sold wine as a supermarket wine specialist, and worked as assistant winemaker for David Lake at Columbia. Although a winery is in the plan, initial vintages are being made at the Coventry Vale custom winery.

The new Chardonnay is quite agreeable, with a good hit of new oak, while the other varietals, fresh and clean in flavor, are fine but unremarkable. Production is planned to increase to around 50,000 cases.

CHARDONNAY ($$) ★★½ Apple and oak flavors, fruity and forward.

FUMÉ BLANC ($) ★★ An aggressive Sauvignon, with slightly harsh, herbal flavors.

RIESLING ($) ★★ Very appley flavors, soft, simple, medium sweet.

PAUL THOMAS
Bellevue (1979)
17,000 cases

The winery has a well-deserved reputation for producing some of the best fruit wines in the Northwest (and probably the United States). But there is a problem: In more recent years it has also established itself as a fine producer of grape wines. As winemaker Brian Carter says, "How do you convince people you can make great Cabernet and great rhubarb wine at the same time?" But owner Paul Thomas, a former schoolteacher, explains his program as making the best wine possible from *all* the fine fruit in the Northwest.

The original premise here was that fruit wines should be taken seriously as dry table wines, and wines like Crimson Rhubarb and Bartlett Pear (the latter goes well with spicy foods and is popular in New Orleans) have a solid following. The fruit comes mostly from western Washington. These are far from the heavy, sweet berry wines of home winemakers—they are crisp, delicate, and balanced.

The vinifera wines from eastern Washington grapes are even better and show the broad range of Carter's talent. The whites are balanced and show good acid; Riesling and Sauvignon Blanc age very nicely and have elegant flavors. Paul Thomas was one of the first in the state to produce a true dry Riesling, which was excellent. Abandoned in the face of consumer apathy, it has now been revived, though the new version is not totally dry. Carter's first Merlot (made as a sort of afterthought in 1984 when Cabernet grapes were not available) was one of the best ever made in the state, and his first barrel-fermented Chardonnay, an understated wine with excellent balance, has walked off with a basketful of gold medals. In fact, each of the wines here is very near the top of its class in the state, making the winery's products a very reliable choice for consumers.

In 1988, Carter, one of the state's most serious talents, left full-time work at Paul Thomas (though he remains consulting winemaker) to branch out into different projects. Paul Thomas has taken over as winemaker, with Mark Cave, formerly at Yakima River, handling day-to-day winemaking chores.

Second-label Rushcutter Bay wines, intended for the restaurant trade, can be good values.

CABERNET SAUVIGNON ($$$) ★★★★ At five years, still youthful, chocolaty nose, with balanced yet intense flavor, well structured, tart, tannic. Very nicely made. Demands aging.

CHARDONNAY ($$) ★★★½ This regular bottling emphasizes fresh fruit, with a hint of buttery oak and a hint of sweetness. The ultimate restaurant Chardonnay.

CHARDONNAY, PRIVATE RESERVE ($$$) ★★★★ An austere nose opens gradually to a nice toastiness; the fruit is restrained, with a good acid backbone, and all is in balance. Lovely.

CHENIN BLANC ($) ★★★½ Light, apple nose, straightforward flavor, slightly sweet—some fresh clove and bread dough in the nose.

MERLOT ($$) ★★★★½ Big plummy nose, lots of raspberry flavors, a soft feel, and a touch of oak. A nicely balanced, very attractive wine—about all one could ask for in Merlot.

MUSCAT CANELLI ($$) ★★★½ Slight spritz on the tongue, lush floral nose with lots of sweet fruit. A lovely dessert wine.

RIESLING ($) ★★★★ One of the best in the state—very fruity (apples), very fresh, a big nose. Most appealing.

RIESLING, DRY ($) ★★½ Apple and grapefruit, just off-dry, not quite the character of the regular bottling.

SAUVIGNON BLANC ($$) ★★★½ Very nice, subtle, grassy aromas with very crisp acidity. More subdued than most—a very good seafood wine. Ages well.

BARTLETT PEAR, DRY ($) ★★★★ Full, rather spicy aroma (not immediately identifiable as pear) and delicate flavors. A viscous feel to it and bone dry.

RASPBERRY ($$) ★★★★ If you have ever wanted to taste essence of raspberry in a wine, this is it. Fresh, lovely fruit, just slightly sweet and not too heavy.

RHUBARB, CRIMSON ($) ★★½ Definite rhubarb flavors, just slightly sweet, light, fresh, very pleasant. A nice alternative to a blush.

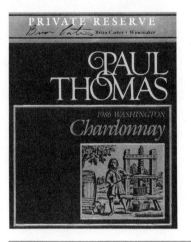

TUCKER CELLARS
Sunnyside (1981)
5,000 cases

The quintessential family fruit operation, the Tucker farm has been producing fruit and vegetables for three generations—the patriarch of the family planted some of the first vinifera grapes (Muscat, Riesling, Semillon) in the Yakima Valley back in 1933. (The grapes were destined for Upland Winery, which went out of business, and the vines were eventually pulled up.) But it wasn't until 1981 that the family added a winery to its burgeoning roadside fresh-produce stand (a valley landmark), using grapes from its sixty-acre vineyard.

Randy Tucker is the winemaker, but lacking technical expertise with wine, he has retained respected consultant Kay Simon for help. All of the wines are made in a straightforward, fruity style, as one might expect, though there's a tendency toward overripeness. Several of the whites lack distinctive varietal characteristics. The tastiest is the Muscat Canelli, with delicate fruit and very fresh flavor—a good value. The wines are all reasonably priced.

CABERNET SAUVIGNON ($$) ★★ Nice berry nose, tart, fruity, with a little tannin.

CHARDONNAY ($$) ★★ Rather light, woody nose. The fruit is like stewed apples and slightly hot.

CHARDONNAY, RESERVE ($$) ★★½ An older wine when released—yellowing, fat and oaky, overripe and rather clumsy. Some varietal character.

CHENIN BLANC ($) ★½ Somewhat weedy nose, light, medium sweet.

MUSCAT CANELLI ($) ★★★ Lovely, fresh, light Muscat nose (not too floral), good fruit. Very pleasant.

PINOT NOIR ($) ★½   Tired and woody, overripe—OK flavors.

RIESLING ($) ★★   Very peachy-apricot nose, heavy, a bit stewed—but just slightly sweet. It doesn't seem to hold up very well.

RIESLING, LATE HARVEST ($$) ★★   Sweet, simple, lacks richness.

VERNIER WINES   *See* SALMON BAY WINERY

MANFRED VIERTHALER WINERY
Sumner   (1976)
16,000 cases (capacity)

Although this winery claims to make white wines in the style of the German Rheingau, most lovers of German Riesling would be disappointed with the results. Owner Manfred Vierthaler does purchase grapes from some local Puget Sound vineyards (he doesn't like grapes from eastern Washington), but most of the wines are made from grape juice obtained from California; these wines are labeled "American." Winemaker Vierthaler has a German background and interest, but the wines, low in both acid and alcohol, lack the fruit and crispness of fine Rieslings. The varietals don't taste much like varietals, and all the wines seem simple, sweet, and often flat and oxidized. The best advice is to avoid the reds and the inexpensive whites—some of the Select Harvest wines are OK.

Most the wines are inexpensive, but hardly worth it; they are available only at the winery.

BARBECUE RED ($) ½   A very light rosé-style wine, innocuous.

Washington Wines and Wineries   339

BURGUNDY, SELECT HARVEST ($$) ½ Interesting—a dark, sweet, smooth wine with decent fruit. Not bad, but most drinkers will find it odd.

GEWÜRZTRAMINER, SELECT HARVEST ($$) ★ Slight apple character, soft, pleasant, sweet.

RIESLING, SELECT HARVEST ($$) ½ Sweet, low in acid, not much character.

WASHINGTON DISCOVERY *See* COVENTRY VALE

WATERBROOK
Lowden (1984)
6,000 cases

Another of the cluster of wineries near Walla Walla, Waterbrook too is taking a handcrafted approach to the making of wine. Like other local winemakers, Eric and Janet Rindal come from farming backgrounds—Janet's family grows alfalfa seed nearby. The energetic Rindals, who pretty much run the winery by themselves, leaped into winemaking feet first. One summer they helped their neighbors the Fergusons with the crush at L'École No. 41; the next year, after a few mini-classes in enology, they bought a couple of tanks and started in on their own. Janet remarks cheerfully that she didn't know anything about wine when they started, but from the beginning the wines have been carefully made and very appealing, no doubt thanks in part to consulting enologist Kay Simon.

They own no vineyards, procuring their fruit from Columbia Valley vineyards, including the well-regarded Moreman Vineyard and Balcom and Moe Vineyard, both near Pasco. Chardonnay will probably end up the specialty here, and the winery is producing several different bottlings, including one entirely barrel-fermented version. (The secondary wine has been labeled Pinot Chardonnay, which may cause some confusion.) Although pleased with the results of their French oak barrels, they are also experimenting with the use of (much less expensive) American oak. Rindal feels he can control the aggressive flavors of American oak by cutting back the time the wines spend in it. Other successful wines here have been Sauvignon Blanc, which sees a little time in oak and ends up soft and not too herbaceous (although the '86 vintage refused to ferment dry, leaving an awkward slight sweetness in the wine), and Merlot, which has a nice balance of berry and sweet oak flavors.

CABERNET SAUVIGNON ($$$) ★★★   Lovely balance of oak and berry flavors, quite tart and hard on the palate, with good spice.

CHARDONNAY ($$) ★★★½   An assertively toasty, oaky style, with pineapple fruit, good acid, and some buttery qualities. The Reserve has even more buttery oak qualities.

MERLOT ($$) ★★★½   Intense, sweetish nose, fairly soft and forward, with slight herbaceousness.

PINOT CHARDONNAY ($) ★★   A straightforward wine with applelike fruit, a hint of sweetness, and decent acid.

SAUVIGNON BLANC ($$) ★★★   Slight grassiness is toned down with rich oak. Usually tart and round, though '86 has some sweetness.

WENATCHEE VALLEY VINTNERS
East Wenatchee   (1986)
20,000 cases

The Wenatchee Valley lies up against the eastern side of the Cascade Mountains, toward the northern end of the

Columbia Valley appellation. A well-known apple-growing region, it has not been home to any wineries until Wenatchee Valley Vintners began. The elevation is higher, the climate a touch cooler, and the harvest a little later than in the Yakima Valley. The Hansens, Mike and Debbie, planted their 18-acre vineyard in 1982 with several varieties, including Sauvignon Blanc and Pinot Noir, and they are also using grapes from Mike's father's 250 acres of vineyard near Zillah, in the Yakima Valley, also the location of a new fermentation facility. (The winery already has considerable tank capacity, and production could grow quickly given the ready source of grapes.)

Mike Hansen is not a winemaker by background (consultant Kay Simon of Chinook Wines provided winemaking expertise when they began), but his training as a biochemist makes him a great quality-control man. His aim is to produce full-flavored varietals; of the initial releases, the Riesling seemed better than the Chardonnay, which didn't show much varietal character.

CHARDONNAY ($) ★★　Light and leafy, this wine is soft and a bit thin.
RIESLING ($) ★★★　Lovely apple flavors—tart and refreshing.

WHITTLESEY-MARK (OREGON CHAMPAGNE CELLARS)
Seattle　(1983)
1,500 cases

Formerly Newton and Newton (the name change resulted from a dispute with California's Newton), this is the Northwest's first exclusive sparkling-wine producer, and the first releases of small amounts of Champagne-method wines have been most impressive. Mark Newton's wine background is primarily as a serious wine consumer—he decided on a career making sparkling wine after a visit to California's Domaine Chandon. He has spent time learning the business at several successful Champagne houses in California, including the large French Deutz concern, and he has several consulting enologists from California. But the Northwest is the place for sparkling wine, he thinks.

Oregon fruit—Chardonnay, Pinot Noir, and Pinot Meunier, the classic French Champagne grapes—is perfect for the wine, ripening with low sugars and high acids. The grapes, from the well-known Hyland Vineyard in the Willamette, are crushed and pressed in Oregon, but the rest of the production process takes place in Seattle, making the winery a true Northwest concern.

Newton has managed to achieve what few others in the Northwest have: a delicately fruity sparkling wine reminiscent of French Champagne. It doesn't have quite the yeasty weight of great Champagne (like most new producers, Newton can't afford to let the wine rest on the yeast for three or four years), but it makes up for that with considerable elegance. The wine is well priced, and production should increase in coming years.

Still Chardonnay will be released under a separate label, diStefano.

BRUT (OREGON) ($$$) ★★★★ Rich, fresh, tart fruit with some depth and lovely rounded elegance. A lively and distinctive wine.

ROSÉ (OREGON) ($$$) ★★★½ Not quite as nice as the Brut. Fresh flavors, some nice Pinot character, quite soft.

WINDY RIVER CELLARS *See* BLACKWOOD CANYON

WOODBURNE *See* COLUMBIA WINERY

WOODWARD CANYON WINERY
Lowden   (1981)
2,400 cases

From its beginning in 1981 this tiny winery near Walla Walla has been one of the state's top producers of both Cabernet Sauvignon and Chardonnay. Owner and wine-maker Rick Small comes from a longtime Walla Walla farming family, but even his relatives numbered among the skeptics in this conservative wheat-and-beef town when Small started his winery. After helping Gary Figgins at Leonetti Cellar (a former fellow drill sergeant in the Army Reserve) make his wines, Small set off on his own, with the same commitment to small quantities of power-ful, top-notch wines.

Rick Small isn't sure what the best grape varieties for the young Walla Walla appellation are, but clearly Char-donnay and Cabernet are among them. His own ten-acre vineyard, on a steep south-facing slope ten miles west of town, is planted with Chardonnay, and he feels Walla Walla's slightly cooler temperatures are ideal for this vari-ety. What's interesting about the finished product, though, is that Small manages to work his magic not just with his own grapes, but with fruit from other sources, drawing from Seven Hills Vineyard across the Oregon border (still part of the appellation), Mercer Ranch, Gordon Brothers Vineyards, and various others.

Small was one of the first in the state to produce a barrel-fermented Chardonnay well aged on the lees: It is consis-tently a big, buttery wine with a soft texture that belies its depth and strength. It has also shown good aging ability. The single-vineyard Chardonnay, from the Roza Bergé Vineyard in the Yakima Valley, shows a slightly different style, with the influence of new oak.

344   *American Wines of the Northwest*

Small's Cabernet is one of the best in the state—a consistent award winner. It's a huge wine, with deep fruit—nearly black in color, and like the Chardonnay aged completely in new French oak. The first vintage, the '81, still looks and tastes young and will take years to develop, but for the patient this is extraordinary wine. The latest Small effort is a blend of 70 percent Merlot and 30 percent Cabernet called Charbonneau (after the Snake River vineyard from which the grapes come). Just released in 1987, this may be the best Merlot-based wine yet from Washington; Small attributes the quality to a meager yield. Riesling is produced for the tourist trade—sold only at the winery. The top wines are expensive and sell quickly but are worth looking for.

CABERNET SAUVIGNON ($$$$) ★★★★★ Big, spicy, oaky nose with tart, lean classic Cabernet fruit. Built for the ages. One of the very best.
CHARBONNEAU ($$$$) ★★★★½ Plummy and rich, with a great whack of oak, extremely tannic, powerful. Exceptional Merlot.
CHARDONNAY (COLUMBIA) ($$$) ★★★★★ Very rich butterscotch-pineapple nose, ripe, round fruit—quite luscious. Lots of fruit and lots of oak. A big style for rich foods. California, watch out.
CHARDONNAY (ROZA BERGÉ) ($$$$) ★★★★½ A lighter, more subtle wine than the Columbia Valley, with a toastier nose and more apparent spicy oak.
RIESLING ($) ★★ Light, tart, apricot flavors.

H.P. ISAACS

woodward canyon

1983

Columbia Valley
Cabernet Sauvignon

Produced and bottled by Woodward Canyon Winery BW-WA-81, Lowden WA 99360
Alcohol by Volume 13.5%

WORDEN'S WASHINGTON WINERY
Spokane   (1980)
18,000 cases

Owner Jack Worden, a longtime fruit grower, has gone through a succession of winemakers, including Mike Conway of Latah Creek and Rollin Soles of Oregon's Crochad operation. The turnover has meant a rather inconsistent style for the wines, though overall quality has improved significantly since the early eighties. (Worden is now making the wines himself.) The winery has had some difficulties in establishing a market niche, but increasing emphasis has been put of late on light, fruity wines, including several pleasant blush-style wines, which have proved to be quite popular.

The winery is outside Spokane, not a grape-growing area, and all the grapes are purchased from Columbia and Yakima Valley vineyards—the majority from the excellent Moreman Vineyard near Pasco. Most of the wines are finished with some residual sweetness and even the reds are made in a soft, forward style, emphasizing fruit. Both the regular and Late Harvest Rieslings are very tasty (the Late Harvest is a sleeper, a very enticing wine at a ridiculously low price), and the various Gamay Beaujolais wines are among the best in their category, with bright flavors and crisp acidity. The leading red wine is a blend of Cabernet and Merlot—Worden likes the effects of blending, with the Merlot softening out the Cabernet. The wines are fairly inexpensive.

The newest marketing effort is the Seafare label, for those wines that the winery feels are particularly suitable with seafood. Of these, the Merlot is the most interesting—almost Beaujolais-like, with light raspberry fruit—though it's a little hard to picture as seafood wine.

CABERNET-MERLOT ($$) ★★½ A light style, with an intense strawberry nose, lots of fruit, and a slight pepperiness. Drink young.

CHARDONNAY ($$) ★★½ Fruity, light, tart, slight oak.

CHENIN BLANC ($) ★★★ Strong nose of apples and wildflowers, slightly sweet, quite soft.

FUMÉ BLANC ($$) ★★★ Definite bell pepper aromas, nicely balanced with a soft finish from French oak.

GAMAY BEAUJOLAIS ROSÉ ($) ★★★ Lovely color, strawberry fruit—delightful flavor and good tartness.

NOUVEAU BLUSH ($) ★★½ Strawberry nose with tart, zippy fruit.

RIESLING, JOHANNISBERG ($) ★★★ It has varied from straightforward, citrusy flavors to a full, peachy style—moderately sweet.

RIESLING, LATE HARVEST ($$) ★★★½ Lovely peach nose, very fresh, balanced, with medium sweetness.

SEAFARE CHARDONNAY ($$) ★½ Light, green flavors, not much interest.

SEAFARE MERLOT ($) ★★½   Beaujolais style, raspberry flavors, light, pleasant.

YAKIMA RIVER WINERY
Prosser   (1979)
18,000 cases

John Rauner loves big red wines, particularly those with a strong oak influence, and that personal preference shows in the wines he makes. Rauner, the owner and winemaker, is a transplanted Easterner and pipe fitter by trade, whose interest in Washington wine was first stimulated when he made wines at home in New York from Washington grapes. One of the older wineries in the Yakima Valley, Yakima River owns no vineyards, preferring to buy grapes from area growers with whom it can build long-term relationships.

There is little pretense in these wines; they are "made with the average consumer in mind," notes Rauner. In fact, they have been fairly rough and ready. Older notes indicate a depressing lack of consistent quality, but in the last few vintages the winery has shown signs of cleaning up its act, especially in the reds. A fairly dull Chardonnay has been dropped and more focus given to red wine. Rauner's current pet project is developing good Pinot Noir in the Yakima Valley—he feels problems with Washington Pinot have been due to poor clonal selection. He has settled on two clones he likes (including the Pommard, well established in Oregon), and initial results look pretty good, though as with Cabernet and Merlot, the use of oak is fairly heavy-handed.

Those who like big, oaky, tannic reds may find some of these wines very attractive, though they often lack depth and complexity. While the Cabernets seem just too tough, the more recent Merlots (like '85) have good fruit, though they are still big wines. There are some decent sweet dessert Rieslings, but here again, they seem to miss out on the fruit and balance that one would like to see. (There is also an occasional Ice Wine.) Moreover, the sweetest are quite expensive.

CABERNET SAUVIGNON ($$) ★★½   Oaky nose and flavors dominate, with some berry qualities. Burly, tannic, rough—but fairly simple.

CABERNET SAUVIGNON, RESERVE ($$$) ★★★   This spent thirty-two months in new oak and shows it. Extremely oaky, lots of vanilla in the nose, spicy, tannic—but not much fruit showing. Will age help?

FUMÉ BLANC ($$) ★★   Very herbaceous, bell pepper nose; aggressive, tart flavors—fairly rough. Good if you like this style.

MERLOT ($$) ★★★   This seems to be lightening up a bit in recent vintages and showing more balance. The '85 had lots of berry fruit, along with a good whack of oak.

PINOT NOIR ($$) ★★½   Nice cherry-oaky nose, lean and tart, with subdued fruit.

PINOT NOIR, WHITE ($) ★½ Pleasant, rhubarby flavors—sweet, clean.

RIESLING, DRY BERRY SELECT ($$$$) ★★★½ Quite yellow, with a spicy, honeyed apricot nose. Very sweet but not terribly rich. Expensive.

RIESLING, SELECT CLUSTER ($$$) ★★ Not as sweet as the Dry Berry, but plenty of sugar. A nice grapefruity nose—but it lacks richness.

ZILLAH OAKES WINERY *See* COVEY RUN VINTERS

WINERIES NO LONGER MAKING WINES
Caroway Vineyards
Cascade Cellars
Daquila Wines
Haviland Vintners
Puyallup Valley Winery
Rainier Valley Cellars

10

IDAHO WINES AND WINERIES

CAMAS WINERY
Moscow   (1983)
1,500 cases

rapes for this tiny winery come from Washington's huge Sagemoor Farms, so the wines don't necessarily represent an "Idaho style." Indeed, the winery is near the Washington border and rather closer to eastern Washington growing areas than to Idaho's Sunny Slope near Boise. The goal of owner-winemaker Stuart Scott (the winery is the Scott basement) is to make fairly light-bodied wines to be consumed young—and Scott likes a soft, slightly sweet style, even in Chardonnay. The most unusual bottling is the Hog Heaven Red, a blend of 60 percent cherry wine and 40 percent Merlot.

CABERNET SAUVIGNON ($) ★½   Light, woody, slightly herbal.
CHARDONNAY ($) ★★   Very oaky, hot, buttery—straightforward and simple.

COVEY RISE
Boise
500 cases

The winery's name is about to change (a result of a dispute with Washington's Covey Run), production is tiny, the owner runs a fish market in Boise, the wines are not generally available, and there is no "winery" (wines are made at another facility). But the Chardonnay under this label, from a small vineyard on the Snake River, is good enough to have attracted the attention of English importer Mark Savage, who is shipping it to the tough English market. Wines not tasted.

DESERT SUN WINERY
Nampa   (1987)
1,200 cases

Owner Brad Pintler is a farmer in the Snake Valley south of Nampa who has converted part of his sugar beet fields into vineyards. The first vintage was crushed at the Stowe Winery in Kuna, but Pintler plans to build his own facility. The first wines were clean and showed good varietal character, especially the Semillon in a fairly aggressive style.

RIESLING ($) ★★   Peachy, soft, clean, off-dry. Very pleasant.
SEMILLON ($) ★★½   Definite Semillon character, with a mixture of citrus and herbaceous fruit. Fairly dry, slightly hot.

LOUIS FACELLI WINERY *See* PETROS WINERY

INDIAN CREEK
Kuna   (1987)
4,000 cases

Indian Creek's twenty-acre vineyard lies south of Boise,
about ten miles east of the established Sunny Slope growing area, and was planted in 1982 to Riesling, Chardonnay,
and Pinot Noir (a variety little grown in Idaho). Owner-
winemaker Bill Stowe says the grapes grow equally well in
his area, the only drawback being greater risk of frost
damage in the spring and fall.

Stowe, a retired air force officer, developed a taste for
wine (especially dry Riesling) while stationed in Germany, where he helped out in vineyard and winery. His
brother Mike, co-winemaker, is a schoolteacher in Davis,
California, where he has had a chance to attend enology

and viticulture classes, and provides Stowe with technical assistance.

The dry Riesling, which Stowe says he makes "out of principle," is the most interesting wine. The other wines seem more problematic, lacking true varietal character, and Stowe admits he is still experimenting with his wine-making (the first Chardonnay was barrel-fermented, but he plans to go to tank fermentation, to emphasize the fruit). A second Pinot Noir, from the Stowe Vineyard, will be released in 1989.

CHARDONNAY (KUNA BUTTE) ($) ★½ Some apple fruit, but woody, leafy flavors—OK.

PINOT NOIR (KUNA BUTTE) ($) ½ This first effort misses the mark, with some off flavors, but the winery gets credit for making the effort with this varietal in Idaho.

RIESLING (STOWE) ($) ★★ Appley, simple, soft—finishes dry.

PETROS WINERY
Boise (1986)

Petros, after an initial splash, is now out of business, though some wines are still available. The winery began life as the project of talented winemaker Louis Facelli, who made a reputation for fine Riesling and Chardonnay under a label bearing his name. Unfortunately, the winery was sold from underneath him to a group of investors, including former Ste. Chapelle winemaker Bill Broich, and renamed Spring Creek. The partnership fell apart under a storm of accusations and lawsuits, and partner Pete Eliopolous, a Boise investor, took control of the winery, which he renamed Petros, in 1987, only to close it under financial pressures in 1988.

CABERNET SAUVIGNON ($$) ★★★½ Dark, with an oaky-vanilla nose, lots of spicy oak, and decent fruit. Tannic, tart, rather rough, but it opens up. One of the Louis Facelli wines.

CHARDONNAY, EARLY SELECT ($) ★★ Very ripe apple nose, with a bit of mushroom, some viscous flavors—a bit hot.

RIESLING, JOHANNISBERG ($) ★★ Pleasant apple-candy nose, lightly sweet, fairly lively.

RIESLING, WHITE ($) ★½ Grapefruity nose, rather herbal on the palate, fairly sweet—not as interesting as the Johannisberg.

SAUVIGNON BLANC ($$) ★½ Light, steely, austere, tart.

PUCCI WINERY
Sandpoint   (1982)
2,000 cases

Sandpoint is several hundred miles to the north of the main grape-growing areas in Idaho (it's not far from Spokane), and the country is more suited to pine than grapevine. In fact, the grapes for these wines come from eastern Washington and from California. Very much a home winery, Pucci is run by Skip Pucci—who comes from a long line of winemakers—in his spare time, using largely homemade equipment. All the wines are fermented and aged in oak, which sets them apart in style from most others in the Northwest. Results have been variable so far.

CHARDONNAY (WASHINGTON) ($) ★ Flavor tends to be a bit cooked and tart, though there is some decent fruit.

RIESLING (WASHINGTON) ($) ★ Not much varietal character—quite light and dry.

ROSE CREEK VINEYARDS
Hagerman   (1984)
4,000 cases

Hagerman is in a picturesque section of the Snake Valley 100 miles southeast of Boise. The forty acres or so of small vineyards in the area are among the most southerly and warm-sited in the Northwest (the town isn't far from the Nevada border), but their high altitude, around 2,800 feet, keeps the fall temperatures cool and the grapes from getting overripe. The local vineyards (some only a few acres) have been developed by Rose Creek owner and winemaker Jamie Martin, who grew up in the area. Martin, who has a viticultural background, has a landscape business and has encouraged clients to plant small vineyards; he manages them and then uses the grapes at his tiny subterranean winery. Pinot Noir grapes come from Oregon and Cabernet Sauvignon from Washington to make the red wines—Martin is happy to go far afield to find what he feels are the best grapes.

The winemaking shows considerable promise. French oak is jammed into the winery, and the partially barrel-fermented Chardonnay is a forward wine with lots of spicy oak. These are not subtle wines (the unfiltered Cabernet is immense and tough), but they have lots of flavor and good balance, and show attention to quality. Idaho has suffered a bit from a reputation for small mom-and-pop wineries, but Rose Creek should be able to compete with the better Oregon and Washington wines; this is the first "boutique" Idaho winery with boutique quality.

CABERNET SAUVIGNON (WASHINGTON) ($$$) ★★★★
Very dark and thick, with herbal-berry-vanilla scents and great depth. Slightly hot. A most impressive first effort.

CHARDONNAY ($$) ★★★★ Ripe, oaky, pineapple nose, viscous, tart, solid. Lovely wine. Should help Idaho's reputation as Chardonnay country.

PINOT ROSÉ VIN GRIS ($$) ★★★ A temporary wine, preceding a red Pinot Noir, but very good anyway. Earthy Pinot fruit, fine backbone—might be a bit drier.

RIESLING ($) ★★½ Interesting peachy-almond nose, tart, off-dry.

ROSE CREEK MIST ($) ★★ Riesling with Cabernet for color. Slightly herbal, crisp, fruity.

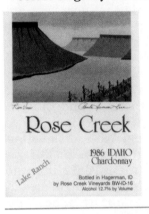

STE. CHAPELLE WINERY
Caldwell (1976)
130,000 cases

For most intents and purposes, Ste. Chapelle *is* Idaho wine. Ste. Chapelle is an offshoot of the Symms family's large fruit business on Idaho's Sunny Slope along the Snake River, which underwrote the fledgling winemaking efforts of Bill Broich in the mid-seventies. The winery has grown quickly, helped along by considerable marketing muscle, and is now not only by far the largest winery in Idaho but one of the largest in the Northwest. Although the winery owns extensive vineyards (about 150 acres), it still buys lots of grapes from other growers, including several in eastern Washington.

The high altitude (around 2,500 feet) of this part of the Snake Valley ensures very cool night temperatures during the critical fall season, which preserves the essential acid content of the grapes even while they ripen. This slow ripening seems ideally suited to Chardonnay, Riesling, and Gewürztraminer. Ste. Chapelle under former winemaker Bill Broich made a reputation for excellent Chardonnay, in a big, oaky, ripe style that was very appealing, though the wines didn't age very gracefully. But as production expanded, quality didn't seem to keep up, and the wines, while clean and well made, haven't stood out in the last several years. The best deal has been a lighter and fruiter Chardonnay than the regular bottling, known variously as Blanc de Chardonnay and Canyon Chardonnay.

Broich has moved on, after problems with mislabeling the wines cost the winery some penalties from the Bureau of Alcohol, Tobacco, and Firearms (the mislabeling was quickly rectified). New winemaker Mimi Mook comes to Ste. Chapelle from J. Lohr Winery in California; her only plans for stylistic changes are with Chardonnay, where she would like to see more fruit and a crisper, less oaky style that will age better. The new Mook-made Reserve Chardonnay, rich and spicy, puts the winery back on the fast track for success with this varietal. She also plans to experiment with a dry but fruity Riesling. Plans call for a red Pinot Noir eventually, as new vineyards come into production—Mook is hopeful that Idaho Pinot can have something of the same success that Oregon Pinot has had, though the climate is hardly the same.

Besides pioneering fine table wine in Idaho, Ste. Chapelle has also made a splash with sparkling wine, produced by the bulk Charmat process (in which the second fermentation, to make the bubbles, takes place in pressurized tanks rather than individual bottles). Ste. Chapelle has the only Charmat line in the Northwest (the equipment is terrifically expensive), and it keeps expanding its production. Both Riesling and Chardonnay "Champagne" have been light and fruity and reasonably priced, and the winery has been hard pressed at times to keep up with demand. (A "Champagne Blush" has been added to the line now.)

Ste. Chapelle has recently introduced a separate label, Chapel Hill, for generic red, white, and blush table wines that the winery promises will be made from a preponderance of top-quality grape varieties (e.g., Chardonnay and Riesling for the white).

CABERNET SAUVIGNON (WASHINGTON) ($$) ★★½
An appealing oaky-vanilla nose, but the flavors are slightly vegetal, and there's no great depth.
CABERNET SAUVIGNON, CANYON ($) ★   Hot flavors, quite vegetal and out of balance.
CHAMPAGNE BLUSH ($$) ★½   Floral-herbal nose, decent fruit.
CHAMPAGNE CHARDONNAY ($$) ★★★   This is the best of these Charmat wines—a pleasant fresh-bread nose, with considerable crisp fruit. Fairly dry. Good value.
CHAMPAGNE RIESLING ($$) ★★   Light bubbles and a light peachy nose; clean, tart flavors. Only slightly sweet.
CHARDONNAY ($$) ★★★   Recent bottlings show a fruity, apple-bready nose, with crisp, understated flavors and a bit of viscosity.
CHARDONNAY, CANYON ($) ★★   Doesn't age long, but it has crisp, applelike fruit.
CHARDONNAY, RESERVE (SYMMS) ($$$) ★★★½
Rich, appley nose, with butterscotch underneath; lots of fruit and some complexity.

RIESLING ($) ★★½   Light, grapefruity nose, good tartness, barely off-dry.

RIESLING, LATE HARVEST ($$) ★★★   Lots of apple and spice flavor in a heavy style. Not as elegant as some.

STOWE WINERY   *See* INDIAN CREEK

WESTON WINERY
Caldwell   (1982)
4,000 cases

Cheyne Weston left Ste. Chapelle, where he worked briefly, feeling that he could make just as good wine as the big boys. The small ten-acre vineyard is claimed to be, at 2,800 feet, the highest-altitude vineyard in the Northwest, though most in Idaho are quite high. While the vines are maturing, wines are being made with grapes from various Idaho and Oregon vineyards—as well as Cabernet Sauvignon from California. Weston, a former cinematographer, is an experimenter—one of his projects is an Idaho cooler called Blue Moon, made from Riesling, fresh peaches, and a bit of ginger for flavor. It's lighter and crisper than California coolers, and Weston figures it should appeal to those who enjoy more natural flavors.

The quality of the wines is variable, though both the Riesling and Chardonnay from Idaho grapes are flavorful in a straightforward fashion. The Chardonnay is barrel-fermented and aged in French oak and shows some promise. There is also a small quantity of Champagne-method sparkling wine. Prices are very reasonable.

CABERNET SAUVIGNON (AMERICAN) ($$) ★★   Cherry nose, soft, fruity—pleasant, but not much to it.

CHARDONNAY ($) ★★★   Very ripe apple nose with some toasty oak—balanced, viscous flavors in a forward, fruity style. Not complicated, but quite nice.

GEWÜRZTRAMINER ($) ★½   Slightly sweet, with pleasant spice and soft fruit.

RIESLING ($) ★★★   Pleasant appley, flowery nose with medium-sweet flavors, clean, fresh.

WINERY AT SPRING CREEK   *See* PETROS WINERY

WINERY NO LONGER MAKING WINE
Petros Winery

APPENDIX A:
RECOMMENDED WINES, BY VARIETAL
(WINES WITH RATINGS OF 3.0 OR ABOVE)

$	$7 OR LESS
$$	$7 TO $12
$$$	$12 TO $20
$$$$	MORE THAN $20

3.0	VERY GOOD QUALITY, WITH SOME DISTINCTION
4.0	EXCELLENT, AMONG THE BEST IN ITS CLASS
5.0	OUTSTANDING, WORLD-CLASS, UNIQUE QUALITIES

CABERNET SAUVIGNON

WINERY	STATE	WINE	PRICE	RATING
Columbia	WA	Cabernet Sauvignon (Red Willow)	$$$	5.0
Leonetti	WA	Cabernet Sauvignon	$$$$	5.0
Leonetti	WA	Cabernet Sauvignon, Reserve	$$$$	5.0
Quilceda Creek	WA	Cabernet Sauvignon	$$$	5.0
Woodward Canyon	WA	Cabernet Sauvignon	$$$$	5.0

WINERY	STATE	WINE	PRICE	RATING
Columbia	WA	Cabernet Sauvignon (Sagemoor)	$$$	4.5
Hogue	WA	Cabernet Sauvignon Reserve	$$$$	4.5
Leonetti	WA	Cabernet Sauvignon (Seven Hills)	$$$$	4.5
Alpine	OR	Cabernet Sauvignon, Vintage Select	$$$	4.0
Arbor Crest	WA	Cabernet Sauvignon	$$$	4.0
Barnard Griffin	WA	Cabernet Sauvignon	$$$	4.0
Chateau Ste. Michelle	WA	Cabernet Sauvignon	$$	4.0
Chateau Ste. Michelle	WA	Cabernet Sauvignon, Reserve	$$$	4.0
Columbia	WA	Cabernet Sauvignon (Otis)	$$$	4.0
Hinzerling	WA	Cabernet Sauvignon	$$$	4.0
Kiona	WA	Cabernet Sauvignon	$$$	4.0
Mercer Ranch	WA	Cabernet Sauvignon (Mercer)	$$$	4.0
Neuharth	WA	Cabernet Sauvignon	$$	4.0
Rose Creek	ID	Cabernet Sauvignon	$$$	4.0
Paul Thomas	WA	Cabernet Sauvignon	$$$	4.0
Columbia	WA	Cabernet Sauvignon	$$	3.5
Columbia Crest	WA	Cabernet Sauvignon	$$	3.5
Covey Run	WA	Cabernet Sauvignon	$$$	3.5
French Creek	WA	Cabernet Sauvignon	$$	3.5
Hinzerling	WA	Cabernet-Merlot	$$	3.5
Mercer Ranch	WA	Cabernet Sauvignon (Sharp Sisters)	$$$	3.5
Petros	ID	Cabernet Sauvignon (Facelli)	$$	3.5
Quarry Lake	WA	Cabernet Sauvignon	$$	3.5
Redford	WA	Cabernet-Merlot	$$	3.5
Valley View	OR	Cabernet Sauvignon	$$	3.5
Bookwalter	WA	Cabernet Sauvignon	$$$	3.0
Champs de Brionne	WA	Cabernet-Merlot	$$	3.0
French Creek	WA	Cabernet Sauvignon, Reserve	$$$	3.0
Hogue	WA	Cabernet Sauvignon	$$$	3.0

WINERY	STATE	WINE	PRICE	RATING
Snoqualmie	WA	Cabernet Sauvignon	$$	3.0
Waterbrook	WA	Cabernet Sauvignon	$$$	3.0
Yakima River	WA	Cabernet Sauvignon, Reserve	$$$	3.0

CHARDONNAY

WINERY	STATE	WINE	PRICE	RATING
Eyrie	OR	Chardonnay	$$$	5.0
Woodward Canyon	WA	Chardonnay (Columbia)	$$$	5.0
Cameron	OR	Chardonnay, Reserve	$$$	4.5
Tualatin	OR	Chardonnay, Reserve	$$	4.5
Woodward Canyon	WA	Chardonnay (Roza Bergé)	$$$$	4.5
Adams	OR	Chardonnay, Reserve	$$$	4.0
Adelsheim	OR	Chardonnay (Yamhill)	$$	4.0
Barnard Griffin	WA	Chardonnay	$$$	4.0
Bonair	WA	Chardonnay (Puryear)	$$	4.0
Cameron	OR	Chardonnay	$$	4.0
Chinook	WA	Chardonnay, Reserve	$$$	4.0
Covey Run	WA	Chardonnay (Willard Farms)	$$	4.0
Hogue	WA	Chardonnay, Reserve	$$	4.0
Kiona	WA	Chardonnay	$$	4.0
Ponzi	OR	Chardonnay	$$	4.0
Rose Creek	ID	Chardonnay	$$	4.0
Shafer	OR	Chardonnay	$$	4.0
Sokol Blosser	OR	Chardonnay, Reserve	$$$	4.0
Paul Thomas	WA	Chardonnay, Private Reserve	$$$	4.0
Adams	OR	Chardonnay	$$	3.5
Amity	OR	Chardonnay, Reserve	$$$	3.5
Bethel Heights	OR	Chardonnay	$$	3.5
Blackwood Canyon	WA	Chardonnay	$$	3.5
Chateau Ste. Michelle	WA	Chardonnay (Cold Creek)	$$$	3.5
Columbia	WA	Chardonnay (Wyckoff)	$$$	3.5
Elk Cove	OR	Chardonnay, Reserve	$$$	3.5

WINERY	STATE	WINE	PRICE	RATING
Girardet	OR	Chardonnay	$$	3.5
Hogue	WA	Chardonnay	$$	3.5
Horizon's Edge	WA	Chardonnay (Fair Acre)	$$$	3.5
Knudsen Erath	OR	Chardonnay, Vintage Select	$$	3.5
Neuharth	WA	Chardonnay	$$	3.5
Oakwood	WA	Chardonnay	$$	3.5
Rex Hill	OR	Chardonnay (Willamette)	$$$	3.5
Ste. Chapelle	ID	Chardonnay, Reserve (Symms)	$$$	3.5
Stewart	WA	Chardonnay	$$	3.5
Paul Thomas	WA	Chardonnay	$$	3.5
Valley View	OR	Chardonnay	$$	3.5
Wasson Brothers	OR	Chardonnay	$$$	3.5
Waterbrook	WA	Chardonnay	$$	3.5
Adelsheim	OR	Chardonnay (Oregon)	$$	3.0
Alpine	OR	Chardonnay	$$$	3.0
Amity	OR	Chardonnay	$$	3.0
Arbor Crest	WA	Chardonnay (Sagemoor)	$$	3.0
Autumn Wind	OR	Chardonnay	$$	3.0
Bonair	WA	Chardonnay (Outlook)	$$	3.0
Broadley	OR	Chardonnay	$$	3.0
Chateau Ste. Michelle	WA	Chardonnay, Reserve	$$$	3.0
Chinook	WA	Chardonnay	$$	3.0
Columbia	WA	Chardonnay	$$	3.0
Columbia Crest	WA	Chardonnay	$$	3.0
Cooper Mountain	OR	Chardonnay	$$	3.0
Covey Run	WA	Chardonnay	$$	3.0
Flynn Vineyards	OR	Chardonnay	$$	3.0
Gordon Brothers	WA	Chardonnay	$$	3.0
Henry	OR	Chardonnay	$$	3.0
Hood River	OR	Chardonnay	$$$	3.0
Hoodsport	WA	Chardonnay	$$	3.0
Horizon's Edge	WA	Chardonnay (McKinnon)	$$$	3.0
Knudsen Erath	OR	Chardonnay	$	3.0
Oak Knoll	OR	Chardonnay	$$	3.0
Preston	WA	Chardonnay	$$	3.0

WINERY	STATE	WINE	PRICE	RATING
Ste. Chapelle	ID	Chardonnay	$$	3.0
Salishan	WA	Chardonnay	$$	3.0
Sokol Blosser	OR	Chardonnay (Yamhill)	$$	3.0
Paul Thomas	WA	Chardonnay	$$	3.0
Tualatin	OR	Chardonnay	$$	3.0
Tyee	OR	Chardonnay	$$$	3.0
Veritas	OR	Chardonnay	$$$	3.0
Weston	ID	Chardonnay	$	3.0
Yamhill Valley	OR	Chardonnay	$$$	3.0

CHENIN BLANC

WINERY	STATE	WINE	PRICE	RATING
Salishan	WA	Chenin Blanc, Dry	$	4.0
Hogue	WA	Chenin Blanc	$	3.5
Latah Creek	WA	Chenin Blanc	$	3.5
Latah Creek	WA	Chenin Blanc, Reserve	$	3.5
Snoqualmie	WA	Chenin Blanc	$	3.5
Paul Thomas	WA	Chenin Blanc	$$	3.5
Blackwood Canyon	WA	Chenin Blanc, Dry	$$	3.0
Columbia Crest	WA	Chenin Blanc	$	3.0
Eola Hills	OR	Chenin Blanc	$	3.0
Serendipity	OR	Chenin Blanc	$	3.0
Worden's	WA	Chenin Blanc	$	3.0

GEWÜRZTRAMINER

WINERY	STATE	WINE	PRICE	RATING
Hinzerling	WA	Die Sonne (Gewürz- traminer)	$$$	4.5
Airlie	OR	Gewürztraminer	$	3.5
Alpine	OR	Gewürztraminer	$$	3.5
Amity	OR	Gewürztraminer	$$	3.5
Callahan Ridge	OR	Gewürztraminer (Elkton)	$	3.5
Elk Cove	OR	Gewürztraminer, Late Harvest	$$$	3.5
Henry	OR	Gewürztraminer	$$	3.5
Hinzerling	WA	Gewürztraminer	$	3.5

WINERY	STATE	WINE	PRICE	RATING
Mont Elise	WA	Gewürztraminer (Mont Elise)	$	3.5
Pellier	OR	Gewürztraminer	$	3.5
Shafer	OR	Gewürztraminer	$	3.5
Woodburne	WA	Gewürztraminer	$$	3.5
Airlie	OR	Gewürztraminer, Late Harvest	$$	3.0
Elk Cove	OR	Gewürztraminer	$	3.0
Hinman	OR	Gewürztraminer	$	3.0
Pacific Crest	WA	Gewürztraminer, Late Harvest	$$	3.0
Staton Hills	WA	Gewürztraminer	$	3.0
Tyee	OR	Gewürztraminer, Reserve	$$	3.0
Wasson Brothers	OR	Gewürztraminer	$	3.0

LEMBERGER

WINERY	STATE	WINE	PRICE	RATING
Kiona	WA	Lemberger	$$	4.0
Mercer Ranch	WA	Limburger (Lemberger)	$$	4.0
Covey Run	WA	Lemberger	$	3.5
French Creek	WA	Lemberger, Reserve	$$	3.5

MERLOT

WINERY	STATE	WINE	PRICE	RATING
Paul Thomas	WA	Merlot	$$	4.5
Woodward Canyon	WA	Charbonneau (70 percent Merlot)	$$$$	4.5
Chateau Ste. Michelle	WA	Merlot, Chateau Reserve	$$$	4.0
Latah Creek	WA	Merlot	$$	4.0
Leonetti	WA	Merlot	$$$	4.0
Arbor Crest	WA	Merlot (Bacchus)	$$	3.5
Chateau Ste. Michelle	WA	Merlot	$$	3.5
Chinook	WA	Merlot	$$	3.5

Appendix A

WINERY	STATE	WINE	PRICE	RATING
Gordon Brothers	WA	Merlot	$$	3.5
Hogue	WA	Merlot	$$$	3.5
L'École No. 41	WA	Merlot	$$$	3.5
Valley View	OR	Merlot	$$	3.5
Waterbrook	WA	Merlot	$$.	3.5
Columbia	WA	Merlot	$$	3.0
Columbia Crest	WA	Merlot	$$	3.0
Covey Run	WA	Merlot	$$	3.0
Hoodsport	WA	Merlot	$$	3.0
Knudsen Erath	OR	Merlot	$	3.0
Lost Mountain	WA	Merlot	$$	3.0
Neuharth	WA	Merlot	$$	3.0
Quarry Lake	WA	Merlot	$$	3.0
Snoqualmie	WA	Merlot, Reserve	$$	3.0
Yakima River	WA	Merlot	$$	3.0
Yakima River	WA	Merlot (Ciel du Cheval)	$$	3.0

MÜLLER-THURGAU

WINERY	STATE	WINE	PRICE	RATING
Airlie	OR	Müller-Thurgau	$	3.5
Johnson Creek	WA	Müller-Thurgau	$	3.5
Tualatin	OR	Müller-Thurgau	$	3.5
Bainbridge Island	WA	Müller-Thurgau	$	3.0
Mount Baker	WA	Müller-Thurgau	$	3.0
Serendipity	OR	Müller-Thurgau	$$	3.0
Siskiyou	OR	Müller-Thurgau	$	3.0

MUSCAT

WINERY	STATE	WINE	PRICE	RATING
Mercer Ranch	WA	Muscat Canelli	$$	4.0
Covey Run	WA	Morio-Muskat	$	3.5
Eyrie	OR	Muscat Ottonel	$$	3.5
Latah Creek	WA	Muscat Canelli	$	3.5
Stewart	WA	Muscat Canelli	$$	3.5
Paul Thomas	WA	Muscat Canelli	$$	3.5

WINERY	STATE	WINE	PRICE	RATING
Arbor Crest	WA	Muscat Canelli	$$	3.0
Columbia	WA	Muscat	$	3.0
Snoqualmie	WA	Muscat Canelli	$	3.0
Tucker	WA	Muscat Canelli	$	3.0

PINOT GRIS

WINERY	STATE	WINE	PRICE	RATING
Adelsheim	OR	Pinot Gris	$$	4.0
Eyrie	OR	Pinot Gris	$$	4.0
Lange	OR	Pinot Gris	$$	4.0
Ponzi	OR	Pinot Gris	$$	4.0
Rex Hill	OR	Pinot Gris	$$	4.0
Tyee	OR	Pinot Gris	$$	3.0

PINOT NOIR

WINERY	STATE	WINE	PRICE	RATING
Adelsheim	OR	Pinot Noir, Elizabeth's Reserve (Yamhill)	$$$	5.0
Amity	OR	Pinot Noir, Reserve	$$$$	5.0
Eyrie	OR	Pinot Noir, Reserve	$$$$	5.0
Knudsen Erath	OR	Pinot Noir, Vintage Select	$$$	5.0
Ponzi	OR	Pinot Noir, Reserve	$$$	5.0
Adelsheim	OR	Pinot Noir (Polk)	$$$	4.5
Amity	OR	Pinot Noir (Estate)	$$$	4.5
Bethel Heights	OR	Pinot Noir	$$$	4.5
Bethel Heights	OR	Pinot Noir, Reserve	$$$	4.5
Cameron	OR	Pinot Noir	$$$	4.5
Cameron	OR	Pinot Noir, Reserve	$$$	4.5
Elk Cove	OR	Pinot Noir (Wind Hill)	$$$	4.5
Eyrie	OR	Pinot Noir	$$$	4.5
Rex Hill	OR	Pinot Noir (Archibald)	$$$$	4.5
Rex Hill	OR	Pinot Noir (Maresh)	$$$	4.5
Adams	OR	Pinot Noir	$$$	4.0
Adams	OR	Pinot Noir, Reserve	$$$	4.0
Broadley	OR	Pinot Noir, Reserve	$$	4.0

WINERY	STATE	WINE	PRICE	RATING
Oak Knoll	OR	Pinot Noir, Vintage Select	$$$	4.0
Panther Creek	OR	Pinot Noir	$$$	4.0
Rex Hill	OR	Pinot Noir (Medici)	$$$	4.0
Rex Hill	OR	Pinot Noir (Wirtz)	$$$	4.0
Sokol Blosser	OR	Pinot Noir (Hyland)	$$$	4.0
Sokol Blosser	OR	Pinot Noir (Red Hills)	$$$	4.0
Sokol Blosser	OR	Pinot Noir, Reserve (Red Hills)	$$$	4.0
Tualatin	OR	Pinot Noir, Reserve	$$$	4.0
Veritas	OR	Pinot Noir	$$$	4.0
Yamhill Valley	OR	Pinot Noir	$$$	4.0
Amity	OR	Pinot Noir	$$	3.5
Arterberry	OR	Pinot Noir, Reserve (Red Hills)	$$$	3.5
Elk Cove	OR	Pinot Noir (Estate)	$$$	3.5
Evesham Wood	OR	Pinot Noir	$$	3.5
Flynn	OR	Pinot Noir	$$	3.5
Glen Creek	OR	Pinot Noir, Whole Cluster	$	3.5
Knudsen Erath	OR	Pinot Noir (Willamette)	$$	3.5
Ponzi	OR	Pinot Noir	$$	3.5
Rex Hill	OR	Pinot Noir (Willamette)	$$$	3.5
Salishan	WA	Pinot Noir	$$	3.5
Amity	OR	Pinot Noir Nouveau	$	3.0
Broadley	OR	Pinot Noir	$$	3.0
Chateau Benoit	OR	Pinot Noir	$$	3.0
Chateau Ste. Michelle	WA	Pinot Noir	$$	3.0
Elk Cove	OR	Pinot Noir (Dundee Hills)	$$$	3.0
Eola Hills	OR	Pinot Noir	$$$	3.0
Glen Creek	OR	Pinot Noir	$$$	3.0
Oak Knoll	OR	Pinot Noir	$$	3.0
Pellier	OR	Pinot Noir	$$	3.0
Rex Hill	OR	Pinot Noir (Dundee Hills)	$$$	3.0
Serendipity	OR	Pinot Noir	$$	3.0
Shafer	OR	Pinot Noir	$$$	3.0
Staton Hills	WA	Pinot Noir (Oregon)	$$	3.0

WINERY	STATE	WINE	PRICE	RATING
Tyee	OR	Pinot Noir	$$$	3.0
Wasson Brothers	OR	Pinot Noir	$$$	3.0
Woodburne	WA	Pinot Noir	$$	3.0

RIESLING

WINERY	STATE	WINE	PRICE	RATING
Arbor Crest	WA	Riesling, Late Harvest	$$$	5.0
Covey Run	WA	Riesling Ice Wine	$$$$	5.0
Stewart	WA	Riesling, Late Harvest	$$$	5.0
Chateau Ste. Michelle	WA	Riesling, Late Harvest (Hahn Hill)	$$$	4.5
Chateau Ste. Michelle	WA	Riesling, Select Cluster	$$$	4.5
Blackwood Canyon	WA	Riesling, Late Harvest	$$	4.0
Blackwood Canyon	WA	Riesling, Ultra Late Harvest	$$$	4.0
Cameron	OR	Riesling, *Botrytis* "Eugenia"	$$$$	4.0
Covey Run	WA	Riesling, White (Mahre)	$$	4.0
Covey Run	WA	Riesling, White (Whiskey Canyon)	$$	4.0
Hogue	WA	Riesling, Late Harvest (Markin)	$$	4.0
Langguth	WA	Riesling, Select Cluster	$$$	4.0
Mount Baker	WA	Riesling, Select Cluster	$$$	4.0
Ponzi	OR	Riesling, Dry	$	4.0
Stewart	WA	Riesling, Johannisberg	$	4.0
Paul Thomas	WA	Riesling	$$	4.0
Alpine	OR	Riesling	$$	3.5
Barnard Griffin	WA	Riesling	$$	3.5
Bookwalter	WA	Riesling	$	3.5
Chateau Ste. Michelle	WA	Riesling	$	3.5
Hinzerling	WA	Riesling, Late Harvest	$$	3.5
Kiona	WA	Riesling, Dry	$	3.5
Kiona	WA	Riesling, Late Harvest	$$	3.5

WINERY	STATE	WINE	PRICE	RATING
Knudsen Erath	OR	Riesling, Vintage Select	$$	3.5
Worden's	WA	Riesling, Late Harvest	$$	3.5
Yakima River	WA	Riesling, Dry Berry Select	$$$$	3.5
Arterberry	OR	Riesling, Vintage Select	$$	3.0
Bethel Heights	OR	Riesling	$$	3.0
Bonair	WA	Riesling	$	3.0
Elk Cove	OR	Riesling, Late Harvest	$$$	3.0
French Creek	WA	Riesling Ice Wine	$$$	3.0
Girardet	OR	Riesling	$	3.0
Hillcrest	OR	Riesling	$	3.0
Hinman	OR	Riesling	$	3.0
Hogue	WA	Riesling	$	3.0
Kiona	WA	Riesling	$	3.0
Oakwood	WA	Riesling	$	3.0
Pacific Crest	WA	Riesling	$	3.0
Preston	WA	Riesling, Select Harvest	$$	3.0
Quarry Lake	WA	Riesling	$	3.0
Salishan	WA	Riesling, Dry	$$	3.0
Seven Hills	WA	Riesling	$	3.0
Snoqualmie	WA	Riesling, Late Harvest	$$	3.0
Ste. Chapelle	ID	Riesling, Late Harvest	$$	3.0
Wenatchee Valley	WA	Riesling	$	3.0
Weston	ID	Riesling	$	3.0
Worden's	WA	Riesling, Johannisberg	$	3.0

SAUVIGNON BLANC (FUMÉ BLANC)

WINERY	STATE	WINE	PRICE	RATING
Hogue	WA	Fumé Blanc	$$	4.0
Arbor Crest	WA	Sauvignon Blanc	$$	3.5
Chateau Ste. Michelle	WA	Sauvignon Blanc	$	3.5
Covey Run	WA	La Caille de Fumé	$	3.5
Paul Thomas	WA	Sauvignon Blanc	$$	3.5
Preston	WA	Fumé Blanc	$$	3.5

WINERY	STATE	WINE	PRICE	RATING
Barnard Griffin	WA	Fumé Blanc	$$	3.0
Cavatappi	WA	Sauvignon Blanc	$$	3.0
Chateau Benoit	OR	Sauvignon Blanc	$$	3.0
Chinook	WA	Sauvignon Blanc	$$	3.0
Hood River	OR	Sauvignon Blanc	$$	3.0
Quarry Lake	WA	Sauvignon Blanc	$	3.0
Shafer	OR	Sauvignon Blanc	$$	3.0
Snoqualmie	WA	Fumé Blanc	$$	3.0
Staton Hills	WA	Sauvignon Blanc	$$	3.0
Waterbrook	WA	Sauvignon Blanc	$$	3.0
Worden's	WA	Fumé Blanc	$$	3.0

SEMILLON

WINERY	STATE	WINE	PRICE	RATING
Blackwood Canyon	WA	Semillon	$$	4.0
Chateau Ste. Michelle	WA	Semillon	$	3.5
Columbia	WA	Semillon	$	3.5
Columbia Crest	WA	Semillon	$	3.0
Latah Creek	WA	Semillon	$	3.0
Snoqualmie	WA	Semillon	$	3.0

SPARKLING WINE

WINERY	STATE	WINE	PRICE	RATING
Hogue	WA	Brut	$$$	4.0
Newton and Newton (Whittlesey-Mark)	WA	Brut (Oregon)	$$$	4.0
Chateau Benoit	OR	Blanc de Blancs	$$$	3.5
Chateau Ste. Michelle	WA	Blanc de Noir Brut	$$$	3.5
Knudsen Erath	OR	Brut (Oregon)	$$$	3.5
Newton and Newton (Whittlesey-Mark)	WA	Rosé (Oregon)	$$$	3.5
Chateau Benoit	OR	Brut	$$$	3.0
Horizon's Edge	WA	Champagne	$$$	3.0

Appendix A

WINERY	STATE	WINE	PRICE	RATING
Mont Elise	WA	Blanc de Noir Brut	$$$	3.0
Ste. Chapelle	ID	Champagne, Chardonnay	$$	3.0

FRUIT AND BERRY WINE

WINERY	STATE	WINE	PRICE	RATING
Hoodsport	WA	Raspberry	$	4.0
Paul Thomas	WA	Bartlett Pear, Dry	$	4.0
Paul Thomas	WA	Raspberry	$$	4.0
Wasson Brothers	OR	Raspberry	$	4.0
Oak Knoll	OR	Raspberry	$	3.5
Shallon	OR	Peach	$$	3.5
Bainbridge Island	WA	Strawberry	$$	3.0
Bjelland	OR	Wild Blackberry	$	3.0
Hoodsport	WA	Loganberry	$	3.0
Oak Knoll	OR	Blackberry	$	3.0
Shallon	OR	Blackberry	$$	3.0
Wasson Brothers	OR	Blackberry	$	3.0

ODDS AND ENDS

WINERY	STATE	WINE	PRICE	RATING
Bainbridge Island	WA	Siegerrebe	$$$	4.0
Bethel Heights	OR	Pinot Noir Blanc	$	3.5
Girardet	OR	Vin Rouge, Reserve	$$	3.5
Mount Baker	WA	Madeline Angevine, Reserve	$$	3.5
Rex Hill	OR	Encore	?	3.5
Adams	OR	Portland's House Wine	$	3.0
Amity	OR	Oregon Blush	$	3.0
Cameron	OR	Red Table	$	3.0
Girardet	OR	Vin Rouge	$	3.0
Kiona	WA	Merlot Rosé	$	3.0
Rose Creek	ID	Pinot Rosé Vin Gris	$$	3.0
Warden's	WA	Gomay Beaujolais Rosé	$	3.0

APPENDIX B: AWARDS

The Wine Festival of the Enological Society of the Pacific Northwest, held in Seattle, is the largest Northwest-only wine competition, and the Oregon State Fair competition (open only to entries from Oregon) is the most important for that state's wines. Both include both local and outside judges. The 1988 results are included here to give the consumer a reference to award-winning wines, although the author does not agree with all the results. Only gold and silver medal winners are listed, and it should be noted that the Enological Society allows only vinifera entries.

Wine judgings are a crap shoot. A great deal depends on the makeup of the judging panel, the prejudices that each judge brings, and the interaction of the different personalities. Northwest wineries have complained consistently, and with merit, that judges from the California industry, no matter how professional, judge Northwest wines by California standards, and therefore frequently "miss the point" of a wine. In addition, some judgings are very liberal with awards (so that a bronze medal becomes almost meaningless), and others quite stingy. The idiosyncrasies of wine judgings are reflected in the widely varying results: Most wineries enter as often as they can, in hopes of hitting an occasional winner. It's a very rare wine indeed that does well in every competition.

ENOLOGICAL SOCIETY OF THE PACIFIC NORTHWEST WINE FESTIVAL, AUGUST 1988

GRAND PRIZES

Gordon Brothers Merlot 1986
Paul Thomas Chardonnay Reserve 1986

GOLD

Amity Estate Pinot Noir 1985
Gordon Brothers Merlot 1986
Hogue Reserve Chardonnay 1986
Hogue Fumé Blanc 1987
Hogue Johannisberg Riesling 1987
Knudsen Erath Vintage Select Pinot Noir 1986
Langguth Late Harvest Johannisberg Riesling 1987
Mercer Ranch Cabernet Sauvignon 1985
Rose Creek Cabernet Sauvignon 1985
Ste. Chapelle Reserve Chardonnay (Symms) 1986
Snoqualmie Late Harvest White Riesling 1987
Tagaris Johannisberg Riesling 1987
Paul Thomas Reserve Chardonnay 1986
Paul Thomas Dry Riesling 1987
Woodward Canyon Cabernet Sauvignon 1985
Worden's Chenin Blanc 1986

SILVER

Airlie Müller-Thurgau 1987
Alpine Chardonnay 1987
Alpine White Riesling 1987
Amity Dry Riesling 1987
Arbor Crest Select Late Harvest Johannisberg Riesling 1987
Arbor Crest Sauvignon Blanc 1987
Bethel Heights Pinot Noir 1986
Blackwood Canyon Chardonnay 1986
Cascade Crest Johannisberg Riesling 1987
Chateau Ste. Michelle Sauvignon Blanc 1986
Columbia Crest Merlot 1984
Covey Run Merlot 1985
Covey Run Morio-Muskat 1987
Covey Run *Botrytis* Affected White Riesling 1986
Desert Sun Semillon 1987
Elk Cove Gewürztraminer 1987
Henry *Botrytis* Affected White Riesling 1987
Hillcrest Riesling 1984
Hoodsport Gewürztraminer 1987
Hoodsport Johannisberg Riesling 1987
Kiona Chenin Blanc 1987

Mount Baker Madeline Angevine 1987
Mount Baker Müller-Thurgau 1987
Neuharth Cabernet Sauvignon 1986
Neuharth Johannisberg Riesling 1987
Oak Knoll White Riesling 1987
Pacific Crest Late Harvest Gewürztraminer 1986
Preston Fumé Blanc 1986
Quilceda Creek Cabernet Sauvignon 1984
St. Josef's Weinkeller Cabernet Sauvignon 1984
St. Josef's Weinkeller "L'Esprit" Gewürztraminer 1987
St. Josef's Weinkeller Pinot Noir 1985
Shafer Gewürztraminer 1987
Staton Hills Pinot Noir 1986
Stewart Late Harvest White Riesling 1987
Paul Thomas Chardonnay 1987
Tyee Gewürztraminer 1987
Tyee Pinot Gris 1987
Woodward Canyon Chardonnay (Columbia) 1987

OREGON STATE FAIR WINE COMPETITION, AUGUST 1988

GOLD

Henry Late Harvest White Riesling 1987 (Governor's Trophy)
Knudsen Erath Vintage Select Pinot Noir 1986
Laurel Ridge Reserve Sauvignon Blanc (Finn Hill) 1987
Wasson Brothers Chardonnay 1986
Wasson Brothers Raspberry (Governor's Trophy)

SILVER

Airlie Müller-Thurgau 1987
Bethel Heights Pinot Noir 1986
Bridgeview "Inspiration" Red Table
Bridgeview Winemaker's Reserve Pinot Noir 1986
Broadley Reserve Pinot Noir 1986
Elk Cove Commander's Cabernet (Dundee Hills) 1985
Elk Cove Pinot Noir (Wind Hill) 1986

Elk Cove Estate Reserve Pinot Noir 1986
Eola Hills Chenin Blanc 1987
Forgeron Pinot Noir 1985
Girardet Chardonnay 1987
Girardet White Riesling 1986
Henry Reserve Chardonnay 1985
Hillcrest Select Harvest White Riesling 1985
Honeywood "Twin Harvest" Peach and Riesling
Knudsen Erath Cabernet Sauvignon 1986
Lange Pinot Gris 1987
Ponzi White Riesling 1987
St. Josef's Weinkeller "L'Esprit" Gewürztraminer 1987
Serendipity Maréchal Foch 1987
Shafer Sauvignon Blanc 1985
Shafer White Riesling 1986
Sokol Blosser Reserve Chardonnay 1986
Sokol Blosser Müller-Thurgau 1987
Tyee Pinot Gris 1987
Wasson Brothers Boysenberry
Wasson Brothers Early Muscat 1987
Wasson Brothers Strawberry

Appendix B   379

INDEX

Index

About the Author

Corbet Clark, a native of Seattle, has spent ten years reporting on the emergence of the Northwest wine region. He writes a weekly column on Northwest wines for the Tacoma *Morning News Tribune.* He lives in Portland, Oregon.